MESSAGE FORM.

System

No.	Date and Time Handed in	Office of Origin		Recd. at		Sent at
fix	3.20 pm	Tralee			From	To
		Service Instructions		By	By

1 MAR 1923

PANOGRAPH PHOTO CO

THE IRISH DEFENCE FORCES

1922–2022

THE IRISH
DEFENCE FORCES
1922–2022

Servant of the Nation

Eoin Kinsella

Four Courts Press
in association with
The Irish Defence Forces

Set in 10 on 14 pt Baskerville

Published by

Four Courts Press, 7 Malpas Street, Dublin 8, Ireland

www.fourcourtspress.ie

and in North America by

Four Courts Press

c/o IPG, 814 N Franklin St, Chicago, IL 60610

A catalogue record for this title

is available from the British Library.

ISBN 978-1-80151-036-3

Book design and typesetting by Anú Design, Tara

Printed in Poland by L & C Printing Group, Krakow

CONTENTS

ABBREVIATIONS AND EDITORIAL NOTE

A list of the most frequently used abbreviations is provided below. To aid the reader, the full names of institutions and military ranks/offices are also given in the text when first mentioned. While a full list of all of the overseas missions in which the Defence Forces have participated is provided at the back of the book, acronyms for those mentioned in the text are also given below. The names and dates of office for all the Commanders in Chief and Chiefs of Staff of the Defence Forces, and of all Ministers and Secretaries/Secretaries General of the Department of Defence, are also found at the back of the book. Where known, an individual's preference for the spelling of their personal name is used.

Since 1946 the Defence Forces has had four main elements: Army, Air Corps, Naval Service, and the reserve (the latter under various names and guises). Though the term Army is frequently used as a shorthand for all of the above elements, after 1924 it properly refers only to the land-based forces, and is used as such below. The military forces of the Provisional Government and the Irish Free State were referred to in a variety of ways between February 1922 and October 1924, including the National Army, the Irish Free State Army, Óglaigh na hÉireann and the National Forces – the National Army has been preferred when referring to that period. The appellation Defence Forces was officially adopted on 1 October 1924.

18MM	18th Military Mission
Brig	Brigadier
Capt	Captain
CMS	Coastal and Marine Service
Col	Colonel
Cpl	Corporal
Comdt	Commandant
DSM	Distinguished Service Medal
EEC	European Economic Community

EU	European Union
FCÁ	Fórsa Cosanta Áitiúil
Gen	General
GHQ	General Headquarters
GOC	General Officer Commanding
GOCF	General Officer Commanding the Forces
LDF	Local Defence Force
LÉ	Long Éireannach ('Irish Ship')
Lt	Lieutenant
Maj	Major
MTB	Motor Torpedo Boats
NCO	Non Commissioned Officer
OC	Officer Commanding
ONUC	Opération des Nations Unies au Congo (United Nations Operation in the Congo)
PDF	Permanent Defence Forces
Pte	Private
QMG	Quartermaster General
RDF	Reserve Defence Forces
Sgt	Sergeant
UN	United Nations
UNDOF	United Nations Disengagement Observer Force
UNFICYP	United Nations Force in Cyprus
UNIFIL	United Nations Interim Force in Lebanon
UNMIL	United Nations Mission in Liberia
UNOGIL	United Nations Observer Group in Lebanon
UNTSO	United Nations Truce Supervision Organization

ACKNOWLEDGMENTS

Writing a centenary history of the Defence Forces has been both a challenging and rewarding experience, and I have many people to thank for their assistance along the way. I am grateful to former Chief of Staff, Vice Admiral Mark Mellett DSM, for entrusting me with the task. Both he and his successor, Lieutenant General Seán Clancy, provided all of the support that I asked for.

Military Archives in Cathal Brugha Barracks became a temporary home for extended periods in 2021 and 2022, and it was a privilege to work closely with Comdt Daniel Ayiotis (Officer in Charge), Capt Sarah Colclough (Second in Command), CQMS Tom Mitchell (Repository Manager), Sgt Matthew Weafer (Records Manager), and Cpl Joseph McDermott (Volunteer Coordinator), and with archivists Hugh Beckett, Lisa Dolan, Noelle Grothier and Linda Hickey. This book simply would not have been possible without the generosity they showed in welcoming me into their space and sharing their knowledge and expertise. Most of my research was completed during the several lockdowns and other public health measures implemented in response to the Covid-19 pandemic, and I witnessed at first hand the extraordinary efforts of everyone at Military Archives to find alternative ways to facilitate researchers.

I am very grateful to Selina Collard, Orna Somerville and Kate McKeown (University College Dublin Archives), Evelyn McAuley (Department of Defence), Natasha Serne (Royal Dublin Society Library and Archives), Clare McNamara and Emer Ní Cheallaigh (National Museum of Ireland), Philip Roe (Hugh Lane Gallery), the National Archives of Ireland, and the United Nations Photo Library, for all of their help. Mary Byrne (née Magennis), Comdt Stephen Byrne (Irish Air Corps Press and Public Relations) and Sgt Rena Kennedy (Defence Forces Press Office) very kindly assisted my efforts to source suitable images. Lt Col Mark Armstrong generously shared material from the archive of the Defence Forces School of Music, and Michael Hayes shared digital images from his personal collection of the first phonographs recorded by the Army No. 1 Band. Paul Manzor and Andrew

Flynn of Eneclann assisted with the scanning of outsize ephemera. Lt Col Richard Cummins (Retd), Sgt Gerry McCann (Retd), and Tony Kinsella, all volunteers in Military Archives, gave me the benefit of their knowledge and good company. Though I didn't work with them directly, I would also like to acknowledge the important work of the team responsible for administering the Military Service Pensions Collection: Cécile Chemin (Senior Archivist), Michael Keane, Robert McEvoy, Sam McGrath, and Leanne Ledwidge.

The Defence Forces convened an editorial board to assist my research and I am very grateful to Comdt Ayiotis, Comdt Shane Conlon, Lt Col Eugene Cooke, Comdt Lar Joye (Reserve Defence Forces and Dublin Port Heritage Director), Dr Michael Kennedy (Royal Irish Academy), Comdt David Kiely, Comdt Stephen Mac Eoin, Lt Col Gareth Prendergast, and Lt Col Gavin Young. Their constructive criticism, guidance, and willingness to engage in robust discussion were vital in shaping my thinking as the project progressed.

Prof Bernadette Whelan very kindly shared documents from the collections in the National Archives and Records Administration, Maryland, as did Michael Kennedy from the collections at the National Archives of the United Kingdom, Kew. Cpl Michael Whelan of the Irish Air Corps Museum shared his vast knowledge of the Air Corps, and steered me through the valuable collection of interviews he has completed for the Military Archives Oral History Project. My thanks to Dr John Gibney and Dr Kate O'Malley of Documents on Irish Foreign Policy for their advice, and to everyone at Four Courts Press and Anú Design. Lastly, my thanks to Lily for her unwavering support throughout.

leanṗam ꝿo ꝺlúṫ ꝺo ċlú áꞃ sinnsiꞃ.

☘ Irish Volunteers. ☘

TICKET OF ADMISSION TO

2764 PUBLIC MEETING

To be held at 8.30 o'clock, in the

CITY HALL, CORK,

ON SUNDAY NIGHT NEXT, 14th DECEMBER,

TO FORM A CORK CITY CORPS OF THE

IRISH VOLUNTEERS

PROFESSOR EOIN MacNEILL, B.A., DUBLIN, and LOCAL
SPEAKERS will address the Meeting.

**Volunteers embrace men of all Creeds, Classes, and Parties.
Only Citizens ready to join should attend, as capacity of hall
is limited to 1,500.**

J. J. WALSH (G.A.A.),
LIAM DE ROISTE (Gaelic League),
DIARMAID FASAIT (I.D.A.),
MAURICE O'CONNOR (U.C.C.)

múscail ꝺo misneaċ a banba.

NB.—THIS MOVEMENT IS STRICTLY
NON-PARTY.

BUREAU OF MILIT R H.
BÚRO S.A. ....ÁRṪA 19'3-21
NO. C. D. 23/2

The Irish Volunteers/Óglaigh na hÉireann were formed in November 1913 in response to the Home Rule crisis, and the earlier formation of the Ulster Volunteer Force. Though the use of the appelation Óglaigh na hÉireann has been disputed since the Civil War, it has been used by the Defence Forces since the beginning of 1922, and was enshrined in legislation as the Irish-language title of the state's military forces in 1923. Above is an admission ticket for a meeting in Cork's City Hall, on 14 December 1913, to establish a Cork City branch of the Irish Volunteers.

INTRODUCTION

The origins of the Irish Defence Forces lie in the formation of the Irish Volunteers/Óglaigh na hÉireann in November 1913, and the political and military revolution that preceded the emergence of the Irish Free State in 1922. The evolution of the Volunteers between 1913 and 1919 was influenced by a number of factors, not least the split within its ranks following the outbreak of the First World War, and the 1916 Rising. In the wake of the disappointment of Easter 1916, reorganization of the Volunteers in the summer and autumn of 1917 was accompanied by a surge in public support for the republican political movement, culminating in Sinn Féin's success at the December 1918 general election.

Refusing to take their seats at the British parliament in Westminster, on 21 January 1919 Sinn Féin established Dáil Éireann, defined in its election manifesto as 'a constituent assembly comprising persons chosen by Irish constituencies as the supreme national authority to speak and act in the name of the Irish people'. That same day the first engagement of the War of Independence (1919–21) took place at Soloheadbeg, Co. Tipperary, when members of the 3rd Tipperary Brigade of the Volunteers ambushed and killed two Royal Irish Constabulary officers. Defence was one of the first four government ministries established by the Dáil, and by August 1919 the Volunteers were essentially regarded as the standing army of the revolutionary government.

As the war with Britain progressed the Volunteers increasingly became known as the Irish Republican Army (IRA). Though IRA members swore an oath of allegiance to Dáil Éireann, and the Chief of Staff required to report to the Minister for Defence, civilian oversight of the IRA during the war was nominal at best. Senior IRA officers also frequently held political office or administrative roles in the Dáil government – a situation that would prove problematic in 1922, when the National Army attempted to exert control over all IRA units, and would later complicate attempts to provide clear lines of separation between the civilian and military elements of the Provisional Government during the Civil War (1922–3).

4

I.—THE COMPANY.

1. The tactical unit of the Irish Volunteers shall be called a Company, and shall consist of four sections numbered 1 to 4.

(a) Four Sections—each composed of 19 or more (but not exceeding 25) men, including two Squad Leaders and one Section Commander.

(b) Sections numbered 1 and 2 shall be the right Half-Company. Sections numbered 3 and 4 shall be the left Half-Company.

(c) Three officers—the Captain, the Right Half-Company Commander (First Lieutenant), the Left Half Company Commander (Second Lieutenant).

(d) One Quartermaster, ranking as Section Commander.

(e) One Adjutant, ranking as Section Commander.

2. In each Section men shall be detailed for the following *Special Services :—*

Engineering	2 men
Scouting and Despatch Riding	2 men
Signalling	3 men
Transport and Supply	2 men
First Aid	2 men
Musketry	1 man

3. As far as possible all men should receive training in these branches, but men as specified above must be specially trained. One man from each Special Service shall be detailed by the Company Commander to see to the training and efficiency of that particular service. As all Volunteers are to be trained as cyclists, a special cyclist section is not considered necessary. It shall be at the discretion of the Company Commander to mount some of his men on horses, and it must be assured that each company shall contain at least a few men proficient in horse-riding.

5

4. A member of the company shall be trained to act as armourer, whose duty it shall be to see that all arms are kept in perfect condition and repair.

5. When a company is below full strength, the Company Commander shall, subject to the approval of Headquarters, use his discretion in determining the strength of each section and special service within the section, *but must in all circumstances see that every prescribed service is represented in his company.* The intention is to empower the Company Commander to reduce the strength of sections and special services when such is found necessary, and further to combine double duties in one individual, or even to distribute, if necessary, the duties of one position between two or more individuals. In this connection it should be remembered that the object is to secure the general efficiency of the company as a fighting unit rather than its conformation to an ideal type.

NOTE—In certain special districts sections shall be recognised by Headquarters as units, and the government of these units shall, as far as possible be modelled on the government of the company.

APPOINTMENT OF COMPANY AND SUBORDINATE OFFICERS.

1. The Company and Half-Company Commanders shall be elected by the Company at a general meeting summoned for that purpose. The election must be by ballot and shall not take effect unless and until ratified by Headquarters. Every Company Officer, upon ratification of his election, shall be given a Commission by Headquarters, such Commission to be his authority to act as a Company Officer of the Irish Volunteers.

2. It shall be within the power of Headquarters to deprive a Company Officer of his Commission, either of its own motion or on the requisition of a majority of the Company.

3. All Section Commanders and other subordinate Officers of the Company shall be appointed by the Company Commander, who shall also have power to dismiss them.

A10033
1

Company...................... No............

Óglaig na h-Éireann—Irish Volunteers.

I, the undersigned, desire to be enrolled in the Irish Volunteers formed to secure and maintain the rights and liberties common to all the people of Ireland without distinction of creed, class, or politics.

Name_____

Address_____

City Ward or Township_____

Date_____

"The Irish Volunteer," 65 Mid. Abbey St., Dublin.

Though hampered by serious deficiencies in arms, ammunition and other warlike stores, by the summer of 1921 the IRA had forced the British to the negotiating table, and a truce was declared on 11 July 1921. The resulting Anglo-Irish Treaty, signed on 6 December 1921, fell short of achieving the ideal of a fully independent Irish republic. The Irish Free State, established under the terms of the Treaty, would be a dominion of the British empire, and the island of Ireland remained partitioned following the creation of Northern Ireland in 1920.

With the terms of the Treaty widely known and fractures among the republican movement already apparent, on 16 December 1921 the newspaper of the IRA, *An tÓglách*, published a call for unity:

> Now as in the past it is the duty of the Army not to allow its discipline or efficiency to be impaired by political happenings. The Army is the servant of the nation and will obey the national will expressed by the chosen representatives of the people and interpreted through the proper military channels ... The strength of the Army lies in its having acted as an organized and disciplined whole, under a single authority, in support of the national will constitutionally expressed. It will continue to act as such. It will never be a menace to the people of Ireland, but a defender of the rights and liberties of the whole nation.[1]

An tÓglách subsequently repeated this theme several times in its attempts to avert civil war, referring in April 1922 to the soldiers of the army as 'the servants, not the masters, in the state'.[2] Yet in the early months of 1922, acceptance of the National Army's status as the servant of the nation, subordinate to the Dáil, had not yet taken hold across the IRA. It would take the fracturing of the organization along pro- and anti-Treaty lines, a bitter Civil War, and an attempted mutiny in early 1924 before the tenet of civil control of the military could be regarded as having been firmly embedded across the National Army.

The National Army, and indeed the Provisional Government of the Free State, were confronted with the crisis of armed opposition to the Treaty and

Opposite page: An extract from the *General scheme of organisation* of the Irish Volunteers, published in late 1914 to establish its military structure, along with a blank enrolment form for the Volunteers.

the outbreak of the Civil War in the summer of 1922. Both sides in the Civil War claimed to be the natural successors of the Volunteers/IRA, and to the name Óglaigh na hÉireann. Yet the Provisional Government's determination to assert the National Army's legitimacy as the inheritors of the revolutionary legacy of the Volunteers was clear from the beginning. Though the name given to the National Army remained fluid for the first half of 1922 – even *An tÓglách* struggled to make up its mind, switching between the Irish Volunteers, the Irish Republican Army and the National Army – the motifs and insignia of the Volunteers were incorporated into the new army's uniforms.

After the Civil War the National Army (renamed the Defence Forces in October 1924) was rapidly reduced both in size and in its prominence within the state. For much of the 1920s and 1930s the Defence Forces suffered from a lack of investment; personnel numbers decreased from the Civil War peak of *c.*55,000 men in April 1923 to just over 5,000 a decade later. That lack of investment, and of a clearly defined policy to guide the development of the Defence Forces, ensured that when a second major European war broke out in 1939 the state's military forces were ill-prepared to face an invasion that, up to 1941, appeared more likely than not.

Known as 'the Emergency' in Ireland, the government's response to the Second World War included a mobilization of military manpower on a scale never seen before or since, and included the creation of a Naval Service that was formally incorporated as a constituent element of the Defence Forces in 1946. The invasion never materialized, and the Second World War marked the last time that the territorial integrity of the state came under threat.

Yet despite the drafting of a comprehensive set of planning documents, and a commitment from the government to avoid a return to the doldrums of the 1930s, within the decade of the end of the Emergency the Defence Forces were once more at a low ebb. All of that changed, however, soon after Ireland's admission to the United Nations in 1955. Ireland's first involvement in UN peacekeeping missions came just three years later, providing a renewed focus for the Defence Forces and inaugurating an unbroken tradition of overseas

Opposite page: The title page of the February 1919 issue of *An tÓglach*, published at the very beginning of what became known as the War of Independence. Its editorial, likely written by Piaras Béaslaí, consciously refers to the Irish Volunteers as 'the Army of Ireland'. By the end of the year the Volunteers were commonly regarded as the army of Dáil Éireann (established in January 1919), and was better known as the Irish Republican Army.

An ⊂-óglác

OFFICIAL ORGAN OF THE IRISH VOLUNTEERS

Vol. I.   No. 10.]   February, 1919.   [Price Twopence.

THE WORK BEFORE US.

The Army of Ireland has passed through more than one critical period since its establishment in 1913. It has sustained many severe trials successfully, has faced and conquered tremendous difficulties and dangers, has maintained its organisation intact and efficient in the face of obstacles such as never before confronted any Army or Volunteer Force in any country in the world. The courage, discipline, and efficiency of the members of the Army of Ireland have been put to the most severe tests, and in nearly every case Volunteers have emerged from the tests triumphantly. To-day the Irish Volunteers are stronger, better organised and disciplined than ever before. The efficiency with which any piece of work is carried out when the arrangements are in the hands of Volunteers has become a proverb with the Irish people. The rescue of the President of the Irish Republic from an English prison is the latest and one of the most striking instances of that efficiency on record.

Properly speaking, the maintaining of a large and well-organised army, in a country held by a huge foreign army of occupation, with its strong places in the hands of the enemy, and all the resources of martial law and a powerful military machine employed against us, is a wonderful achievement. All the efforts of the enemy to break up our ranks have failed. The prisons of the enemy have been filled with our officers, but good men have always been forthcoming to take their places. In a sense the conduct of our Volunteers when captured by the enemy and when in prison should be one of our greatest sources of pride. They have behaved like true soldiers; they have shattered the prestige of British law, "civil" or "martial," they have smashed up the British prison system, they have faced the tortures and brutalities of the enemy with an unflinching spirit which again and again has won them the victory. At present Irish Volunteers are lying handcuffed day and night in cells devoid of furniture in Belfast, Mountjoy and Cork prisons. This has gone on for weeks, but there is no sign of surrender on their part. The Volunteers are watching the fate of their imprisoned comrades with the most earnest attention, and are prepared to take the most drastic action should circumstances render it necessary.

We have paid the officers and men of the Volunteers a tribute for the courage, discipline, efficiency and military spirit displayed by them on so many a trying occasion. We wish, however, to point out that these qualities will be more called for than ever in the service of Ireland in the immediate future. It would be impossible to expect that in so large an Army, many of whose members have only recently "joined up," the same high standard would prevail everywhere. The Conscription danger brought a large accession of strength to our ranks. Many of the newcomers were undoubtedly men whose eyes had been opened to the necessity of the Irish Volunteers by this moment of national peril and who joined to take their part in the defence of the Irish people. Some, it is to be feared, were influenced by most selfish considerations, and were more affected by the sense of personal peril than the danger to the nation. If there are any such who, believing the immediate danger to be past, have relaxed their attention to Volunteer duties, they must be spoken plainly to and made to "get on or get out." We have no time for shirkers or slackers. The period of crisis and danger is *not* over. Never were we at a more critical period in the fate of Ireland than to-day. Never were we facing a time more fraught with possibilities in which the courage and discipline of the Volunteers will be more severely tried, and the fate of Ireland will depend upon their activities.

It is the will of Ireland, expressed by her responsible Government, that the state of war between this country and England shall be perpetuated until the foreign garrison have evacuated our country. It will be the duty of the Volunteers, acting in accordance with the will of our Government and the wishes of the Irish people, to secure the continuance of that state of war by every means at our disposal and in the most vigorous way practicable. Every Volunteer must be prepared for more drastic actions, more strenuous activities, than ever before since Easter, 1916. As has several times been stated before, Volunteer officers must contemplate the possibilities of offensive as well as defensive action. What form our offensive activities will take depends upon the responsible leaders of the Irish Army, acting in consultation with the Irish Ministry, under the direction of the Minister of Defence. It should be recognised that the establishment of a National Government elected by and responsible to the Irish people enormously strengthens the hands of the Irish Volunteers. This Government claims the same power and authority as any other lawfully consti-

Michael Collins, photographed in the Gresham Hotel, Dublin, on the evening of 7 January 1922 – the day the Dáil narrowly voted to ratify the Treaty. Collins appears content, if exhausted.

deployment on peacekeeping and peace support missions that has stretched for more than six decades.

Alongside overseas deployment, the outbreak of the Troubles in Northern Ireland redefined the duties and priorities of the Defence Forces. Membership of the European Economic Community brought renewed focus on fisheries protection and led to the first major period of investment in the Naval Service since the 1940s, supported by European funding. For the Air Corps, the acquisition of helicopters in the 1960s and consequent development of its air ambulance service and search and rescue capabilities provided a welcome focus, as did its evolving role in maritime surveillance and patrol.

Following the turn of the century, a national defence policy was defined for the first time in the state's history with the landmark publication of a White Paper on Defence. Deployment on peacekeeping and peace enforcement missions remains at the centre of Defence Forces' operations in the twenty-first century, while serious organizational and operational challenges have emerged at home.

This book explores the history of the military forces of a small island state situated at the westernmost edge of Europe, a location of immense geopolitical importance. It offers a broad chronological overview of all elements of the Defence Forces, adopting a thematic approach to topics that thread through several of the chapters. It is also intended to be a visual history, illustrated with photographs, documents and other ephemera, accompanied by captions that provide additional detail and nuance to the narrative. Together, the text and images offer an insight into the development of the Irish Defence Forces over a century, from the crisis of the Civil War through to the complex, globalized security environment of the twenty-first century.

CHAPTER 1

1922–3

RAISING THE NATIONAL ARMY

Large crowds lined the streets of Dublin's city centre on the early afternoon of 1 February 1922, straining to catch a glimpse of the 'first regular unit of an Irish Army swing by on its way to occupy the first stronghold taken over from the British ... uniformed and fully accoutred'.[1] Down Dame Street, through College Green and on towards Haddington Road, fifty men from the Dublin Guard were cheered en route to accept the handover of Beggars Bush Barracks from the British Army. They had marched from a temporary barracks established in a vacant workhouse in Celbridge, Co. Kildare, where preparations for the takeover of Beggars Bush had not been completed until 4 a.m. that morning. Largely composed of members of the Dublin Active Service Unit and Michael Collins' 'Squad', the Dublin Guard represented the first step in the transformation of the Irish Republican Army (IRA), and the raising of the National Army of the Provisional Government of the Irish Free State. Though that process began in earnest in the days and weeks that followed the handover of Beggars Bush, it was hampered by the divisive aftereffects of the Treaty split. When Dáil Éireann ratified the Treaty on 7 January, it set in motion a chain of events that resulted in the formal establishment of the Irish Free State on 6 December 1922 – the first anniversary of the signing of the Treaty. That anniversary fell, however, amid an increasingly bitter civil war, a physical manifestation of the split in Irish society engendered by the Treaty, and fought between an evolving National Army and the anti-Treaty elements of the IRA.

'The direct and legitimate descendant of the Irish Volunteers of 1916 and the IRA of 1920'[2]

Richard Mulcahy's appointment as the Provisional Government's Minister for Defence on 10 January 1922 saw him relinquish his role as Chief of Staff of the IRA. The future of the IRA was raised in the Dáil later that day, with Éamon de Valera inferring that its loyalty to the government of a state that fell short of the ideal of an Irish republic was far from certain: 'I am anxious myself as an individual who knows the Army ... What I am anxious about is that orders given to the Army will be given in the name of the Government of the Republic; otherwise I fear there might be some trouble.' Mulcahy's response, that the Provisional Government intended to keep the IRA intact 'as the army of the Irish Republic', was to prove overly optimistic.[3]

The evacuation of British troops from Ireland began shortly after the Dáil's ratification of the Treaty, a process that incorporated the handover of military infrastructure and equipment to the Provisional Government. As many as 57,000 British troops had been stationed in Ireland at the end of 1921; apart from those that remained in the Treaty Ports of Queenstown (Cobh), Berehaven and Lough Swilly, the last British troops departed the Free State in December 1922. Beggars Bush was not the first; barracks were surrendered to local IRA units in Clogheen, Co. Tipperary, on 25 January, quickly followed by Michelstown (26 January), Bandon (27 January), and Cahir (30 January).

Assuming control of former British barracks presented an enormous logistical challenge, with the task made even more difficult by the uncertain loyalties of so many IRA units, especially in the south and west. Tense confrontations ensued at several locations when National Army troops were

The pro-Treaty members of the 2nd Dáil. Seated in the front row (*left to right*), Patrick Hogan, Eoin Mac Neill, Fionán Lynch, Michael Collins, Arthur Griffith, W.T. Cosgrave, Kevin O'Higgins, Eamon Duggan, and Desmond FitzGerald. Ernest Blythe is standing directly behind FitzGerald.

prevented from entering barracks by IRA units and commanders with anti-Treaty sympathies. Ensuring that arms and equipment were transferred directly to the Provisional Government required close liaison with departing British forces.

Two key dates in February 1922 may be taken as the foundation stones of what would become the Irish Defence Forces. As well as marking the first appearance of soldiers in uniform, 1 February was also the date from which public funds were first made available for the National Army. The first recorded date of payment for troops was 4 February 1922. Pay records provide a useful method of tracking development, and demonstrate that recruitment was frequently haphazard for the next eight months, a situation exacerbated by the outbreak of the Civil War. Periods of enlistment were often not defined for these first recruits. The split within the ranks of the IRA also dictated a cautious approach, with enlistment in some areas initially restricted to members of Active Service Units recommended by their commanding officers. The reliability of such recruits proved vital early on;

Col Jeremiah 'Ginger' O'Connell, appointed General Officer Commanding (GOC) of the Curragh Camp in 1922, later claimed that the recruits of February, March and April 1922 were 'the only dependable instrument the government possessed'.[4]

The creation of a National Army presented any number of logistical challenges, not least of which was the requirement to transform the pro-Treaty IRA from a force of semi-autonomous units accustomed to guerrilla-style operations into a disciplined whole. Administrative structures suitable for a professional army, centrally controlled by a general headquarters and regional command staffs, were virtually non-existent. The initial formation of the National Army was thus a haphazard affair, built on the pre-existing, localized structures of the IRA but conducted at a time when fractures in that organization inhibited recruitment and organizational reform. Command structures remained in flux for much of 1922.

The scale of opposition to the Treaty within the IRA ensured that the task of creating an army loyal to the Provisional Government would be far from easy. Edited by Piaras Béaslaí, *An tÓglách* aligned with the pro-Treaty side and evolved into the National Army's newspaper; a week after the Dáil's ratification of the Treaty it urged its readership to maintain their discipline:

> The situation as far as the Army is concerned remains unchanged … The Army will remain in command of the same officers as heretofore and any attempt to impair its discipline and solidarity by introducing political controversies into its work will be sternly resisted … The country is at the present time … in a chaotic state, exposed to danger from foreign and domestic enemies of peace and its great hope in this moment of need is the splendid discipline and ordered organization which has characterized the Irish Volunteers. The British forces are preparing to evacuate Ireland; the duty of securing public order and public safety will rest on the Irish Army and all its units must co-operate loyally in this work.[5]

That editorial was drafted in response to clear signs of dissent within the ranks of the IRA. On 12 January Mulcahy had received a letter from senior IRA officers, including Liam Mellows (GHQ), Rory O'Connor (Director of Engineering) and Oscar Traynor (OC Dublin Brigade). Mulcahy was urged

Barely visible in the centre of the photograph, but distinguishable as one of the few hatless men in the huge crowd and with a path to the car before him, Michael Collins makes his way from the Mansion House to a waiting car. It is possible that this photo was taken on 16 January 1922, as Collins and the other members of the Provisional Government departed for the ceremonial handover of Dublin Castle from the British administration.

to call an IRA convention, similar to previous Volunteer conventions held between 1913 and 1917, for the purpose of electing an executive that would exercise 'supreme control' of the Army.[6] The complete list of signatories to the letter brought home the uncomfortable reality that opposition to the Treaty was the prevailing sentiment within the rank and file of the IRA, as well as among some of its most experienced and well-regarded officers. Yet despite these defections, the majority of the IRA's senior staff accepted the Treaty and would go on to join the National Army's General Staff, including Michael Collins, Richard Mulcahy, Seán Mac Mahon and Gearóid O'Sullivan.

Mulcahy's initial discussions with the discontented officers suggested he was amenable to a convention, subject to certain conditions, and up to late February the proposal had the tacit agreement of the government. That

23

The first unit to wear the uniform of the National Army, known as the Dublin Guard, marched through Dublin on 1 February 1922 to take possession of Beggars Bush Barracks from the British Army. This photograph of the unit was taken in the barracks on 4 February 1922.

agreement was withdrawn in early March, however, and the government banned the convention.

Disaffected IRA officers nonetheless convened in Dublin's Mansion House on 26 March. Delegates from 52 of the IRA's 73 brigades attended, and voted to repudiate both the Treaty and the Provisional Government. Two weeks later, on 9 April, the convention elected an army executive with Liam Lynch as Chief of Staff. The split among the IRA had been formalized, and the distinction between the National Army and the anti-Treaty IRA had hardened – the latter would typically from that point be referred to as Irregulars. *An tÓglách* labelled the convention 'an act of military despotism. Its promoters have acted as the masters, and not the servants, of the Irish Nation.'[7]

Anti-Treaty soldiers occupied several buildings in Dublin city centre on 13 April, including the Four Courts, setting the stage for what seemed an increasingly inevitable clash between the National Army and anti-Treaty IRA. After several weeks of escalating disorder, culminating in the assassination of Sir Henry Wilson in London on 22 June and the kidnap of 'Ginger' O'Connell by the anti-Treaty Four Courts garrison, the Provisional Government took the decision to shell the Four Courts. The decision was not taken lightly, and was a result not just of increasing lawlessness in the city, but also of

FEBRUARY· 4ᵀᴴ 1922·

immense pressure from the British government. In fact, the British had gone as far as issuing instructions in early April to the commander of the British forces in Ireland, General Cecil Macready, to prepare for a possible military intervention, including the unilateral declaration of martial law in Dublin.

On the morning of 28 June the National Army began shelling the Four Courts garrison with 18-pdr field guns. In a major boost for the Provisional Government, control of Dublin was established by 5 July, after several days of intense fighting in the city centre. The following day the Provisional Government issued a 'national call to arms', appealing for new recruits to the Army. Crowds of young men eager to sign up were reported at each of the Dublin recruiting stations over the following days: 'Dublin's answer to the Government's call to arms has been magnificent. It was much greater and more spontaneous than could have been expected'.[8]

Clothing and equipping the new recruits created more logistical problems, including procurement of sufficient numbers of uniforms. Manufacturing the uniform in large numbers had proven difficult even before the Civil War, and indeed from an early stage the Department of Defence drew criticism for contemplating tenders for military clothing from British companies. Challenged in the Dáil about the provenance of the Army's uniforms, Mulcahy argued that the majority still came from Irish business: ' ... of all the uniforms used in the Army, 85% are of Irish manufacture, and I can assure the Dáil that everything is done to give our work to Irish manufacturers.'[9]

25

Though Mulcahy acknowledged that an order had been placed in England by Briscoe Importing, a Dublin-based firm, he did not reveal that it was for as many as 10,000 uniforms and greatcoats.

Fashioning a 'fabric of organization'

Throughout the summer of 1922, Collins and his headquarters staff issued a series of general orders, intended to provide structure and stability to the National Army. There was little scope for sweeping changes to the existing military infrastructure. General Order No. 1, issued on 5 July, created three district commands: Eastern, Western and Southern. There was otherwise neither the time nor supporting administrative framework available to attempt any kind of restructuring of the forces. General Order No. 5, also issued in July, declared that it was of 'utmost importance that the Old Company Battalion, etc., organization should be clearly retained'.[10]

Following the success of the national call the Provisional Government approved an Army establishment of 35,000: 15,000 regular troops and 20,000 reserves. Enlistment escalated rapidly through July, and on 5 August Collins was able to inform the government that the Army's strength stood at just under 15,000 regulars and 15,700 reserves. Recruitment levels in the summer of 1922 were all the more notable for the fact that the Army had no 'fabric of organization' in – and was therefore unable to recruit from – large parts of the country, including most of Munster, as well as Sligo, Mayo, Leitrim, Louth, Offaly, and south Wexford.[11]

Collins based his report on information received from Mulcahy, who had added the caveat that the figures were imprecise. Mulcahy instanced a report he had received from Maj Gen Seán Mac Eoin, GOC of Western Command, who admitted that he was uncertain as to the whereabouts of as many as 1,000 men under his command. Efficient administration of an Army whose exact numbers and distributions were unknown was next to impossible.

On 12 July 1922 GHQ issued instructions dividing the country into five military commands: Western (Maj Gen Seán Mac Eoin), South Western (Gen Eoin O'Duffy), Eastern (Maj Gen Emmet Dalton), South Eastern (Comdt Gen John Prout), and Curragh Command (Lt Gen J.J. O'Connell). On the same day the cabinet authorized the establishment of a War Council,

National Army recruits receiving their uniforms at Beggars Bush Barracks in early 1922.

consisting of Michael Collins (appointed as Commander in Chief of the Army), Gen Richard Mulcahy (Chief of Staff and Minister for Defence), and Gen Eoin O'Duffy. The War Council's powers were never clearly defined, and O'Duffy's immediate departure for South Western Command ensured that the council never properly functioned before Collins' death on 22 August.

Collins died at Béal na Bláth during an ambush by anti-Treaty troops, less than two weeks after the death of the Provisional Government's chairman, Arthur Griffith. With William T. Cosgrave taking up the mantle of leader of the government, the cabinet appointed a new Army Council, notice of which was formally promulgated on 28 September. The new council included Mulcahy, who replaced Collins as Commander in Chief while retaining his ministerial portfolio, along with Gen Seán Mac Mahon (appointed as Chief of Staff), Maj Gen Joseph McGrath (Director of Intelligence), Comdt Gen Diarmuid O'Hegarty (Director of Organization), and Lt Gen Gearóid O'Sullivan

Members of the Dublin Guard in Portobello Barracks on the day of its handover by the British Army, 17 May 1922. The men are holding a tricolour embroidered with the names of nine men killed during the War of Independence; the flag was known as the Banner of the Patriots and is now on display in Kilmainham Gaol Museum.

(Adjutant General).[12] By the end of the year, however, the directorships of intelligence and organization had been abolished, and the Council – whose powers were also never formally defined by government – consisted of Mulcahy and Mac Mahon. Seán Ó Muirthuille joined following his appointment as Quartermaster General in January 1923.

'The Finance Department of the Army itself should hold a strong position'

Alongside its efforts to construct a fighting force in the first half of 1922 and to establish a viable command structure once the Civil War began, the National Army also faced the task of standardizing its administrative processes. Efficient administration was hampered rather than helped by the prior existence of the IRA, on which the National Army initially based its organization, but which had (for obvious reasons) little in the way of a centralized bureaucracy. The civil branch of the Department of Defence was slowly established during the war, with two distinct offices and staffs: Secretary and Army Finance Officer.

Mulcahy had established ministerial offices at Portobello Barracks, alongside GHQ, and was joined there by Cornelius O'Connor, a civil servant in the Department of Labour seconded to the Department of Defence on 4 August 1922. Educated in Dublin, O'Connor had joined the civil service in 1902, later serving with distinction as an infantry officer with the British Army during the First World War. Formally appointed Secretary of the Department of Defence in June 1923 on Mulcahy's recommendation, O'Connor had already played an integral role in building the administrative structures of the department.

O'Connor worked alongside Thomas Gorman, who in late May 1922 had been appointed Accountant General (a title soon changed to Army Finance Officer), the first step in standardizing procedures for pay, procurement and day to day accounting. Concerned at the latitude granted to Mulcahy in terms of expending the National Army's budget, the Department of Finance had welcomed Gorman's appointment:

We contemplate that in the near future Army expenditure, like all other public expenditure, will require to be supported by written authority from the Minister of Finance ... But until very effective control is applied by the Minister of Finance, it seems specially necessary that the Finance Department of the Army itself should hold a strong position ... The appointment of the Accountant General is a necessary administrative improvement, due largely to the growth of the Army, and his introduction cannot in the least be regarded as a reflection on any of the existing military staff. At the present time the Army is getting funds from the Exchequer (£550,000 to date) which are being expended apparently according to the discretion of the Minister of Defence.[13]

Burned out houses on Antigua Street, Belfast, pictured on 17 April 1922 and destroyed during a sustained period of sectarian violence and murder in the city. Sectarian tensions had been escalating since the expulsion of Catholic workers from shipyards and docks in 1920, and the scale of murder and intimidation in the early months of 1922 prompted hundreds of Catholics to flee south of the new border. Efforts to mount a joint offensive in Northern Ireland, combining both pro- and anti-Treaty units, were unsuccessful.

Gorman formally assumed the role of Army Finance Officer on 1 August 1922. The scale of the challenge facing both Gorman and O'Connor was readily apparent, and the handover of accounting duties from the Quartermaster General's department to Gorman's office was not without its hitches, particularly in relation to oversight of Army pay. The office previously responsible for pay, the Army Pay Corps, had been overwhelmed from July 1922 as recruits poured in, often with little or no enlistment documentation. In September 1922 the paymaster at Wellington Barracks (later renamed Griffith Barracks) told Gorman's office that he had great difficulty regarding arrears of payment, and was forced to issue pay based on the word of individual soldiers as to the date of their last payment. Frustrated at the widespread inability of (and occasional refusal by) pay officers to adopt the procedures he had mandated, Gorman voiced his concerns to Mulcahy: 'The attached report from Mr O'Sullivan illustrates the somewhat hopeless position of affairs in so far as control of Army funds by this office is concerned.'[14] Though progress was gradual, Gorman's office exerted increasing levels of control as the war progressed. The Army Census, carried out on 12 and 13 November, was a vital step in regularizing Army establishments, supplies and pay roll, as it allowed GHQ to take stock of the Army's strength and establish its precise disposition around the country.

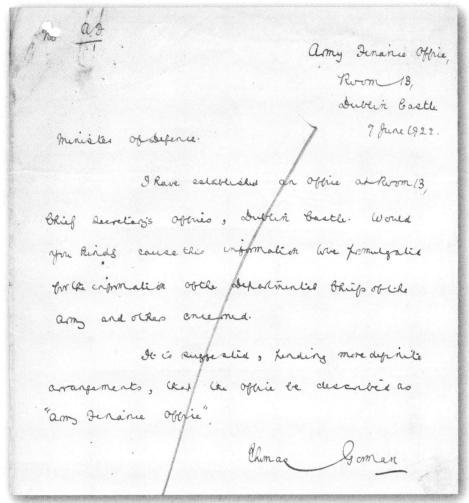

Army Finance Memo No. 1, dated 7 June 1922, from newly appointed Army Finance Officer, Thomas Gorman, to the Minister for Defence.

LONDON & NORTH WESTERN RAILWAY

HOLYHEAD, KINGSTOWN & DUBLIN EXPRESS STEAMERS.
ROYAL MAIL ROUTE.
S.S.

Recd 122
27/7/1922
@ 2.30 P.M.

WESTPORT.

To. M.D.

25/7/22.
19

The troops under Col. Comd't O'Malley left Wellington at 3.30 P.M. on Sat 22nd

Arrived at North Wall at 4.30 P.M. We here encountered some delay in getting the "Whippet" aboard as the 100 ton Crane was out of order.

At 8 P.M. we left North Wall. After an uneventful voyage we arrived at WEST PORT BAY at 2.A.M on Monday 24th. We immediately signalled for pilot. Pilot arrived at 4. A.M He stated it was imposible to proceed further as vessel was 100 ft too long.

We then tried to get in touch with Portobello. [By wireless] We failed to do this up to 12 noon (monday). Another pilot came aboard at 5 A.M. He also stated vessel was too long. On account of this we missed the morning tide.

At 4 P.M (Monday) a British destroyer answered our wireless message. At 4.15 P.M. a food ship SS. 'ADMIRAL' was bound for WESTPORT QUAY was ordered by Col Comd't. O'Malley to come alongside. She did so. We then tried to get the "whippet" aboard her. We intended if successful in this to land our men, under cover from ear in small boats. However we failed to get the whippet transferred so things remained at a standstill. (over)

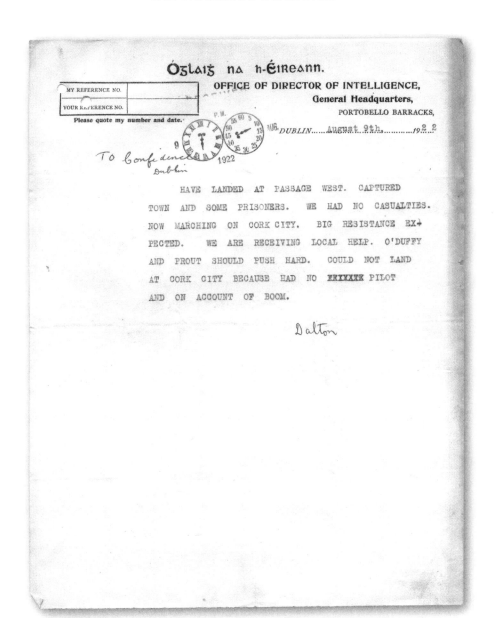

Opposite page: First page of a report from Col Comdt O'Malley to Gen Richard Mulcahy, dated 25 July 1922, on the successful landing of National Army troops at Westport. This was the first seaborne operation undertaken by the National Army, soon followed by landings at Fenit, Co. Kerry, and Passage West, Co. Cork. **Above:** Telegram of 9 August 1922 from Maj Gen Emmet Dalton, informing GHQ that National Army troops had abandoned attempts to land at Cork city but had successfully disembarked at Passage West, and were marching on Cork city.

'The Staters were not expected so soon and there was a panic'[16]

Under the terms of the Treaty, the Provisional Government were permitted to maintain 'such vessels as are necessary for the protection of the revenue or the fisheries.' Early consideration of the establishment of a naval service was evident when the Provisional Government sanctioned the purchase, in May 1922, of four ex-Royal Navy motor launches (designated ML–1 to ML–4) equipped with Lewis machine guns. The motor launches, however, got off to an inauspicious start. While journeying in convoy from England they were separated in heavy seas, with ML–2 sinking en route while ML–4 was diverted to Southampton after suffering heavy damage.

ML–1 and ML–3 required extensive overhaul but were finally ready to enter service at the end of September. Maj Gen Joseph Vize, an experienced mariner and later appointed GOC of the Coastal and Marine Service, appears to have been given some form of responsibility for the motor launches: 'Vize has been foustering about [them] for weeks … The crews should be fixed up and rates of wages suggested for them, and authority got, and they should be sent to the Limerick command, where they have been pressing for them for some time.'[17] The problem of insuring the launches further delayed their use until 30 October, when they were sent to Kerry, and ML–4 finally arrived from Southampton on 10 November. Once operational the launches were quickly found to be unsuitable for general coastal patrol and largely confined to working in harbours, estuaries and rivers.

By that stage of the war, seaborne operations had already played a crucial role in establishing the National Army along the south and west coasts. Following a successful if protracted battle for Limerick in July, Maj Gen Emmet Dalton urged the use of seaborne operations to attack remaining anti-Treaty strongholds on the south and west coasts. Though Dalton's plans met with some resistance, GHQ recognized the potential to avoid difficult advances over land, through territory controlled by anti-Treaty forces.

Under the command of Col Comdt O'Malley, 400 troops accompanied by a Rolls Royce 'Whippet' armoured car and 18-pdr field gun sailed for Westport aboard the *Minerva* and landed on 24 July, meeting little resistance. One week later a similarly sized and equipped force boarded the *Lady Wicklow* in Dublin, en route for Fenit, Co. Kerry. On 8 August the largest operation of this type saw more than 800 troops, aboard four ships, land in Cork with the main concentration at Passage West. Three days later Cork city was fully under National Army control, with the anti-Treaty garrison electing to burn the barracks and retreat into the countryside rather than mount a defence of the city.

Though the landings at Westport, Fenit and in Cork were daring and important elements of the National Army's strategy during the summer of 1922, their success relied on more than a little luck. Planning and intelligence in each location focused on the strengths of the anti-Treaty garrisons and paid little attention to logistics. As a result, the ship used to transport troops to Westport was 100 feet too long for the harbour's pier, causing confusion and a delay of several hours before the troops and equipment could disembark. Here, as would be the case for later seaborne operations, anti-Treaty forces failed to take advantage of these poor preparations, overlooking several opportunities to stop the landings.

Transportation of troops was usually achieved by cargo ships and cross-channel ferries commandeered for the purpose. In addition to *Minerva* and *Lady Wicklow*, troops were also transported on *Alexandra*, the Commissioners of Irish Lights' tender. Infamous for its use by the British to shell Dublin during the 1916 Rising, HMS *Helga* was also pressed into service as a troop transport.

Despite their evident utility in allowing National Army troops to rapidly deploy to the west coast, and importance in driving anti-Treaty forces from Cork city, the seaborne operations of summer 1922 were dismissed as incidental to the National Army's early successes. Recalling the progress of the war in 1924, Seán Mac Mahon (QMG in summer 1922) merely mentioned them in passing: 'Early in August ... small expeditions were despatched from Dublin by sea and landed at different points in Cork as also did a small force land at Fenit.'[18] Yet the landings on the west and south coasts in July and August allowed the National Army to build pressure on anti-Treaty forces, and their proven potential to surprise anti-Treaty garrisons almost certainly caused some to withdraw from some coastal positions that were never actually threatened. James Moore, lightkeeper at Dungarvan Lighthouse, reported in August 1922 that anti-Treaty troops had been camped around the lighthouse for several days, 'watching Free State troops to come by sea and have Helvick Pier heavily mined. After they burned [the] Coast Guard Station they left this locality and I have not seen them since.'[19]

Coastal patrols, mounted with commandeered commercial vessels, occasionally with discreet assistance from the Royal Navy, further disrupted

MINISTRY FOR DEFENCE

"Civil Aviation Dept."

Minutes

Minutes of a Meeting of Members of the Government, Members of the
General Staff, and Officers from the Military Aviation Department,
held at Beggar's Bush Barracks, Thursday, 23rd March, 1922.

The following were present at the Meeting :-

    Mr. R. Mulcahy, T. D., Minister for Defence. -- Chairman --

    Mr. M. Collins, T. D., Minister for Finance.

    General O'Duffy, T. D., Chief of the General Staff.

    Lieut. General J. O'Connell, Assistant Chief of Staff.

    Major General J. E. Dalton, Director of Training.

    Commdt. General W. J. Mc Sweeney, Director of Military
       Aviation.

    Mr. C. F, Russell, Director of Civil Aviation and Secretary
       to the Air Council.

    (Mr. Russell acted as Secretary to the Meeting.)

The Agenda for the Meeting was as follows:-

(1) "Recommendations made by Sub-Committee with regard to Schemes 1.
and 2. for the control of Aeronautical matters in general."

The Meeting having considered both Schemes in detail, adopted the
recommendations made by the Sub-Committee, which were as follows:-

    (1) That Aviation be divided into two sections, namely, Military
        and Civil.

    (2) That Officers be appointed to direct the two branches. -
        The Military Director being responsible to the General
        Headquarters Staff - The Civil Director being respons-
        ible to an Air Council.

    (3) That the Air Council be constituted as follows:-

        Minister for Defence.
        Minister for Finance.
        Minister for Trade.
        Chief of the General Staff.
        Director of Military Aviation
        Director of Civil Aviation.
        Representative from Land & Survey.

anti-Treaty plans and movements. By February 1923 GHQ was sufficiently convinced of the value of naval capabilities to authorize the formation of the short lived Coastal and Marine Service.

'The military air authorities should aim at the organization of one Air Squadron'[20]

While the National Army was being built from the ground up, by far the greatest amount of time, energy and resources were devoted to the Infantry Corps. Aviation, both military and civil, was still in its infancy, though the utility of aircraft in wartime had become apparent during the First World War.

The Army Air Service (renamed the Air Corps in 1924) was formally established in March 1922, but traces its history to October 1921, when its first two aircraft were purchased in England. Those machines, a decommissioned Martinsyde Type A Mk II and an Avro 504K, were evaluated in England and their purchase recommended by Charles F. Russell and William 'Jack' McSweeney.

Opposite page: Minutes of a meeting, held on 23 March 1922, of members of the Provisional Government, the National Army's General Staff and the Aviation Department, at which Comdt Gen William J. McSweeney was appointed Director of Military Aviation, with Charles F. Russell appointed Director of Civil Aviation. This meeting is regarded as the foundation date of the Army Air Service, reorganised and renamed as the Air Corps in July 1924. **Below:** The Martinsyde Type A, Mk II, purchased in late 1921 and shipped to Ireland in crates in June 1922. Named 'The Big Fella', it became the first aircraft to fly with the Army Air Service. It was renamed 'City of Dublin' before being retired from service in the late 1920s.

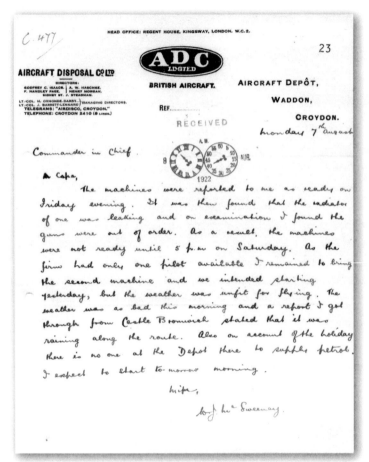

On 30 July 1922 Comdt Gen William J. McSweeney, Director of Military Aviation, travelled to London to purchase two aircraft from the Aircraft Disposal Company (ADC Ltd). In this letter, dated 7 August, McSweeney informs Michael Collins that he and one of the pilots attached to ADC Ltd would fly the aircraft to Ireland the following day. McSweeney had purchased a Martinsyde F4 (Buzzard) and an SE 5A. ADC Ltd supplied the Air Corps with several aircraft during the 1920s.

Russell and McSweeney were the perfect candidates to supervise the nascent development of aviation in Ireland. Both were former RAF pilots who later joined the Dublin Brigade of the IRA during the War of Independence. A kind of mythology has grown around the rationale behind the acquisition of the Martinsyde and Avro, that the Martinsyde in particular was purchased solely to provide a potential escape route for the Irish plenipotentiaries should the Treaty negotiations in London break down. Its potential use in bombing British positions and forces should negotiations break down and hostilities resume also appears to have been considered.

On 23 March 1922 Russell and Sweeney were appointed as Directors of Civil and Military Aviation, respectively. The Air Service's first plane arrived

Sir John Lavery's *Blessing of the Colours*, painted in 1922, depicts the Archbishop of Dublin blessing the National Colours, held by a National Army soldier who kneels with his head bowed, symbolising allegiance both to the new state and to the Catholic Church.

Between 4 and 10 May 1922 eleven meetings were held between representatives of the National Army and the Army Council of the anti-Treaty IRA. These meetings were among the last concerted efforts to heal the split in the IRA and avoid civil war. Pictured here in a relaxed moment prior to discussions are (*left to right*) Seán Mac Eoin, Seán Moylan, Eoin O'Duffy, Liam Lynch, Gearóid O'Sullivan and Liam Mellows. British Pathé newsreel footage of this meeting exists, with the title card: 'First rays of hope – Army chiefs agree to a truce'.

in June 1922 when the Martinsyde, which had remained in England, was shipped to Ireland in crates and reassembled at Baldonnel. Over the next year the Air Service obtained eight Bristol F2B fighters, six Avro 504Ks, six Airco DH9s, four Martinsyde F4 Buzzards and an SE 5A, either from the departing Irish Flight of the Royal Air Force or from the Aircraft Disposal Company, a British firm that sold surplus aircraft.

Though anti-Treaty forces had no aerial capability, leaving the skies uncontested, the potential for the Air Service to make a material difference to the war was never fully realized. But speedy communications were facilitated, while aerial reconnaissance supplemented troop movements and the retaking of strategically important towns, including Cork; a reconnaissance mission

Ðáil éireann.

| aireaċt cosanta | Department of Defence |

Ar fhreagairt duit luaidh
Tagra Uimh. A. 3790.

25th., May, 1922.

TO;

Commdt. Liam Lynch.

A Chara,

DEFENCE COUNCIL.

RETREATS, ETC., FOR SOLDIERS.

I would like to take early action in this matter along such lines as, perhaps, the following:-

1. To arrange a week-end Retreat for Officers at Rathfarnham Castle on two succeeding week-ends, so as to give two re-lays of Officers a chance of attending.

2. Then, a week or so later a weeks Retreat for the men of Wellington Barracks, to be held either in Wellington Barracks or possibly in St Kevin's Church – preferably in the Barracks. It would consist of Mass and lecture in the morning and evening devotions and sermon in the evening. The 4th. Battalion Companies, both G.H.Q. and Executive might possibly be associated with the Wellington Barracks men for this Retreat.

3. On the following week a similiar Retreat for the Portobello men, to be held either in Portobello Barracks or in Rathmines Church, and if possible the 3rd. Battalion Volunteers, both G.H.Q. and Executive to be associated in the matter.

Beir Beannacht,

AIRE CHOSANTA.

Letter from Richard Mulcahy, Minister for Defence, to Liam Lynch, Chief of Staff of the anti-Treaty IRA, 25 May 1922. Despite the failure of talks aimed at healing the divide within the IRA, and the ongoing occupation of several buildings in Dublin's city centre by the anti-Treaty IRA, efforts to reconcile both sides continued. In this letter, one of a number exchanged between the two men, Mulcahy informs Lynch of his plans to hold a series of religious retreats for men and officers of the Army.

Comdt Gen William J. McSweeney (*left*) was appointed as the first Director of Military Aviation, with Col Comdt Charles F. Russell (*right*) appointed as Director of Civil Aviation. Both men were former RAF pilots who joined the IRA during the War of Independence, and both served as OC of the Air Corps during the 1920s.

National Army troops operating an 18-pdr field gun during the shelling of the Four Courts in late June 1922. Two 18-pdr guns were placed on the southside of the River Liffey, opposite the Four Courts, at the junctions of Winetavern Street and Bridge Street. The shelling of the Four Courts, which began early on the morning of 28 June, marked the formal beginning of the Civil War.

flown on 10 August by Comdt Russell, accompanied by Capt Stapleton as observer, reported that the seaborne landing at Passage West had been successful, with no visible resistance met. There was no opportunity to complete one of the mission's objectives, to provide aerial machine gun fire in support of ground troops.

Basic operation bases were established at Kilkenny and Waterford in August 1922, and a detachment of Bristol Fighters deployed to Fermoy airfield, Co. Cork, in October. As the National Army established a more secure foothold in the south-west at the end of the year, the Air Service began operating from a former RAF airfield near Tralee, Co. Kerry. The SE 5A

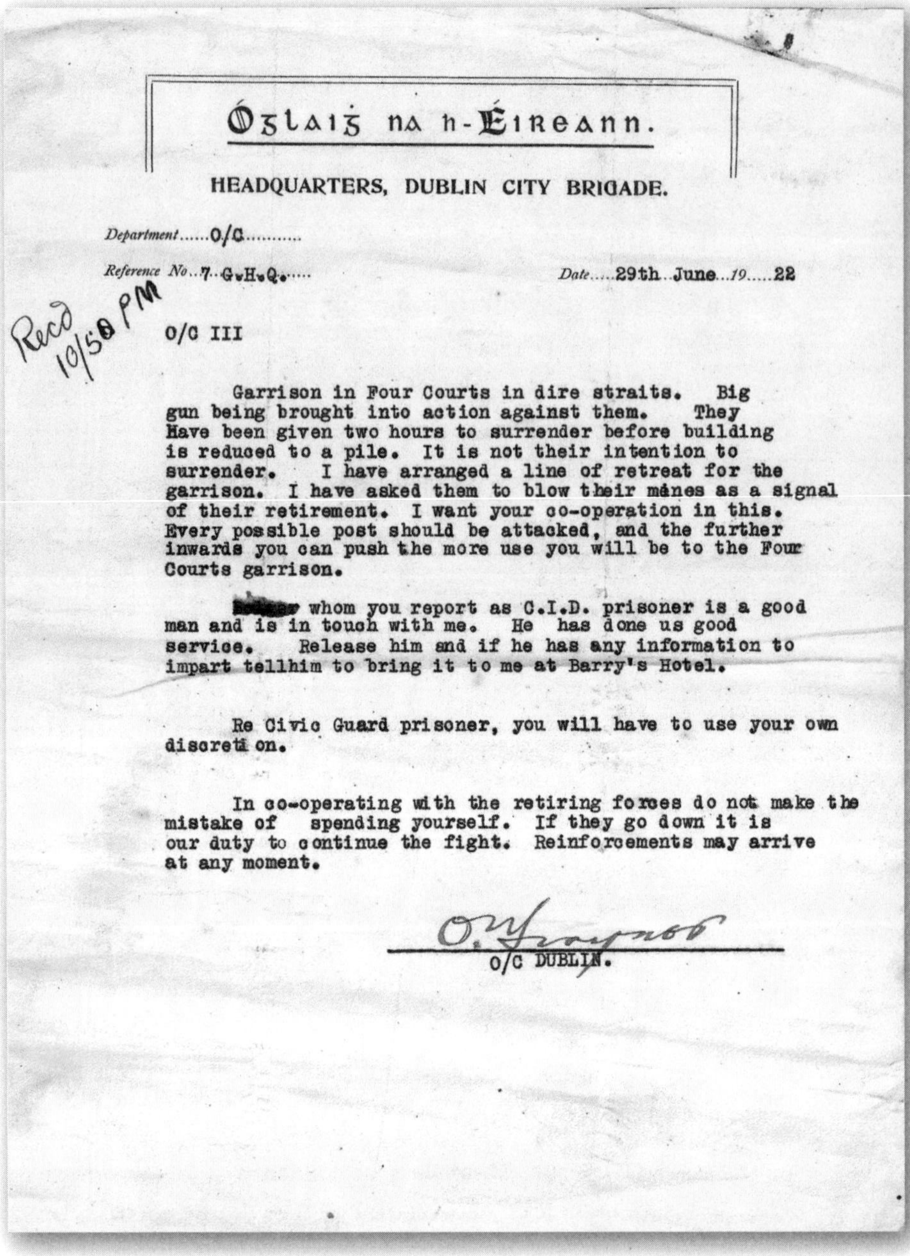

Óglaiġ na h-Éireann.

HEADQUARTERS, DUBLIN CITY BRIGADE.

Department......O/C..........

Reference No..7..G.H.Q......   Date......29th..June...19.....22

Recd 10/50 PM

O/C III

     Garrison in Four Courts in dire straits. Big gun being brought into action against them. They have been given two hours to surrender before building is reduced to a pile. It is not their intention to surrender. I have arranged a line of retreat for the garrison. I have asked them to blow their mines as a signal of their retirement. I want your co-operation in this. Every possible post should be attacked, and the further inwards you can push the more use you will be to the Four Courts garrison.

     whom you report as C.I.D. prisoner is a good man and is in touch with me. He has done us good service.   Release him and if he has any information to impart tellhim to bring it to me at Barry's Hotel.

     Re Civic Guard prisoner, you will have to use your own discretion.

     In co-operating with the retiring forces do not make the mistake of spending yourself. If they go down it is our duty to continue the fight. Reinforcements may arrive at any moment.

O/C DUBLIN.

Orders issued on 29 June 1922 by Oscar Traynor, Officer Commanding the anti-Treaty Dublin Brigade, noting that the Four Courts garrison were under heavy fire and that he had instructed them to blow their mines once they began their retreat.

was technically the only aircraft lost in combat operations during the Civil War, when in September 1922 its pilot, Lt Crosseley, was forced to land near Macroom, Co. Cork. The aircraft was subsequently burned by the IRA.

'The resulting state of discipline is not to be wondered at'[21]

Faced with the prospect of an interminable, costly and protracted war against forces well-versed in guerrilla warfare, the state implicitly condoned the use of intimidation and terror in its efforts to bring the anti-Treaty forces to surrender. The Army Emergency Resolution, presented to the Dáil on 27 September and more commonly known as the Public Safety Bill, gave extraordinary powers to the Army to allow it more effectively suppress anti-Treaty forces. Derided by Thomas Johnson, leader of the Labour Party, as akin to the establishment of a 'military dictatorship', the resolution introduced military tribunals and state-sanctioned executions to the Civil War. The reaction from the anti-Treaty side was to threaten summary reprisal executions, marking a new phase in the conflict characterized by an escalating willingness on both sides to commit atrocities.

On the National Army's side, executions of captured prisoners – some summarily shot – became a tacitly accepted tactic in the attempt to force the

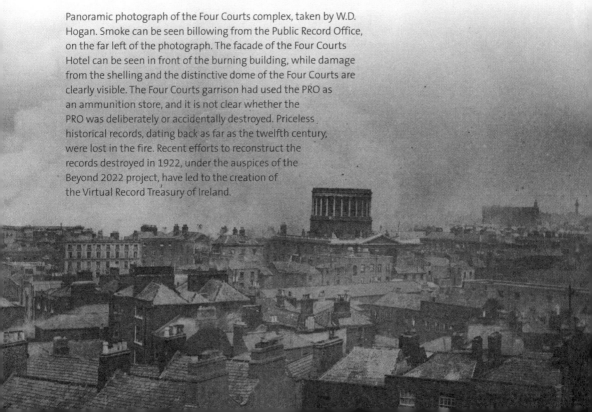

Panoramic photograph of the Four Courts complex, taken by W.D. Hogan. Smoke can be seen billowing from the Public Record Office, on the far left of the photograph. The facade of the Four Courts Hotel can be seen in front of the burning building, while damage from the shelling and the distinctive dome of the Four Courts are clearly visible. The Four Courts garrison had used the PRO as an ammunition store, and it is not clear whether the PRO was deliberately or accidentally destroyed. Priceless historical records, dating back as far as the twelfth century, were lost in the fire. Recent efforts to reconstruct the records destroyed in 1922, under the auspices of the Beyond 2022 project, have led to the creation of the Virtual Record Treasury of Ireland.

During the battle for Dublin, anti-Treaty forces occupied buildings across the city. Here a Rolls Royce armoured car is parked on O'Connell Street. Smoke billows from the building beside the Hibernian Bible Society, while the façade is riddled with bullet holes from the intense fighting. A man in what appears to be a National Army uniform strolls away calmly. The National Army acquired fourteen Rolls Royce armoured cars (1920 pattern, also known as 'Whippets') from the British Army between the beginning of 1922 and August 1923.

surrender of the anti-Treaty forces. Beatings and the torture of anti-Treaty prisoners were also prevalent, with Portobello Barracks, Wellington Barracks and the Curragh Camp gaining particular notoriety. Executions carried out on 8 December 1922, as a retaliation to the murder of Seán Hales, TD, the previous day, prompted widespread shock. Reacting to the executions of Joseph O'Connor, Liam Mellows, Joseph McKelvey and Richard Barrett at Kilmainham Gaol, Labour Party leader Johnston told the government that 'I am almost forced to say you have killed the new State at its birth'.[22]

January 1923 saw the first large-scale, centrally co-ordinated reorganization of the National Army, based in part on a scheme drafted by Maj Gen Emmet Dalton and given effect by a series of General Routine Orders. The country was divided into nine regional commands: Dublin, Waterford, Cork, Kerry, Limerick, Claremorris, Donegal, Athlone and the Curragh. General Routine Order No. 16, dated 24 January 1923, rearranged the Army's infantry into 58 battalions, while a further three garrison and seven reserve battalions were stationed at the Curragh. Only 3 Infantry Battalion of the current Defence Forces can trace its origins directly to January 1923.

Following his assumption of the role of Commander in Chief alongside his brief as Minister for Defence, Richard Mulcahy's relationship with several of his cabinet colleagues deteriorated. Kevin O'Higgins, Minister for Home Affairs, emerged as a particularly vocal critic of Mulcahy's tendency to secrecy regarding the Army. O'Higgins was not alone in his belief that the Army was operating without sufficient oversight from the government, an impression bolstered by resistance within GHQ, led by Chief of Staff Seán Mac Mahon, to deeper integration with the fledgling Department of Defence.

Matters came to a head at a meeting of the Executive Council (the name given to the cabinet of the Irish Free State) on 27 March 1923, at which the National Army's conduct and Mulcahy's reluctance to share detailed reports on its activities came in for sustained criticism. In response Mulcahy tendered the resignation of the entire Army Council: 'The Executive Council must take the opportunity at once to secure the control over the Army they allege they are deprived of'.[23] With the Civil War yet to be concluded and the need for stability within the Army as great as ever, the Executive Council backed down, rejecting the resignation in favour of establishing a Council of Defence.

The confrontation came at the end of a particularly grim month, characterised by murders, ambushes and outrages. Maintaining and enforcing discipline within the National Army had been a challenge throughout the war. There was little opportunity to train recruits or IRA veterans, and minor mutinies were frequent. Maj Gen Seán Mac Eoin, GOC of Western Command, wrote to Mulcahy in early September, informing him that there was 'serious trouble with some of the men – in fact mutiny in some cases for want of pay. Owing to this mutinous spirit Dromahaire has been lost this morning, as far as I can see handed over to the enemy ... Do something about pay for Regulars at once.'[24]

Mac Eoin's report was followed two weeks later by a similar missive from Maj Emmet Dalton, GOC of Southern Command, following the shooting dead of an anti-Treaty prisoner by former members of Collins' 'Squad'. The

A Peerless armoured car (1919 pattern) being unloaded from the *Arvonia* at Passage West, Co. Cork, 8 August 1922. Due to its weight, the unloading had to be postponed until the tide had gone out, lowering the *Arvonia* and allowing the car to be pulled onto the dock. The insignia of the National Army is visible on the turret. Seven Peerless armoured cars were acquired by the National Army from the British in 1922 and 1923, and were equipped with two Hotchkiss .303 inch machine guns, housed in separate turrets. The Peerless cars remained in service until 1932.

killing was carried out in response to an ambush at Rathmore, Co. Kerry, in which seven National Army troops died:

> Now I personally approve of the action but the men I have in my command are of such a temperament that they can look at seven of their companions being blown to atoms by a murderous trick without feeling annoyed – but when an enemy is found with a rifle and ammo they will mutiny if he be shot. On this account I think it would be better if you kept the Squad out of my area.[25]

There were other serious incidents involving officers and soldiers engaged in reprisals, the violent intimidation of civilians, sexual assault of women and murder. Several of the worst atrocities of the conflict took place during March 1923 in Co. Kerry, where Gen Paddy O'Daly was General Officer Commanding. When five National Army soldiers died in a trap mine explosion at Knocknagoshel on 6 March, their colleagues responded in kind. Seventeen anti-Treaty IRA prisoners were murdered in gruesome fashion over the following days, at Ballyseedy, Killarney and Bahaghs. On each occasion the prisoners were incapacitated around a mine, which was then detonated.

Violence against women, very often sexual in nature, is one of the more prominent characteristics of the dark underbelly of armed conflicts. Aided by the ongoing release of witness statements and other material relating to those who participated in, or were affected by, the revolutionary conflicts, recent research has revealed incidents of sexual and gender-based violence that accompanied the revolution, committed by British forces and later both by the National Army and the anti-Treaty IRA.

The Peerless armoured car unloaded from the *Arvonia* is here pictured in action in Passage West, Co. Cork. A National Army soldier is crouching in front of the car holding a revolver, while behind him several of his fellow soldiers peer around the corner of Fitzgerald's general store in the direction of anti-Treaty troops. The photograph was taken by W.D. Hogan and appeared in the *Sunday Independent* on 13 August 1922.

Michael Collins (*left*), Commander in Chief, and Richard Mulcahy, Minister for Defence, lead the National Army's General Staff through the streets of Dublin in the funeral procession of Arthur Griffith, 16 August 1922. Collins was killed at Béal na Bláth less than a week later.

Two of the most notorious instances of sexual violence committed by National Army personnel involved officers and occurred in May and June 1923, after the Civil War had ended. On 27 May 1923, Margaret Doherty of Foxford, Co. Mayo, was assaulted and raped in her home by three National Army officers. The following month three other officers, including Paddy O'Daly, assaulted Flossie and Jessie McCarthy in Kenmare, beating them with belts and smearing their faces and hair with dirty grease.

In many instances, ensuing disciplinary action was perfunctory. The officers accused of raping Doherty faced a general court martial in July 1923 and were given an 'honourable acquittal'. The victim's fate was much

National Army officers, some of whom are visibly emotional, salute at the grave of Michael Collins during his burial on 28 August 1922. A gravedigger stands in the foreground of the picture, while the chief mourners are behind the officers.

starker; she died on 28 December 1928, having spent the intervening years in Castlebar Mental Hospital. A military court of inquiry, presided over by John Hearne, recommended proceedings be brought against the officers accused of assaulting the McCarthys, as did Cahir Davitt, the National Army's Judge Advocate General:

> The whole affair is horrible and distressing, but a straight and courageous course is bound to be the best in the long run for all concerned. If 'irregularism' within the Army itself is not checked at once, it is good bye to any hope of ever making anything out of the Army.[26]

Those recommendations were ignored both by Mulcahy and the Executive Council. The actions of O'Daly and the men under his command were not

Seán Mac Mahon, Richard Mulcahy, Diarmuid O'Hegarty, Michael Brennan and Seán Ó Muirthuille, pictured at what is likely the handover of Parkgate Barracks on 17 December 1922. Mac Mahon was appointed Chief of Staff in August 1922 following Michael Collins' death, with Mulcahy appointed Commander in Chief in addition to his duties as Minister for Defence. O'Hegarty was Director of Organisation in the National Army from July to December 1922, and Director of Intelligence from December 1922 to May 1923 before leaving the Army. Michael Brennan later served as Chief of Staff (1931–40), while Seán Ó Muirthuille was appointed Quartermaster General in January 1923. Both Mac Mahon and Ó Muirthuille were dismissed from their posts during the crisis provoked by the Army Mutiny of March 1924.

unique, though among the worst examples. Few faced serious repercussions, and Mulcahy's instinct to protect the National Army's reputation had the opposite effect and undermined his own standing with some of his colleagues in government, a major factor in his sudden fall from grace in March 1924.

Davitt, who was appointed Judge Advocate General in August 1922 and was the main architect of the National Army's code of discipline, later outlined what he believed to be the root of ill-discipline during the Civil War:

> When it is recollected that recruiting for the National Forces during the period from June '22 till the end of the year was free and unchecked, and that men were taken without any strict enquiries as to character, it will be readily realized that a large proportion of the criminal element found its way into the Army. To put the matter bluntly nearly every criminally disposed person had a gun either from the Government or from Mr de Valera, and needless to say the Government service, on account of the pay involved, was the more attractive. Old soldiers, experienced in every kind of military wrongdoing, were placed under the command of officers necessarily inexperienced and the resulting state of discipline is not to be wondered at.

Yet Davitt was also quick to identify a rapid improvement in general discipline in the year that followed the war's end, with demobilization and peacetime conditions allowing for more effective training amid the ongoing professionalization of the Army: 'In my opinion it is a matter for congratulation that for a year past discipline has been steadily improving. It is now excellent.'[27]

'Am I working in the steady spirit of service of Pearse and Tom Clarke and Seán MacDermott?'[28]

The Civil War ended between 30 April 1923, when Frank Aiken, anti-Treaty IRA Chief of Staff, issued an order to suspend all operations, and the subsequent order to dump arms on 24 May. The latest research on the number of deaths during the conflict indicates that the total number of casualties, including civilians, was approximately 1,600, below previous estimates of between

Transcript of wireless message sent by Maj Gen Patrick O'Daly, GOC of Kerry Command, informing GHQ of the condition of Joseph O'Brien, survivor of the incident at Knocknagoshel when five officers and men of the National Army were killed by a mine laid by anti-Treaty forces. O'Brien was the only survivor. National Army troops carried out a number of reprisals in the following days.

3,000 and 4,000, and also below the number that died during the War of Independence. Civilian deaths are estimated at between 300 and 400. Anti-Treaty casualties are likely to have been approximately 500, with as many as 180 of these killed either by firing squad or in extra-judicial reprisals.

Approximately 800 National Army soldiers died in the thirteen months between the death of Company Adjutant Patrick Columb in Mullingar on 27 April 1922, and the end of May 1923. James Langton's comprehensive survey of National Army casualties shows that 488 of these deaths came in combat, while the remainder died as a result of natural causes or accidents, especially the mishandling of weapons and explosives.[29]

That the National Army appear to have lost more men in combat than anti-Treaty forces is unsurprising, even with their superiority in equipment. In the first weeks of fighting, especially in Dublin, the Provisional Government's forces were generally attempting to dislodge well-entrenched garrisons in urban settings, increasing the likelihood of casualties. During the second phase of the war the adoption of guerrilla tactics meant that the initiative in combat often lay with the anti-Treaty side.

Even though the war had ended, challenges remained both for the government and the National Army. The January 1923 reorganization had given rise to disaffection among a small cadre of officers who, though prominent during the War of Independence, had been identified by GHQ as unsuited to professional military life and shunted into positions with little influence. Careful management of the demobilization of at least 30,000 men was also required, given the potential for widespread unemployment and consequent potential for a resurgence in support for subversive republican forces. Despite these looming difficulties, there was optimism about the National Army's future. The building blocks of a modern military were in place, with a stable structure, well-defined corps, and the necessary administrative services and supports. It was an extraordinary organizational feat, all the more so given the loss of so many of the leaders of the pre-Treaty IRA in the aftermath of the Treaty, the schism within the IRA, the descent into Civil War, and the death of the Commander in Chief in August 1922. During the final weeks of the war, an editorial in *An tÓglách* paid tribute to the achievement:

> Few people outside the Army realize what a vast amount of work has been accomplished in the face of enormous difficulties, and what an elaborate and effective machinery has been built up, starting *de novo*. The Army is now a big new fact in the life of the Nation, a thing with many facets ... What the Army is destined to be in the future remains to be seen, but that it must play a big part in the national existence is certain.[30]

The prediction that the National Army would continue to hold a prominent place in Irish society, was, however, woefully misplaced.

SPECIALIST CORPS OF THE CIVIL WAR

The civilian police force created to replace the Royal Irish Constabulary, initially known as the Civic Guard and renamed An Garda Síochána in 1923, was unarmed and generally ill-equipped to tackle criminality related to republican activities. For this, the government were almost wholly reliant on the National Army, which in turn created specialist units to counter specific problems, whether engendered by the activities of the anti-Treaty IRA or more general lawlessness.

An Ordnance Survey map with manuscript annotations, dated 26 January 1923, by the Railway Repair, Protection and Maintenance Corps, indicating which railway lines had been damaged. These summaries were prepared on a daily basis.

Commanded by Col Patrick Dalton, the Special Infantry Corps was formed in January 1923 in response to an urgent appeal from the Minister for Agriculture, Patrick Hogan, who warned of an increasingly dangerous 'land war'. According to Hogan, a co-ordinated campaign of land seizures had been instigated by anti-Treaty forces as a corollary to its campaign to disrupt railway transport. Agrarian agitation was rather simplistically identified as merely another tactic of anti-Treaty forces, and a fundamental challenge to the authority of the state that required a military response: 'The problem can only be dealt with by the Army, and that the measures adequate to cope with it are measures which the Government could defend only on the ground of military necessity. The Civil Authorities … would be quite powerless.'[1] Effectively a military police force, the activities of the Special Infantry Corps in rural areas often proved controversial, with the army's own intelligence suggesting that it was having a 'bad effect' on local populations and likely to

A flat wagon with armoured protection housing a J15 0-6-0 steam locomotive. Members of the Railway Protection, Repair and Maintenance Corps can be seen along the train. A hand-painted sign attached to the rear carriage shows that the train has been christened 'Noah's Ark'. This photo was likely taken along with others that appear in a special report on the Corps published in the 21 April 1923 issue of *An tÓglách*.

Members of the Railway Protection, Repair and Maintenance Corps pose on two armoured cars. Seven Lancia armoured troop carriers were assigned to the Corps during the Civil War, and were extensively remodelled for use on the railway, including the addition of a closed top for added protection. The car on the left appears to carry the serial number AL23.

incite local resentment.[2] Kevin O'Higgins, Minister for Home Affairs, would later defend its conduct, praising the Corps for its effectiveness in 'stamping out agrarian anarchy and other serious abuses'.[3] In July 1923 the Corps had a strength of just over 2,700, including a Border Unit, headquartered at Dundalk and tasked with liaising with the customs officials of the Irish Free State and of Northern Ireland. The Corps was disbanded in November 1923.

Other special purpose units established during the war included the Railway Protection, Repair and Maintenance Corps (raised in September 1922), the Works Corps and the Salvage Corps (both raised in January 1923). The Salvage Corps assumed responsibility for deconstruction of British Army camps while salvaging as much building material as possible, which was often then repurposed by the National Army. The Corps also surveyed barracks destroyed since 1919, salvaging thousands of pounds worth of material that it stored in two dumps, in Cork and Dublin, the latter in the hangars of Tallaght Aerodrome. At its peak, the Salvage Corps' strength reached 540 men. The Works Corps was best known for its reconstruction of the bridge on Ferryquay, Co. Wexford, and was disbanded in September 1923. Its men formed the nucleus of the Army Corps of Engineers, which was established in the same month by Defence Order No. 26.

The Railway Protection, Repair and Maintenance Corps, under the command of Maj Gen Charles Russell, provided the vital service of protecting and repairing the country's most important transport infrastructure. Railways were a frequent target of the anti-Treaty IRA during the guerrilla phase of the war, with the intention of disrupting the National Army's distribution of men and supplies. The impact on local economies was severe, while several railway workers were also shot and killed. With virtually every railway line affected by sabotage during the war, many of the recruits to the Railway Corps were unemployed railwaymen, who were said to be 'ideal soldiers'.[4] By April 1923 nearly 5,000 men had been recruited to and served with the Corps, though as rail services gradually returned to normal there was a continual process of demobilization of men back to their original employment throughout 1923. The Corps protected rail services by using armoured trains and seven Lancia armoured cars specially modified at Inchicore Railway Works, in conjunction with approximately 50 blockhouses and gun posts across the rail network.

The Railway Protection, Repair and Maintenance Corps, and the Salvage Corps, were respectively disbanded in September and November 1923. *An tÓglách* featured special reports on their activities in its issues of 21 April 1923 and 5 May 1923, and on the Works Corps on 7 April 1923.

The Salvage Corps dismantling a British Army rest camp, located at the back of the London and North Western Hotel, North Wall, Dublin, in early 1923. Photo printed in the 5 May 1923 edition of *An tÓglách*.

CHAPTER 2

1923–32
REORGANIZATION, PROFESSIONALIZATION
AND RETRENCHMENT

The end of the Civil War and restoration of relative peace and stability allowed the General Staff to prepare ambitious plans to professionalize the force, to transform it into a modern army capable of defending the state against both internal and external threats. Those plans were, however, hampered both by lack of investment and the Cumann na nGaedheal government's reluctance to elaborate on the vague defence policy it outlined in 1925. Even so, several important principles and systems were embedded during the 1920s, creating the foundations on which the Defence Forces would be built.

By the end of the decade the Army's national status had dramatically receded from its former prominence as one of the most visible and important institutions of the state. That diminution in status was measurable in various ways, not least the precipitous decline in the public finances allocated to defence, from close to £11m in 1924 to slightly more than £1m six years later. While the former figure was inflated by the expense of the Civil War, and the state's financial position remained perilous throughout the decade, such a severe fiscal correction starved the Defence Forces of resources at a crucial stage in its development. Declining investment was just one of a cascade of challenges presented over the remainder of the decade. The most pressing concern in the immediate aftermath of the Civil War was the fraught task of demobilizing at least half its force and reorganizing yet again.

'To be regulated in a proper manner'

One of the anomalies of the Civil War is that the National Army operated within a loosely defined legal framework, having never been formally constituted by the Oireachtas. Richard Mulcahy conceded the ambiguity when introducing the Defence Forces (Temporary Provisions) Bill to the Dáil in July 1923: 'The accomplishment of the entire submission of the Army to the Civil Power has to be regulated in a proper manner, and all powers

A large group of
National Army soldiers
and civilians run towards
the camera, clearly celebrating.
None of the soldiers carry weapons.

to establish, maintain, organize, discipline and control the Defence Forces must be sought from the Oireachtas in the ordinary way.'[1] Modelled on British legislation, the Bill was approved by the Oireachtas in August and subsequently renewed annually, providing the legal basis for the Defence Forces until replaced by new legislation in 1954.

As the title indicates, the resulting 1923 Defence Forces (Temporary Provisions) Act formally bestowed the designation 'Defence Forces' on the state's military. Control was vested in the government, exercised through the Minister for Defence. The minister was not, however, permitted to wield executive military command or to be a member of the forces on full pay, ending the anomalous position whereby Mulcahy served as both Minister for Defence and the Army's most senior officer. The Act also created the unusual – and problematic – position that command authority over the forces was vested in General Officers Commanding (GOCs), who derived their authority from the minister. As a result, the Chief of Staff, the most senior military officer in the Defence Forces, had no command over the force.[2]

Following a proclamation by the Executive Council the Defence Forces were legally established on 1 October 1924. The Act also enabled the creation of a new Council of Defence, to advise the minister and assist in administering the department. Membership consisted of the minister (as chairperson), the Chief of Staff, Adjutant General, Quartermaster General, and the secretary of the department. The council has never been formally abolished, though it has long since ceased to be an important forum for discussion of military affairs and policy.

August 1923 also saw the Oireachtas approve the Indemnity Act, which provided legal protection – with some very limited exceptions – for all actions taken by the National Army 'during the suppression of the state of armed rebellion' between 27 June 1922 and 3 August 1923.[3] That protection extended to all military tribunals and the carrying out of their verdicts, thus preventing any civil or criminal legal suits arising from, or formal investigation of the executions carried out by the state during the Civil War.

'Drifting Towards Another Mutiny'

The drafting of the Defence Forces (Temporary Provisions) Act took place during the summer months of 1923, at a time when the government was searching for ways to reduce expenditure and address its mounting debt. The Civil War had placed an enormous strain on public finances, with the combined Army budget for 1922 and 1923 totalling £17.9m. Also looming on the horizon was the issue of property losses sustained during the war, with compensation payments exceeding £10m by the end of 1924. While the cost of the war was largely covered by the flotation of a national loan in early 1924, the Department of Finance vigorously pursued urgent reductions in public expenditure. From December 1922 new recruits had been enlisted for a period of just six months, but recruitment only ceased at the end of April 1923, with approximately 55,000 men then in uniform.[4] Targeting a reduction of at least 30,000 all ranks by March 1924, GHQ began planning for mass demobilization and a second reorganization in a matter of months.

Implementation of those plans proved problematic. A scheme of reorganization circulated to GOCs in November provoked a storm of protest. The reaction of Seán Mac Eoin, GOC of Western Command, was typical: 'To my mind the scheme is so preposterous that one could speak on the matter for days.'[5] An occasionally bad-tempered consultation process followed, before an agreed scheme was submitted to the Executive Council for approval in early 1924.

The challenge of finding jobs for demobilized men at a time of widespread unemployment was never satisfactorily met, despite inter-departmental co-operation and the implementation of several employment initiatives. Demobilization payments provided some small help. More dangerous problems arose with the General Staff's attempts to demobilize some of its higher-ranking and more volatile officers, exacerbating pre-existing tensions. The January 1923 reorganization had sidelined several officers with pre-Treaty IRA service records. Liam Tobin, Tom Cullen and Charles Dalton responded by establishing the IRA Organization (IRAO). According to Army intelligence, the organization's intention was

> to get in touch with all IRA men serving in the National Army and, if they believed in our ideals, to link them together in an organization which when strong enough would demand a strong voice in Army policy with a view to securing complete independence when a suitable occasion arose.[6]

DEFENCE ORDER No. 38.

AIREACHT CHOSANTA,

1st December, 1923.

Duties of Military Members of the Council of Defence.

1. The Command of the National Forces is vested in the Executive Council and exercised through the Minister for Defence in accordance with the following Section 236 of the Defence Forces (Temporary Provisions) Act, 1923:—

" The Command-in-Chief of and all executive and administrative powers in relation to the National Forces (including the power to delegate authority to such persons as may be thought fit) shall be vested in the Executive Council and exercised through and in the name of the Minister."

2. A Council of Defence has been created for the purpose of assisting the Minister for Defence, in accordance with the following paragraph 2 of Executive Council Order, No. 11, of 1923:—

" There shall be and there is hereby constituted a Council of Defence to assist the Minister for Defence in the administration of the business of the Department of Defence but without derogating from the responsibility of the Minister for Defence to the Executive Council and to the Oireachtas respectively for all the administration and business of the Department of Defence and for the exercise and performance of all the powers, duties, and functions connected therewith."

3. The Military Members of the Council of Defence are:—

> The Chief of Staff.
> The Adjutant General.
> The Quartermaster General.

They are the heads of Departments for the proper administration of which they are respectively responsible direct to the Minister for Defence. Their Departments collectively constitute the General Headquarters of the Army and are at the same time branches of the Ministry of Defence.

Defence Order No. 38, issued on 1 December 1923, outlining the duties of the military members of the Council of Defence.

DISPERSAL CERTIFICATE.

A.F. 173c.

Report to be sent by Officer i/c Army Records to the Secretary, Ministry of Industry and Commerce, Dublin, on Soldiers discharged or about to be discharged.

Soldier's Surname.....................................Christian Names (in full)...

Unit from which discharged or about to be discharged...

Army No...Rank on discharge...

Married or Single...

Home Address...

Military Character...

Anything against the Soldier to render his recommendation undesirable.................................

Date of proposed discharge...

Officer i/c Records..

Date...

(1234.) Wt. 1431. 50,000 6/23—G.P.D.

More than 30,000 officers and men were demobilised from the National Army between the end of the Civil War and early 1924. Despite the introduction of several special programmes, many were left unemployed following their discharge.

Convinced that the Army Council had strayed from the revolutionary ideal of an Irish Republic, the IRAO also accused the Council of casting aside its members in favour of officers with links to the IRB or who had previously served with British forces.

Mention of the revival of the IRB and the whiff of impropriety within the Army Council caught the attention of Kevin O'Higgins (Minister for Home Affairs) and Joseph McGrath (Minister for Industry and Commerce), who persuaded the government to consider the IRAO's grievances. Led by Tobin, an IRAO deputation met with W.T. Cosgrave and Mulcahy on 25 June, at which it gave full vent to its grievances. A document outlining the IRAO's position was also presented at the meeting, which included an extraordinary threat: 'Unless satisfactory arrangements are come to between us, our organisation will take *whatever steps they consider necessary* to bring about an honest, cleaner and more genuine effort to secure a Republic.'[7]

That threat laid bare the government's strategic error in agreeing to meet with the IRAO. As Minister for Defence and (until the legislation of August 1923) the Army's most senior officer, Mulcahy could not countenance any

Copy of the 'Document' outlining the IRAO's demands, read at a meeting between representatives of the IRAO, W.T. Cosgrave (President of the Executive Council) and Richard Mulcahy in June 1923.

"DOCUMENT"   B.

1.   Previous to the negotiations with the British which ended in the signing of the Treaty we all had one outlook and common aim, viz., "The setting up and maintaining of a Republican form of Government in this Country". In this ideal we followed the late C. in C. and accepted the Treaty in exactly the same spirit as he did. We firmly believed with him that the Treaty was only a stepping stone to a Republic.   The late C. in C. (Mick Collins) told us that he had taken an oath of allegiance to the Republic and that oath he would keep Treaty or no Treaty – this is our position exactly.

2.   The actions of the present G.H.Q. Staff since the C. in Cs. death their open and secret hostility towards us, his Officers has convinced us that they have not the same outlook as he had. We require a definite "Yes" or "No" from the present C. in C. if this be so.

3.   Does the C. in C. understand the temper of the old I.R.A. who are now in the National Army? He does not! Your Army is not a National Army. It is composed of 40% old I.R.A. 50% Ex-Britishers and 10% Ex-civilians. The majority of the civilians were and are hostile to the National Ideals. In the Army you have men who were active British Secret Service agents, previous to the Truce and who have never yet ceased their activities.

4.   We ask that a Committee of Inquiry be set up at once to investigate the advisability of retaining or dispensing with the services of any Officer gazetted or otherwise. The findings of this Committee to be accepted and acted on by the staff. We require equal representation on this Committee.

5.   We wish to bring to your notice the following facts on which we will have we hope a full and frank discussion.

        1. The Composition of the Dublin Command
        2. The recent appointment of the D.M.P. Commissioner
        3. The staffs peace overtures to the Irregulars
        4. The setting up of an S. S. Dept.

6.   It is time that this state of affairs ended , we intend to end it . Unless satisfactory arrangements are come to between us. Our Organisation will take whatever steps they consider necessary to bring about an honest, cleaner and more genuine effort to secure the Republic.

7.   It is not our intention to cause any rupture which would give satisfaction to the enemies of Ireland. We ask the C. in C. to meet our efforts in the same spirit which he would have regarded them in 1920 and 1921.

Finis.

effort to have military policy and plans dictated by subordinates. Despite indicating that he would continue to engage with their concerns, by the end of July Mulcahy had cut communications with the IRAO.

The pace of demobilization accelerated from September 1923, with the result that the IRAO's membership dwindled. Matters came to a head in November when seven officers based at the Curragh refused to accept their

Charcoal portrait by Frank Leah of Maj Gen Peadar MacMahon, General Officer Commanding, Curragh Command. Published on the front page of *An tÓglách* on 1 September 1923. MacMahon was appointed Chief of Staff in March 1924 and remained in post until March 1927; he was then appointed Secretary of the Department of Defence, where he remained until his retirement in 1958.

demobilization orders, a number that soon rose to sixty. Each was forcibly removed from the camp and their demobilization payments withheld, but a tipping point had been reached. At the Executive Council the Minister for Defence was becoming increasingly isolated. Mulcahy's relations with O'Higgins and McGrath deteriorated, a situation not helped by Mulcahy's refusal to assist a cabinet committee established in December to examine the cases of the Curragh officers.

Aware of the growing crisis, Mulcahy was either unable or unwilling to defuse matters. He was, however, determined that the principle of military obedience to the civil authority should be copper fastened:

> We are drifting at present and drifting towards another mutiny ... The Army must not be involved in any political crisis, even if that crisis develops from the mutiny, but must be forced into a military machine that will be the right arm of any Government that the people wish to place in power.[8]

Open mutiny loomed when, at 10 p.m. on 6 March, the IRAO submitted an ultimatum to the government, signed by Tobin and Dalton, demanding the dismissal of the Army Council and the immediate suspension of demobilization and reorganization. A deadline of 10 p.m. on 10 March was set for the government to respond.

Events moved quickly. Reports were received that army officers had abandoned their posts, taking with them arms and ammunition. The government ordered the arrest of the IRAO's leaders and condemned their actions in the Dáil. Fault lines that had been evident in the Executive Council for several months emerged into full view. McGrath resigned as Minister for Industry and Commerce in protest at the arrests, declaring in the Dáil that the mutiny was the inevitable result of 'muddling, mishandling and incompetency' at the Department of Defence.[9]

Electing to negotiate with the mutineers, the government entrusted matters to Kevin O'Higgins and by 12 March the crisis seemed to have been averted. In return for a promise that weapons and ammunition would be returned, the government released Tobin and Dalton and made a public commitment to inquire into the administration of the National Army. Army intelligence suggested, however, that the mutineers were still intent on staging a coup d'état. On 18 March GHQ received information that a meeting of mutineers was underway at Devlin's Hotel on Dublin's Parnell Street. Mulcahy and Adjutant General Gearóid O'Sullivan ordered an army raid. Eleven armed army officers were arrested, while several others escaped.

By failing to consult the government before ordering the raid, Mulcahy seemed to confirm fears, often expressed by O'Higgins, that the National Army could not be controlled. Led by O'Higgins in the absence of the apparently ill Cosgrave, the Executive Council demanded the immediate resignation of Chief of Staff Seán Mac Mahon, O'Sullivan and Quartermaster General Seán Ó Muirthuille. O'Sullivan and Ó Muirthuille resigned immediately. Mac Mahon's treatment was particularly harsh, as he had been visiting troops in Cork on 18 March and was unaware of the raid. He refused to resign until given a clear explanation for the request and was peremptorily dismissed. Mulcahy in turn resigned as minister in protest; had he not done so, the Executive Council was prepared to remove him.

When compared with its response to actual mutiny, the government's treatment of the National Army's senior staff was spectacularly heavy-handed. As the *Irish Times* remarked in an editorial, 'Mutiny has been condoned'.[10] In its disciplined acquiescence to the government's actions and Mulcahy's resignation, the officer corps indicated that obedience to the civil authority was now firmly entrenched, offering a counterargument to the government's conclusion that its will had been intentionally subverted.

THE IRISH DEFENCE FORCES, 1922–2022

SAORSTÁT ÉIREANN.

Reference No.

RA.

TELEPHONE 5166.

OIFIG AN UACHTARÁIN
(The President's Office),

SRÁID MHUIRBHTHEAN UACH.
(Upper Merrion Street).

BAILE ÁTHA CLIATH
(Dublin).

5th April, 1924.

J. Creed Meredith, Esq., K.C.

A Chara,

   With reference to my statement to
the Dail on Thursday last announcing the personnel
of the Committee of Enquiry into Army Administration
it is very desirable that the Committee should
commence its deliberations at the earliest possible
date. I venture to suggest, therefore, that a
preliminary meeting be held on Monday next at 12 noon,
and I would be glad if you would inform me whether
this date and time would be suitable to you.

   I have arranged to place the Council
Chamber, Government Buildings, at the disposal of the
Committee for their meetings and I have asked
Mr. Banim, my Assistant Secretary, to act as Secretary
pro tem. to the Committee.

   If it is possible for me to further
facilitate the Committee in their work I shall be only
too happy to do so.

   The following are the Terms of Reference

               for

2.

for the purposes of the Enquiry:-

"To enquire into and report to the
Executive Council upon the facts and
matters which have caused or led up to
1, the indiscipline and mutinous or insubordinate
conduct lately manifested in the National
Army and generally to investigate and report
2, upon the state of discipline prevailing
amongst all ranks in the Army and any facts or
X circumstances adversely affecting discipline,
as for example the existence of factions,
3, conspiracies, secret societies, or political
organisations, or groups amongst the officers
and men, the considerations determining and
making of promotions or appointments. And to
enquire and report whether the discontent
amongst certain officers and men shown in the
4. recent threat of mutiny and insubordination is
justly and fairly attributed to "muddling,
mismanagement and incompetence in the
5. administration of the Army". And in addition
to report on such specific matters and reply
to such specific queries as may from time to
time be referred to the Committee by the
Executive Council".

Mise le meas,

W.T. Cosgrave to Justice James C. Meredith, 5 April 1924, enclosing the terms of reference for the Army
Inquiry Committee and urging a speedy start to the committee's work.

Honouring a commitment made in the Dáil on 12 March, Cosgrave established an inquiry into the circumstances surrounding the mutiny. Chaired by Justice James Meredith, the Army Inquiry Committee met on forty-one occasions between 7 April and the beginning of June, with detailed testimony presented by twenty-seven witnesses, including Mulcahy, O'Higgins and the dismissed Army Council officers. Seán Mac Mahon's opening statement offered some insight into the shock of their dismissal:

> I cannot help feeling a sting of degradation when I reflect on the work of the years that have passed and sit here now accused of having done something – although that something is not quite clear to anybody – to disrupt the Army and pull down the edifice we have spent so many years and so much energy in building up.[11]

The committee worked quickly and submitted its report to the Executive Council on 7 June, which was published and presented to the Dáil ten days later. Its main conclusion, that there was no evidence to justify the charge of 'muddling, mishandling or incompetence', appeared to vindicate the Army Council. Referring to the selection process governing demobilization of officers, the committee found that the Army Council 'honestly endeavoured to deal fairly' with the issue.[12] It also concluded that many of the officers selected for demobilization had become a problem even before Michael Collins' death, and were too ill-disciplined and temperamentally unsuited to the demands of peacetime and of a professional military – one of the principal reasons they had been sidelined in the first place. Mulcahy's failure to inform the government of the reorganization of the IRB, and his decision to drop the Kenmare assault case, were heavily criticized – both in the report and in an unpublished reservation submitted by Meredith that was even more trenchant in its criticism of the former Minister for Defence.

By the end of June the controversy had largely abated. Intent on drawing a line under the mutiny and its fallout, Cosgrave declared: 'That particular incident which occurred three months ago is an incident which in my opinion, ought to be dead and buried and ought not to be resurrected, no matter what its influence was either at that time or now.'[13] His eagerness to move on was motivated by a number of factors, not least the plummeting market value of the government stock issued as part of the state's first national loan.

The mutiny's potential to destabilize the state quickly receded. Confined mostly to a small group of senior officers, the mutineers found little support among junior officers or NCOs. The government's first instinct, of negotiating with the IRAO, arose partly from its fears that disaffected officers might join subversive organizations. Equally, its forceful handling of the Army Council was, perhaps, an inevitable result of the tension between Mulcahy and other members of government, and a general – if unfounded – insecurity within the Executive Council that the National Army had yet to be brought fully under its control.

At first glance the mutiny's overall impact on the Army's future seemed minimal, yet the inquiry's proceedings had revealed glaring weaknesses in the administrative practises of the civil and military branches of Defence, particularly procurement and financial oversight. Over the following weeks and months, the Department of Finance and the civil side of the Department of Defence increased their control and influence on the Army's affairs. Cornelius O'Connor, Secretary of the Department of Defence, began administrative reforms that had long been delayed, first by war, and then by disagreement with the General Staff. Increasingly tight management of financial expenditure, with all items requiring approval first by the Army Finance Officer and then by the Department of Finance, substantially decreased the Army's autonomy. Cost rather than value became the overarching criteria by which expenditure on the Defence Forces would be assessed.

In a bid to ensure its control of the Army during the mutiny crisis, the government temporarily appointed Eoin O'Duffy, then Garda Commissioner, as Inspector General and General Officer Commanding the Forces (GOCF). O'Duffy moved quickly to select a new General Staff and to draft and implement yet another new scheme of organization. Peadar MacMahon, Hugo MacNeill and Felix Cronin were appointed as Chief of Staff, Adjutant General and Quartermaster General, respectively. Due in no small part to O'Duffy's remarkable energy and formidable administrative skills, a revised scheme of organization was presented to the Executive Council and approved by July.

The Army that emerged from the Civil War had been hurriedly built to meet that crisis, but found to be 'crude because of its precocious growth and defective because of its limited purpose'.[14] Under O'Duffy's approved scheme, seven brigades of twenty-seven battalions were distributed across four new commands: Western, Southern, Eastern and the Curragh Training

OFFICE of the GENERAL OFFICER
COMMANDING THE FORCES,
Royal Hospital,
KILMAINHAM.-

CONFIDENTIAL.

7th April, 1924.

To The President and
Members of the Executive Council.

          I have the honour to submit my first
Confidential Report in accordance with instructions received.
This report must be viewed in the light of:-

(1)   The resignation of the Minister for Defence.
(2)   The resignation of the Chief of Staff, the Adjutant
      General and the Quartermaster General.
(3)   The recent demobilisation of 1,000 Officers.
(4)   The big reduction in the rate of pay in the N.C.Os and
      Privates.
(5)   Threatened mutiny on the part of 100 Officers serving
      in the Army.
(6)   Transition stage in Army organisation involving transfer
      of personnel, warlike and other stores.
(7)   The debates in the Dail on the Army position as reported
      in the Press and read by Officers and men.

          All these things added very considerably to my
responsibilities, and were I not buoyed by the confidence of
the Government, the co-operation of the responsible officers of
the Army and the loyalty of the rank and file, I would have been
unable to bear the strain. Since I accepted military control
of the Army I am glad to say no untoward incident occurred, and,
with a few exceptions, the different Departments are getting
after their work. There are, however, Officers in the Army who,
if not politicians, may be designated as diplomats. These work
in little circles, and, while their intentions may be good, their
actions are unsoldier like and harmful. They sometimes get
audiences from members of the Oireachtas, but what is more
dangerous they have approached Officers of lesser rank than
themselves, painted certain pictures for these officers and
attempted to have certain interpretations put on the decisions
of the G.O.C.F. Such conduct on the part of officers has been
brimful of bad results in the past and is indiscipline of the
grossest type. While I am entrusted with control of the Army
I will not tolerate such conduct and it is my intention to
suspend any officer, of whatever rank, who is reported to me for
attempting to cause disaffection or distraction, discussing Army
matters with non-members of the Army, or who attend mixed
meetings of members and non-members for such purposes. The name
of any officer so suspended will be forwarded to the Executive
Council with a recommendation for the withdrawal of his
Commission. This matter has not gone far as yet, but if not
checked, might become a serious menace to me. I should say that
it has no connection, so far as I am aware, with the recent
mutiny or with Irregularism.

RECENT MUTINY IN ARMY. 96 Officers have resigned and a further
Officers deserted and did not yet send in their resignations.
According to my reports none of the Officers concerned handed in
their uniforms or revolvers, and I think that demobolisation
grants should not be considered until these are forthcoming.

                   (over)

The first page of Gen Eoin O'Duffy's report to the Executive Council, delivered on 7 April 1924, following
his apppointment as GOCF, offered a stark overview of recent events.

Camp. The retained corps were Armoured Car; Engineers; Signals; Transport; Artillery; and Military Police. The Army Air Service officially became the Air Corps. The recently established Army School of Music was retained and headquartered at Beggars Bush Barracks before moving to Portobello, while the Army Medical Service was kept busy assessing claims under the Army Pension Act (1923) and the Military Service Pensions Act (1924).

O'Duffy served as GOCF until 30 September, during which time he displayed an astonishing attention to detail. In a series of detailed reports to the Executive Council he offered a string of recommendations to improve discipline and morale, from overhauling the chaplaincy to reducing rates of venereal disease. Monitoring subversive factions was also a priority, conforming to the government's growing conviction that the National Army's primary role lay in maintaining internal security. His final report suggested that work remained to be done before it could be regarded as a cohesive force, and urged the government to inculcate martial pride in the civilian population:

> At the present time, I fear that our Army is Irish in name only, and that any sign of esprit de corps is confined to a few scattered units ... To be frank, we have a mercenary Army pure and simple. This is really not to be wondered at when you consider the composition of the Forces. Our officers are mainly drawn from the ranks of the old IRA, our NCOs from the British Army, while the majority of the rank and file served in neither armies ... Day after day for the past few years, we have listened to the Irregulars declaring that they are the rightful successors to every Irish soldier that ever fought in the Nation's cause, to every military force that ever battled for Irish freedom; while the first Irish regular army since the days of Sarsfield or indeed of Eoin Ruadh, remain silent, apparently admitting the fact.[15]

'An expensive luxury to the state'

Long before the July 1924 reorganization, it had become clear that there was no future in the Defence Forces for any form of navy. Several of the specialist corps formed during the Civil War were disbanded shortly after its

THE IRISH DEFENCE FORCES, 1922–2022

conclusion. Some, such as the Salvage Corps and the Railway Protection, Repair and Maintenance Corps, had been created to perform specific roles that were no longer required. Others simply presented too much of a financial burden. As the country gradually moved to peacetime conditions the nascent Coastal and Marine Service (CMS), which had only begun to take shape in the early weeks and months of 1923, struggled to justify its existence.

Apart from the obvious consideration that the state was an island, the successful transportation of troops by sea to the south and west coasts in summer 1922 hinted at the benefits of a small naval force, while very limited coastal patrol capabilities were provided by the motor launches purchased from the British Admiralty in May 1922 and other vessels commandeered during the war. GHQ initially proved willing to invest in further seagoing capabilities; twelve armed trawlers were purchased from the British Admiralty in February 1923 at a cost of £87,000. Headquartered at Portobello Barracks, the CMS consisted of three elements – coastal infantry, coastal patrol, and the marine investigation department – with bases in Killybegs (Donegal), Galway, Dún Laoghaire, and the former Royal Navy base at Haulbowline, Cork. Maj Gen Joseph Vize, already familiar with naval operations, was appointed GOC.

The service got off to an unfortunate start, from which it never recovered. Each of the newly acquired trawlers required an extensive overhaul, originally to be completed in England before handover to the CMS. A political decision was later made to have all the work undertaken at Haulbowline, which proved disastrous. The necessary expertise was unavailable, and the trawlers languished in dry dock. Vize visited Haulbowline on 16 May to check on progress and found work at a virtual standstill:

> Six of the ships are required urgently for the protecting of fisheries and the prevention of smuggling, etc ... the fishing grounds are being destroyed by illegal trawling, seals, etc. Smuggling is going on and we are powerless to prevent same, as long as our ships are tied up.[16]

Delay was the last thing that Vize needed, as attitudes towards the CMS had already begun to change at the Department of Defence, under considerable pressure from Finance. The capability of intercepting potential gun runners

The SS *Dainty*, flagship of the CMS, with its crew gathered on the foredeck and Tricolour hanging to the aft. The photo was originally published in the 6 October 1923 issue of *An tÓglách*.

and smugglers, or indeed to protect Ireland's fisheries, was now considered surplus to requirements.

Poor organization also undermined the case for retaining the service. Its duties and functions were never satisfactorily outlined and occasionally duplicated pre-existing arrangements – responsibility for coast watching, for example, was split between Defence and the Revenue Commissioners. An analysis of the personnel within the marine investigation department showed that the majority had little or no technical qualifications, and only 12 per cent had pre-Truce service records.

By the end of the summer the mood had turned decisively against retention of the CMS. Mulcahy notified the Executive Council in August that preparations to decommission the entire fleet were underway. His rationale suggests a haphazard, slapdash approach not just to the original decision to create the service, but also to future planning: 'We would never have suggested purchasing twelve trawlers and setting up a Naval establishment such as we have now if it were not for the necessity and special circumstances of controlling

Pictured aboard Motor Launch 1 (ML–1) in Cork Harbour are (*left to right*): Capt Francis O'Connor, Capt Liam O'Connor (shore captain, Haulbowline), 2nd Engineer R. Heffernan and First Officer M. Bradley. Originally published in the 6 October 1923 issue of *An tÓglách*.

the coast and of despatching troops by water to the different parts of the coast.' Noting that these services were unlikely to be needed in the immediate future, Mulcahy pointedly ignored Vize's advice on smuggling and fisheries:

> It would be a great mistake to keep on a costly service not very pointedly applied to definite and required work. It would be more satisfactory, and more administratively healthy to get rid of all those vessels, even if we had to start in two or three years' time to rebuild the service. We would probably save much more in the meantime than would purchase boats for a new, well thought out service subsequently.[17]

The heavy costs associated were certainly resented within GHQ. Seán Mac Mahon scathingly dismissed the marine investigation department, which had an annual budget of £36,000, as a 'perfectly useless department, constituting an expensive luxury to the State and calling for immediate disbandment'.[18]

The financial argument, while undoubtedly short-sighted and for once largely driven from within the Defence Forces, proved persuasive. On 6 October *An tÓglách* published an extensive profile of the CMS; four days later the Executive Council effectively ordered that it be disbanded. All remaining boats and men were to be demobilized as soon as possible, and by 31 March 1924 the CMS no longer existed. Responsibility for fisheries protection, along with a single armed vessel (the *Muirchú*, formerly the infamous *Helga*, the Royal Navy vessel that shelled Dublin during the 1916 Rising), was handed over to the Department of Agriculture. All armed trawlers were handed over to the Office of Public Works and the state was left without a naval service for the next sixteen years.

'To train a sufficient number of flying officers'

The crisis in the public finances and the 1923/4 demobilization and reorganization process also posed an existential threat to the Army Air Service. In August 1923 Finance bluntly declared that its retention was difficult to justify. As with the CMS, concerns about the Air Service's cost and effectiveness were also prevalent among senior officers.

In a December 1923 submission to Mac Mahon, proposing an alternative organization scheme for the Army, Maj Gens Peadar MacMahon, Seán Mac Eoin, Joseph Sweeney and Dan Hogan (all of whom would serve as Chief of Staff before the end of the decade) argued that the Air Service had not justified its existence during the Civil War. Moreover, it was too weak to defend the state's airspace and the cost of bringing it up to the required scale was prohibitive. Most importantly, unfamiliarity with the concept of air power was considered an insurmountable obstacle, rather than a challenge to overcome: 'Having regard to our inexperience in matters relating to aircraft and the state of national finances, we recommend that the Air Service be abolished.'[19] Arguments such as this, and indeed those that resulted in the disbandment of the CMS, were made by officers and civil servants convinced that the greatest threat to the state lay internally, best countered by a highly-trained, mobile infantry. Little thought seems to have been given to the reconnaissance and transport potential of the Air Service.

In what appears to be a staged photograph, a group of Army Air Service mechanics service a Bristol F2B Fighter at Baldonnel Aerodrome.

The actual cost of the Air Service was, in fact, a very small proportion of the overall National Army budget of £17.9m for the Civil War years. As much by luck as by design, the Air Service survived the 1924 reorganization and emerged as the newly named Air Corps, headquartered at Baldonnel Aerodrome with twenty-two aircraft and an initial establishment of 155 all ranks – less than one per cent of the total establishment proposed for the Defence Forces. A new GOC was, however, required, following the resignation of General William McSweeney and twelve other officers during the mutiny.

Throughout the 1920s the Air Corps struggled to achieve full integration with the Army. The piloting skills on display during an aerial show in the Phoenix Park in August 1924 drew favourable comments from observing British and American officers. A cadet training system was introduced in 1925, while six new Bristol Fighters were delivered that year, intended for a

The Bristol F2B Fighter, pictured in flight. Eight of these aircraft were acquired for the Army Air Service from the Royal Air Force and the Aircraft Disposal Company, Ltd, between July and November 1922, and saw active service during the Civil War. Six further Bristol F2B (Mk II) were purchased in 1925; all had either been crashed and written off or withdrawn from service by May 1935.

fighter squadron that never materialized. Four De Haviland Moths arrived at Baldonnel on 12 July 1926. Major refurbishment of the aerodrome commenced in 1929, including construction of quarters for married and single men and an officers' mess with recreation, reading and writing rooms.

Uncertainty regarding its proper development plagued the Air Corps well into the 1930s. The limited ambitions of developing a technical support staff and of training 'a sufficient number of flying officers for peace-time coast defence' guided early thinking.[20] In 1926 the Army Organization Board noted that it had experienced 'particular difficulty in putting forward any scheme of organization' for the Corps. At issue was the extent to which civil and military aviation should be developed in tandem:

> It is felt that civil aviation can only be assisted to birth and maturity through the medium of the Army, and, on the other hand, adequate and efficient air defences can only be assured as a result of the proper development of civil aviation. The two are absolutely interlocked, and for this reason the Board strongly recommend that all aviation in this country – civil and military – be placed under the supervision of the Minister for Defence.[21]

That recommendation was not acted upon, though earlier in the year Charles Russell, OC of the Air Corps, had been appointed to an inter-departmental

Recruitment poster designed and printed in May 1924. Even though the National Army had just completed a major demobilization scheme that had reduced the army's strength from more than 50,000 to c.15,000, a recruitment drive was launched in late May 1924. This was because the majority of soldiers had less than a year remaining in their service periods and would soon need to be replaced. The response to the recruitment campaign was not as good as hoped. By 8 September the drive had attracted 3,263 new recruits, though 3,849 were discharged from the army during the same period.

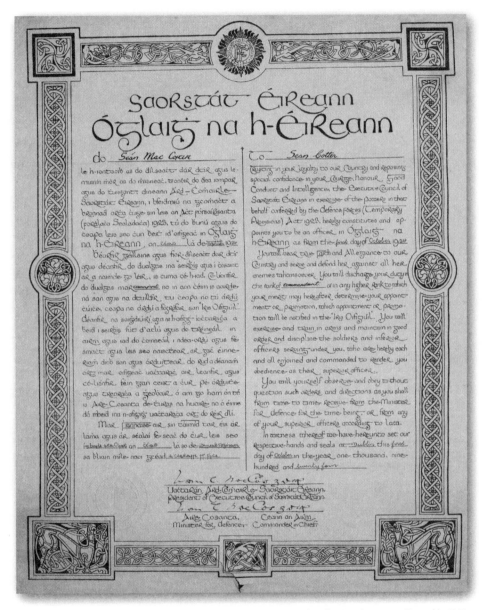

Certificate of commission in the Defence Forces for Seán Cotter, dated 1 October 1924. Signed by W.T. Cosgrave as both President of the Executive Council and Minister for Defence. Cosgrave took over as acting Minister for Defence following Richard Mulcahy's resignation in the midst of the Army mutiny crisis in March 1924. Cosgrave held the ministerial brief until November 1924, when Peter Hughes was appointed to the post.

A Defence Forces soldier pictured in regulation drill dress, with 1908 pattern webbing and Lee Enfield rifle. This was one of a series of photos of the various uniforms of the National Army, taken by Training and Operations Branch on the grounds of General Headquarters, Parkgate Street, in the winter of 1924/5.

committee on the future of Irish aviation. Otherwise, the policy adopted for the remainder of the decade was to maintain the smallest corps possible, principally to give infantry troops a passing knowledge of the value of aerial co-operation. How that was to be accomplished was never fully teased out and interactions between the Army and Air Corps were intermittent, largely confined to annual manoeuvres.

Towards the end of the decade Comdt James Fitzmaurice, appointed OC in April 1927, brought international attention and renown to the Air Corps as co-pilot on the *Bremen*, the first aircraft to successfully complete an east to west trans-Atlantic flight. Crewed by Fitzmaurice (acting as co-pilot) and German aviators Capt Hermann Köhl and Baron von Hünenfeld, the

Bremen took off from Baldonnel on 12 April 1928, and landed at Greenly Island lighthouse, Canada, the following day. That stunning success led to extended periods on leave, and Fitzmaurice retired as OC Air Corps in March 1929, less than two years after taking up the post. Six months later the Chief of Staff, Joseph Sweeney, stressed that

> a more progressive and well defined policy in regard to the Air Corps is an urgent necessity. The provision of a definite programme for some years ahead, the organization of the Corps, and the formation of a Reserve, are matters calling for early and earnest consideration. Technical and Administrative control of the Corps in its present depleted condition is extremely difficult.[22]

Shortages of mechanics frequently hampered flying time, with all Bristol Fighters grounded in 1929 pending reconditioning. Nonetheless, integration of aerial photography into the training programme proved successful. In November 1929 the Council of Defence approved a significant investment of £25,000 on equipment for aerial photography and the purchase of seven new aircraft, which were delivered the following year. Training standards were further improved in 1929 in co-operation with the RAF, who provided a limited number of places on their courses for Air Corps officers.

'To fulfil the functions of a modern army'

By early 1925 it was clear that the Defence Forces had weathered the storm of demobilization. For the first time since January 1922, time and space were available for a comprehensive review of the state's defensive needs. With O'Duffy having returned to his role as Garda Commissioner, Peadar MacMahon's tenure as Chief of Staff was characterized by a more expansive approach to reform. Following a conference with his General Staff in April 1925, MacMahon convened an 'organization board', with a remit to advise on the modernization necessary 'to fulfil the functions of a modern army in relation to national defence'.[23]

To do so effectively, some indication of the government's defence policy was required. In July 1925 the Council of Defence presented a memo to the government, outlining the 'urgent and absolute necessity' of providing the council with 'at least the outlines' of a defence policy. The memo warned that not only were the Defence Forces entirely dependent upon the British government for equipment, they were incapable of providing any effective defence against a modern army, navy or air force. In the event of war between Britain and another powerful nation, Ireland was likely to become a 'cockpit for the belligerents.' Assuming that the state would remain neutral in any international conflict while preventing the use of its territory to attack Britain, the council proposed developing forces 'sufficient of a hornet's nest to any outsider' to deter invasion. Three main policy options were offered for the government's consideration:

1. the development and organization of Irish military resources into a complete defensive machine, including aerial and naval capabilities, and the fostering of industrial capacity to manufacture military equipment;
2. the development of Defence Forces which would be an integral part of the British Imperial forces and would, in the event of war, be controlled by the Imperial General Staff;
3. complete reliance on Britain for defence from external threats, and the maintenance of Defence Forces solely to deal with internal threats.

The government's response, delivered in November, was to confirm its commitment to neutrality. The Defence Forces were to consist of between 10,000 and 12,000 all ranks and be capable of 'rapid and efficient expansion' in time of need. In addition to an ability to defend the state's territorial integrity against internal or external aggression, the Defence Forces were to be 'so organized, trained and equipped as to render it capable, should the necessity arise, of full and complete co-ordination with the forces of the British government in the defence of Saorstát territory.'[24] The brief document merely sketched the outlines of a defence policy, but at least offered a framework around which the Defence Forces could plan.

Problems arose immediately. Rapid expansion implied reserve forces, which would not be organized for another two years. The practicalities of effective co-ordination with British forces, either from a military or political perspective, were not specified. While the Anglo-Irish Treaty stipulated that a joint conference on coastal defence should be convened by the end of 1926, neither government was inclined to press the matter and the conference never

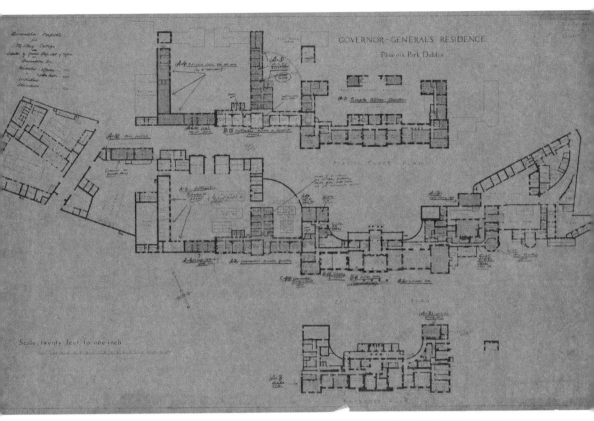

Plans for the proposed conversion of the Governor General's Residence, Phoenix Park, into a Military College, drawn up by the Defence Forces' General Staff in December 1924. These plans were never acted upon, and the residence became home to the President of Ireland from 1938.

materialized. A handful of spaces were made available for officers to attend courses each year at British military schools and colleges, but such courtesies were a long way from active co-operation.

The Army Organization Board received submissions from every corps and service, as well as staff and technical officers, and reviewed the structures of various other military forces. Delivered in June 1926, its report recommended the conversion of the Defence Forces 'from its present semi-immobile basis, designed to deal with internal disorder solely, to a mobile basis'. A volunteer force and reserve officer corps would be necessary to supplement the regular army, which would provide a 'skeleton or scaffolding from which the main body of the Defence Forces would be built up in time of war'.[25]

The Cork Command hurling team, who defeated GHQ in the semi-final of the Army Chaplain's Cup, on a scoreline of 6-3 to 2-7. The match was played in Croke Park on 1 January 1924, with a report carried in the 12 January 1924 issue of *An tÓglách*.

In an effort to broaden the General Staff's knowledge of military matters beyond its familiarity with British systems, and to expand on the Board's work, the government sanctioned the departure of six officers on a military mission to America. Their remit was to conduct a general study of the legislation governing American defence and its military system, with a particular focus on military education. First mooted in 1925 but delayed by scepticism from several quarters, including the Department of Finance, the mission proved to be an important milestone in the modernization process, particularly the subsequent establishment of the Military College.

Assistant Chief of Staff Maj Gen Hugo MacNeill and Col Michael J. Costello were first to depart, in July 1926, followed by Maj Joseph Dunne, Capt Patrick Berry, and Lts Seán Collins-Powell and Charles Trodden a month later. There was palpable excitement at the mission's potential for shaping the future of the Defence Forces: 'For the first time in our lives we will be able to estimate exactly on our requirements in accordance with a definite programme.'[26] All returned in October 1927, having studied tactics and troop dispositions at Fort Leavenworth, Fort Benning and Fort Sill and completed tours of inspection of several other American military schools and installations.

Shortly after their return the Temporary Plans Division was established at the Hibernian Schools, Dublin, with MacNeill as director and a staff of fifteen officers, including Costello. Structured as an experimental general staff, the division was presented with an ambitious brief: to devise a doctrine of war that would form the basis of the state's defence policy; to formulate tactical doctrines to govern the deployment of the Army and its corps in line with that policy; to propose a suitable organization and devise tables of equipment and supply; and to outline the best methods for educating officers and men on the doctrine of war. Its work commenced on 6 February 1928 and was completed the following year. Daniel Hogan, who replaced Peadar MacMahon as Chief of Staff in 1927, was cautiously optimistic that, given time and resources, the division's recommendations could transform the Defence Forces:

> The problems confronting us are so tremendous, and varied in
> scope, that the task of solving them satisfactorily in the manner laid
> down by this Division may sometimes seem practically impossible
> of attainment ... the lines we are working on are the same lines on

Defence Forces soldiers, pictured on 20 June 1926 at the annual military ceremony at Bodenstown, Co. Kildare, in honour of Theobald Wolfe Tone, one of the founders of the United Irishmen. Approximately 1,400 troops were present at the ceremony, which included a flyover from Baldonnel Aerodrome by an Air Corps squadron of Bristol F2B fighters.

which the modern Armies of France, Germany and America at least were built up, they are the same lines that were followed by the Prussian General Staff after 1806, by Foch and his comrades after 1870, and by the American Naval and Military War Plans Section prior to the entering of the United States into the World War.[27]

The division's proposals on military doctrine were endorsed, though it generated some internal opposition with its recommendation to adhere

A firing party from An Chéad Chath under the command of Lt Seán O'Connor, accompanied by buglers, during a ceremony on 21 August 1927 to commemorate the deaths of Arthur Griffith and Michael Collins. More than 4,000 troops assembled at McKee Barracks before parading to the ceremony, which took place on the lawn of Leinster House in front of the Collins-Griffith Cenotaph – a concrete-covered wooden structure unveiled in August 1923 that contained plaster medallions of both men. The National Army played an important role in symbolically projecting the legitimacy of the Irish Free State during the 1920s, particularly at sites such as Bodenstown, which continued to be a focal point for republican opponents of the Treaty and of the Free State. An Céad Chathlán Coisithe (1 Infantry Battalion) was established on 10 March 1924, with recruitment initially confined to fluent speakers of Irish, preferably from a Gaeltacht area – a policy that continues in operation to this day.

closely to British doctrine. In reality there was little alternative, given the government's previous indication of its preferences, the state's reliance on Britain for virtually all its military supplies, and the British government's willingness to facilitate training of Irish officers. The cost, both financial and political, of pursuing closer links with the American or any other military were simply too high.

On a technical level, the work of the Army Organization Board and Temporary Plans Division demonstrated the increasing confidence and professionalism of the General Staff. Submission of the Division's final recommendations in 1929 marked the end point of nearly four years of continuous study, during which a plethora of plans and advice were presented to the Minister for Defence. Many were simply too ambitious, paying no heed to the economic and political realities that prevailed. Virtually all were ignored, or accepted but later quietly shelved.

The government seemed content to allow personnel numbers to diminish so long as a vibrant public facade was maintained. In 1926 the Army Equitation School's show jumping team placed second at the Aga Khan trophy, in its first appearance at the Royal Dublin Society's annual horse show, and began competing internationally. Military tattoos in 1927 and 1929, featuring as many as 1,500 all ranks and hosted as part of Civic Week festivities in Dublin city, brought public acclaim and short-term boosts in recruitment. The Army No. 1 Band regularly toured the country and released several records on the Velvet Face and HMV labels, providing a useful, if limited, source of revenue. That there was deep unhappiness with the limited scope for evolution of the forces might be inferred from the appointment of three separate chiefs of staff in 1929, following the early retirement of Daniel Hogan in February and the sudden departure of his successor, Seán Mac Eoin, after just three months.

'A further degree of training is advisable'[28]

Though the Defence Forces now had a structure around which it proposed to develop, it lacked the men and the money to do so. Replicating the same standards of professionalism that had been achieved among the officer corps across the entire Defence Forces proved difficult. In addition to declining numerical strength, the equipment available for training and manoeuvres was deeply inadequate.

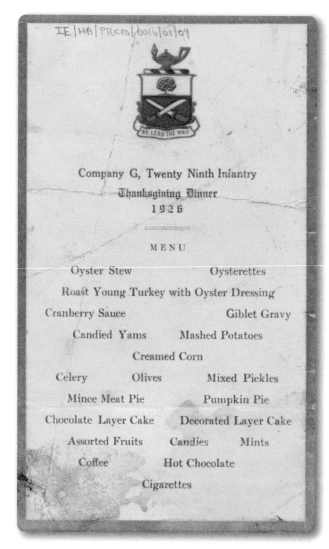

IE|MA|PRCNo|0016|01|09

Company G, Twenty Ninth Infantry

Thanksgiving Dinner

1926

MENU

Oyster Stew   Oysterettes

Roast Young Turkey with Oyster Dressing

Cranberry Sauce   Giblet Gravy

Candied Yams   Mashed Potatoes

Creamed Corn

Celery   Olives   Mixed Pickles

Mince Meat Pie   Pumpkin Pie

Chocolate Layer Cake   Decorated Layer Cake

Assorted Fruits   Candies   Mints

Coffee   Hot Chocolate

Cigarettes

Menu for the Thanksgiving Dinner hosted by Company G, 29th Infantry of the United States Army and attended by Lt Seán Collins-Powell while on the Military Mission to America.

Maintaining morale across all ranks proved difficult. Among the concerns of the officer corps was a lack of legislation providing for and safeguarding pensions. That there were too many officers also created unease, with opportunities for promotion limited. A voluntary redundancy scheme for officers followed in 1928, with up to two years' pay and allowances on offer for senior ranks. The result was a further hollowing out of experience at a time when the Defence Forces' strength was declining precipitously. Further

'Training of Infantry Companies' was the first in a series of training memoranda issued by the National Army in 1923.

redundancies followed in 1929. From a post-demobilization high of 17,439 in November 1925, just 5,294 men were in uniform at the beginning of 1930. The twenty-seven battalions stipulated in the July 1924 reorganization had been reduced to a mere five just six years later.

This steady drain of manpower placed significant obstacles in the way of modernization. Ambitions to develop a well-equipped, highly trained force were rendered impractical by plummeting strengths and strangled budgets.

Collective training, a key element for moulding a cohesive force, was virtually impossible. Personnel were dispersed around the country in barracks and small posts, stretched too thinly to allow battalions train together. The tedium of constant guard and fatigue duty meant that few chose to extend their stay in the army once their initial period of enlistment had expired.

The importance of officer education, and the need for guidance from foreign militaries, had been recognized while the Defence Forces was in its infancy. Though an attempt to arrange a military mission to Switzerland in August 1922 was unsuccessful, in July 1923 a delegation of five officers, including Chief of Staff Seán Mac Mahon, were invited to France and granted permission to inspect the École Spéciale Militaire, Saint-Cyr, and the Centre d'Étude d'Infanterie at Versailles. A review of British military academies followed in 1928. The opening of the Army School of Instruction, which welcomed its first students in April 1924 under the command of Michael Hogan, was a vital step in the professionalization of the army's officer corps. Attempts to decentralize the training of NCOs by opening regional Command Schools were, however, soon abandoned.

Infantry practising their tactical drills while training at the Curragh in 1927. This formation was known as the 'V-shape' or 'Arrow Head', and was used while crossing open ground to provide maximum security to the front and to the rear.

Refinement of officer training and education, guided by the work of the Temporary Plans Division, saw the school absorbed into the newly established Military College in October 1930. Located in the Curragh Camp, the college's first commanding officer was Maj Gen Hugo MacNeill, one of its most vocal proponents after his return from America. A few training manuals were developed in 1926 by the No. 1 (Training) Bureau, though British manuals for specialist corps, such as artillery and engineers, had to be acquired and adapted. Large-scale Army exercises were relatively rare. When held at the Curragh in September 1925 and in the Wicklow Mountains in September 1926, they provided tantalizing glimpses of what could be achieved when collective training was possible.

Much to the chagrin of the General Staff, the demands of internal security and guard duty continued to dominate, especially after the assassination in July 1927 of Kevin O'Higgins, Minister for Justice and Vice President of the Executive Council. The resulting creation of a special protection unit of more than 100 men, detailed to provide additional security to government ministers, was a further unwelcome drain on manpower. Even though responsibility for domestic intelligence had been entrusted to An Garda Síochána in 1926, attempts to similarly hand over responsibility for ministerial protection were blocked at cabinet level, and the unit remained in existence into the 1930s. Successive Chiefs of Staff urged the government to abolish the unit and to close smaller and less important outposts, but progress was slow. Despite persistent efforts to persuade them otherwise, government ministers continued to regard security against internal dissent as the Defence Forces' *raison d'être* until the eve of the Second World War.

Regulations for the raising of a reserve force were finally prepared and distributed in 1927. Soldiers whose period of enlistment had ended became eligible for reserve service, with thirty days of paid training per annum, theoretically providing the Defence Forces with 'an easily mobilized *trained* fighting force … part complementary and part supplementary to the regular force'.[29] Initial plans envisaging a reserve of 20,000 men by 1940, based on the assumption that the regular force would be maintained at 10,000, soon proved unfeasible. By the late 1920s the Defence Forces scarcely had the resources to train its regular forces, never mind allocate time and equipment to the reserve. To make matters worse, no less than five separate reserve forces were established between 1927 and 1931, including a Volunteer

Reserve and Reserve Officer Training Corps in October and November 1929 respectively. The Officer Training Corps was to be recruited from among third-level students, and despite the establishment of corps in each of the main universities, less than 20 per cent of those who enrolled during their university studies took out commissions after graduation.

'A spirit of efficiency and corporate pride'[30]

The Defence Forces began the 1930s with a hint of controversy attached to some senior officers. Two incidents, one that played out in public, the other in the shadows, represented a final attempt to exert some political influence by an officer corps who had come to prominence between 1919 and 1923.

Formed in 1929, the National Defence Association (NDA) was established as a response in part to the declining fortunes of the Army journal, *An tÓglách*,

Supervised by an officer, National Army soldiers practise their shooting skills at a firing range at the Curragh Camp. One appears to be glancing nervously over his shoulder.

and to provide a forum for officers. Led by Hugo MacNeill and Michael Costello, its aims were to foster and maintain discipline, esprit de corps and efficiency among officers, to ensure that the Irish Army developed as a bulwark of Irish nationality, and to educate the Irish people as to the 'great problem' of defence.

Rebranded as the Association's journal in October 1929, *An tÓglách* began to print articles and editorials that frequently questioned and were occasionally critical of government policy. It was not long before the Association's activities raised the hackles of senior ministers, including Ernest Blythe, Vice President of the Executive Council and acting Minister for Defence in the absence of Desmond FitzGerald. Blythe raised the government's concerns at a Council of Defence meeting in January 1930, registering his objections to the 'type of matters' being raised by the Association, but also his disappointment that they 'were being put forward over the signature of [MacNeill], a serving officer, from his official residence'.[31] Despite the removal of Costello as editor of *An tÓglách* in the aftermath of the meeting, the journal continued its provocative editorial stance. The Association's tactics proved counter-productive and approval for its existence was withdrawn by the government in October 1930, precipitating an acrimonious dissolution that was played out in pages of the national press, though with far less controversy than the 1924 Mutiny.

If the 1924 Mutiny had stress-tested the National Army's commitment to the democratic principles of the state, and its willingness to serve whatever government was chosen by the electorate, the final test of this commitment was still to come. Less than a decade after the end of the Civil War, the general election of February 1932 placed Fianna Fáil – the party founded in 1926 by Éamon de Valera and other anti-Treaty TDs – in government. The political atmosphere in which that election took place was febrile. For the second time in less than a decade, military courts dealing with internal political disorder had been established.

Any hint of nervousness within the Defence Forces' senior ranks at the prospect of a Fianna Fáil government was perhaps understandable. Several of the most prominent leaders of the anti-Treaty IRA were now bound for ministerial office. While in opposition Fianna Fáil had frequently declared its intention to further reduce an already severely understrength army. Rumours circulated that officers would be replaced by anti-Treaty republicans. In

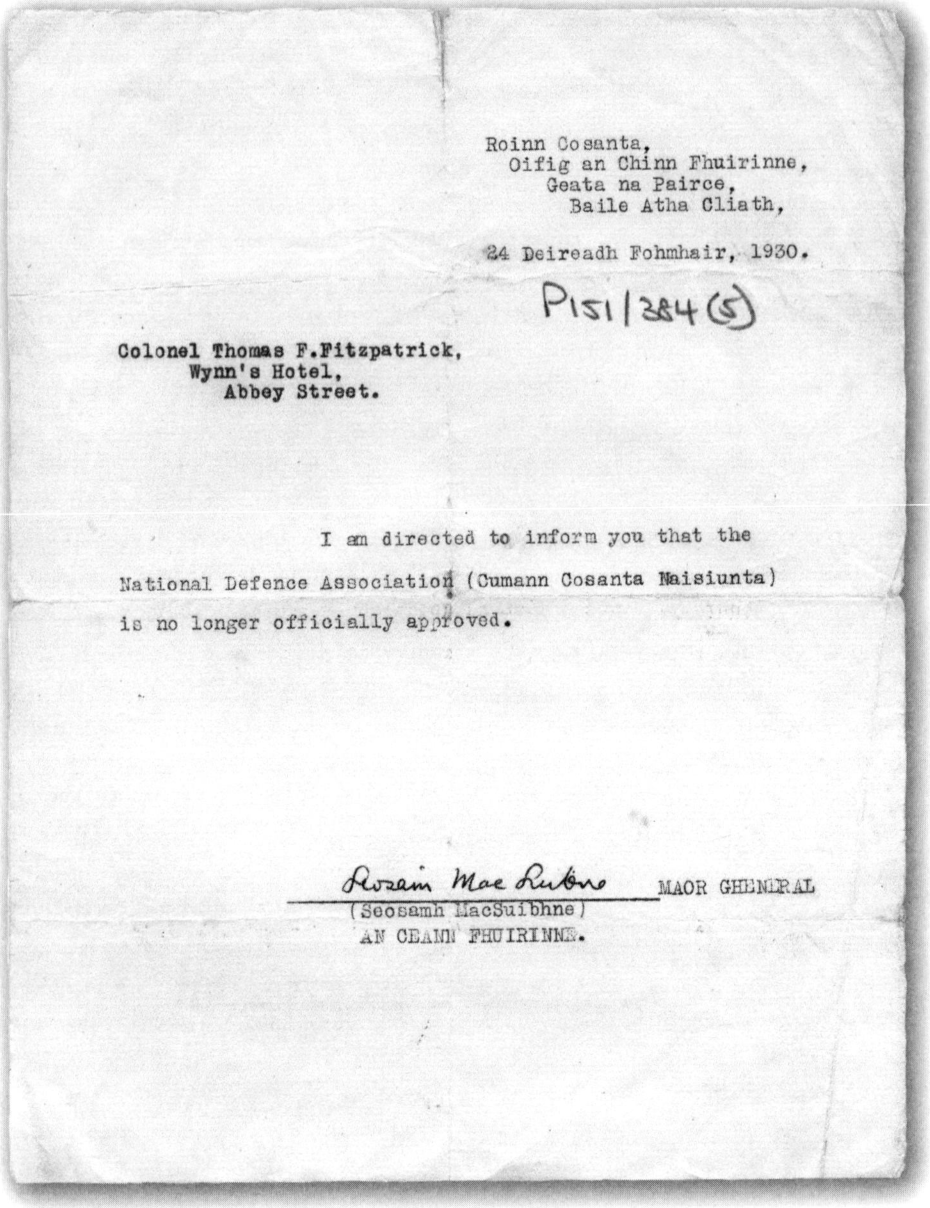

Roinn Cosanta,
Oifig an Chinn Fhuirinne,
Geata na Pairce,
Baile Atha Cliath,

24 Deireadh Fohmhair, 1930.

P151/384(5)

Colonel Thomas F.Fitzpatrick,
Wynn's Hotel,
Abbey Street.

I am directed to inform you that the National Defence Association (Cumann Cosanta Naisiunta) is no longer officially approved.

Seosamh Mac Suibhne MAOR GHENERAL
(Seosamh MacSuibhne)
AN CEANN FHUIRINNE.

The National Defence Association, established in 1929 as an officers' forum, soon ran afoul of senior government ministers, due to its perceived attempts to influence the government's defence policy. In October 1930 the government withdrew its approval for the NDA, which was communicated by Chief of Staff Joseph MacSweeney to its vice president, Col Thomas Fitzpatrick, on 24 October.

anticipation of reprisals, particularly for the state-sanctioned executions, some records dating from the Civil War were quietly destroyed.

There were certainly elements within the state's security forces, both civil and military, that considered an attempted coup against a Fianna Fáil government. Little direct evidence exists that would shed light on how advanced plans were and who was involved, though some plotted more openly than others. Garda Commissioner and former GOCF, Eoin O'Duffy, canvassed army support for a military dictatorship, with O'Duffy at its head. Maj Gen Michael Brennan, appointed Chief of Staff in October 1931, swiftly stifled O'Duffy's efforts and reaffirmed the army's intention to support the newly elected government. Fellow officers and senior Cumann na nGaedheal politicians did their part to hold any potential mutineers in check, and on 9 March 1932 the peaceful transfer of power was completed.

The Mutiny of March 1924 had marked the end of the National Army's transition, at times a painful one, to a formal, state-controlled army. Professionalization followed within the constraints of falling personnel numbers and limited budgets, and in the absence of a clearly defined defence policy. The General Staff frequently found itself out of step with a government increasingly content to maintain the smallest possible force. There was simply no appetite within Leinster House to divert scarce financial resources to the Defence Forces. Proposals that emanated from the Army Organization Board and Temporary Plans Division anticipated a larger army and far greater levels of investment than actually materialized, and apathy soon set in. The Ministers and Secretaries Act of 1924 limited the terms of office for each of the military members of the Council of Defence to just three years. Yet between 1922 and 1932 only Peadar MacMahon served as Chief of Staff for the full three years. His predecessor Seán Mac Mahon was forced out of office, while neither Dan Hogan (1927–9), Seán Mac Eoin (1929) or Joseph Sweeney (1929–31) completed a full term. Such a high rate of turnover is striking among men who had come to prominence during the War of Independence and were still relatively young. The government's willingness to allow the Defence Forces shrink to the barest possible minimum was underpinned by several assumptions, not least a firm belief that Britain could be relied on for military assistance in the event of a threat from a belligerent power. As authoritarian governments tightened their grip on Europe and the continent inched closer to war, the Defence Forces nonetheless turned its focus to external threats.

THE CARTOONS AND CARTOONISTS OF *AN tÓGLÁCH*

First published on 31 August 1918, *An tÓglách* ('The Soldier') was styled as the official newspaper of the Irish Volunteers and a continuation of the *Irish Volunteer* newsletter, published from February 1914 to April 1916. *An tÓglách* evolved to become the journal of the Defence Forces and remained in print, in various formats, until 1933. The journal served many purposes and after the formation of the National Army in early 1922 printed a wide variety of material, from Defence Forces Regulations and General Orders to editorials, training guides, historical essays, and in-depth features on units and general military life. Maj Gen Piaras Béaslaí, Col Jeremiah 'Ginger' O'Connell and Comdt William J. Brennan-Whitmore were among its most frequent contributors. Administration of the journal fell under the Chief of Staff's Branch from 1922, and a grant-in-aid was provided from the Army's budget until October 1923.

As the journal grew in confidence and length in the early and mid-1920s, a lighter side to its content began to emerge, often expressed in

Cartoon by GA (Fr Tom Grogan), depicting an armoured car carrying three Defence Forces officers and men, asking a young boy: 'Did you see an aeroplane coming down here my lad?' The boy, who can be seen dropping a pebble and hiding a catapult behind his back, replies: 'Er, n-no sir, I was only shooting at sparrers!'

Cartoon by GA (Fr Tom Grogan) titled 'Company Formation' depicting Defence Forces troops marching with their partners, no. 3 in the 'Military Terms Illustrated' series. This cartoon was reprinted on the June 1979 cover of *An Cosantóir*, along with an appeal for help identifying the artist. Lt Gen M.J. Costello wrote to the journal to identify the artist as Fr Grogan, a letter that was published in the October 1979 issue.

cartoons. *An tÓglách* debuted cartoons on 1 December 1923, with a cover and internal illustrations by Lt P. Collins depicting a boxing tournament held in Cork Command the previous month. The cover of the next issue carried the debut of Capt B.S.C. Thomson. A staff officer at the Army School of Instruction, Thomson became *An tÓglách*'s regular cartoonist for the next three years. His sketches are dotted throughout each issue, alongside a long-running series about the adventures of 'Private Murphy' and humorous illustrations of current events.

1923 was also the year that well-known artist Frank Leah (1886–1972) was commissioned to provide pen portraits of officers and men in the various corps and commands. His portraits graced fifteen covers that year, with many more sketches printed within the journal.

Cartoon by B.S.C. Thomson, printed in the 9 October 1926 edition of *An tÓglách*, titled 'More artistic impressions of the Manoeuvres', referring to Defence Forces manoeuvres undertaken in the Wicklow Mountains in September 1926. In his report to the Minister for Defence, Chief of Staff Peadar MacMahon noted that the exercises imposed on the troops a 'severe test of stamina', and also incorporated the use of machine gun blank ammunition for the first time, introducing a sense of realism to the exercises previously unobtainable. British Pathé filmed the manoeuvres.

In January 1926 *An tÓglách* moved to a more demanding weekly publication schedule, and responsibility for cover illustrations was soon shared between Thomson and Fr Tom Grogan. Ordained in 1922, Grogan was a talented musician, portrait artist and prolific cartoonist. Appearing under the nom de plume 'GA' (an effort to evade detection by his religious superiors), Grogan was a regular contributor to the satirical magazine *Dublin Opinion*. Beginning on 5 June 1926, *An tÓglách* began publishing a series of Grogan's cartoons on its cover, collectively titled 'Military Terms Illustrated' – twenty-eight appeared in total. Grogan's well-established satirical style was on full view, displaying humour more risqué than might have been expected from 'The Army Journal'. Throughout 1926 Grogan also provided illustrations for *An tÓglách*'s serialization of *Clementina*, a historical novel by Alfred E.W. Mason first published in 1901.

An tÓglách experienced periodic financial troubles and underwent significant reorganization after publication of its Christmas 1926 issue. When it reappeared in October 1927, after a ten-month hiatus, there were precious few photographs and no cartoons. From October 1927 to its demise in 1933, *An tÓglách* adopted a more sober editorial tone and, despite an increase in page length from twenty to more than one hundred, no longer had room for the antics of Private Murphy, or Grogan's satirical takes on military life.

A brief history of *An tÓglách*, with a particular emphasis on the 1918–22 period, was published in the April 1932 issue. In addition to its near complete run of issues (which are available to view online), Military Archives holds a collection of original cartoons and sketches by Leah, Thomson, and Grogan (some unpublished), as well as a handful of cartoons by other contributors.

CHAPTER 3

1932–9
HOLDING PATTERN

By the time Fianna Fáil – supported by the Labour Party – took office in March 1932, the storm clouds of another European war were gathering. The strength of the Defence Forces was now at an all-time low. Despite regular and vociferous criticism of Cumann na nGaedheal's defence policy, once in power Fianna Fáil adopted largely the same approach – maintenance of the Defence Forces in the smallest form possible. As a result the 1930s were largely years of stasis, with few developments of note before the sudden rush in 1938 and 1939 to expand the Defence Forces and prepare for war in Europe.

Frank Aiken's appointment as Minister for Defence in March 1932 was an important step in defusing any potential tension with the Fianna Fáil administration. Though he had succeeded Liam Lynch as leader of the anti-Treaty IRA in 1923, that appointment came in the final weeks of the Civil War and Aiken had been prominent in efforts to avoid conflict in April and May 1922. The military forces he now inherited were in poor condition; under strength, ill-equipped and dispersed across nearly thirty barracks and posts. Rationalization of personnel in a more suitable, smaller number of barracks was desirable and a long-standing military request. Yet the local economic cost of barracks closures was a political landmine that Aiken was unwilling to approach; indeed, it remains a sensitive topic.

'The primary purpose ... is a political one'

Aiken's main innovation was to reform the reserve forces. Government policy since 1925 had ostensibly been to develop the regular Army as a small cadre of well-equipped troops, around which a large, trained reserve could coalesce in a time of crisis. The main problem with this policy – in addition to the ongoing failure to properly fund the Army – was that no coherent scheme for raising a reserve force had yet been implemented.

Aiken announced the creation of a new Volunteer Force in April 1934, alongside a new tactical and territorial organization for the Defence Forces, which came into effect in July 1934. Named in a deliberate homage to the Irish Volunteers of 1913, the new Volunteer Force was expected to attract 20,000 recruits by 1936, complementing or absorbing existing reserve detachments.

Taken at face value, the creation of the Volunteer Force was a welcome attempt to bolster the regular Army. In truth, Aiken's motivations were political rather than military, and he pressed ahead with the formation of the Volunteer Force despite the objections of the General Staff. Twenty-one Fianna Fáil supporters were commissioned into the Defence Forces as Area Administrative Officers to help administer the force, while local committees (known as 'Sluagh') were created to assist Volunteer units. The Volunteer Reserve, established by Cumann na nGaedheal in 1929 and regarded by Fianna Fáil with suspicion, was disbanded without ceremony in March 1935.

Seán Lemass, Minister for Industry and Commerce, outlined the policy underpinning the Volunteer Force in a memorandum to his cabinet colleagues:

> The primary purpose of any Volunteer scheme in the present circumstances of the Saorstát is a political one, i.e. the provision of an opportunity of military training in a manner beneficial to the State to young men to whom military manoeuvres are an attraction

(*left to right*): Chief of Staff Maj Gen Michael Brennan, Minister for Defence Frank Aiken, Taoiseach Éamon de Valera, and Charles Lindbergh, pictured at Baldonnel Aerodrome on 21 November 1936. During his visit Lindbergh took de Valera into the air for his first ever flight. Lindbergh's Miles Mohawk monoplane is pictured in the background, with the registration number G-AEKN partially visible.

and who if they do not get the association they desire in an official organization may be induced to seek it in illegal organizations.[1]

The Volunteer Force thus had the dual purpose of bolstering the Defence Forces and combating the attraction to the young men of Ireland of the IRA, the Blueshirts or any other organization deemed subversive to the state.

An initial rush of enthusiasm saw 11,594 men enlist in the first twelve months, allowing Aiken to continue to insist that the regular army would be maintained as a small highly trained force, 'which would serve as a pivot around which might, if necessary, be organized, developed, and trained, the entire man-power of the State.'[2] However, that early flush of success soon proved to be a false dawn.

The tunic and shako cap of Maj Gen Michael Brennan's dress uniform, which is preserved in the National Museum of Ireland. New dress uniforms for officers were introduced in 1935. The uniform for general officers, seen here, was predominantly black, with gold and scarlet facings, while the shako was crowned with matching scarlet. Gold aguilettes were worn on the right shoulder, while the collar and cuff patches were decorated with gold oak leaves.

Recruitment after the initial wave was hampered by problems equipping, training, and administering the force. Removal of unemployment benefits to Volunteers attending training camps and mobilizations affected morale and quickly dampened enthusiasm. More than half of those who enlisted between 1934 and 1939 were discharged for failure to attend training. The Volunteer Force stood at less than 10,000 men in April 1938, with attendance at local training dropping to just 29 per cent. When the Volunteer Force was reorganized in March 1939, all 7,278 then left were discharged with the option of re-enlisting – just 3,731 chose to do so. Strength had risen to just under 7,000 by September 1939, half of whom were not yet fully trained.

Perhaps the central problem to Aiken's vision of the regular Army as a highly trained core, around which an enlarged force could quickly coalesce, was that the regular Army itself was poorly equipped and poorly trained. The Volunteer Force merely exacerbated existing problems. Maj Gen Michael Brennan, Chief of Staff, left Aiken in no doubt of the folly of expecting the main force to cope with the additional burden of training the Volunteers:

The Regular Army ... is not in any way capable of discharging its theoretical function of providing a highly trained cadre for expansion in emergency. Since the creation of the Volunteer Force the administrative and guard duties have very much increased owing

108

to the re-opening of closed barracks and posts and also because of week-end camps, additional training camps, etc. In addition an enormously increased amount of duty has to be performed in connection with training of the Volunteers but this is largely of the barracks square or elementary type in which the regular troops are already proficient. The training and administrative duties described have however entirely destroyed the few opportunities the regular troops previously had of obtaining any more advanced training.[3]

'The Saorstát can hardly be said to have a Defence Force at all'[4]

Brennan's warning reflected the fact that, for much of the 1930s, the Defence Forces were placed in a holding pattern. Some stability in the General Staff was finally achieved by Brennan's reappointment as Chief of Staff on two occasions; he held the position until January 1940. Otherwise, the new government's treatment of the Defence Forces was virtually indistinguishable from its predecessor, an irony that can hardly have been lost on those who recalled the fears regarding the handover of power to Fianna Fáil in 1932. Financial investment remained static up to 1938, fluctuating between £1m

A Volunteer Force platoon conducting foot drill on a parade square.
The Volunteers are carrying Lee Enfield rifles with bayonets fixed.
The photo was possibly taken in Portobello Barracks,
Dublin (renamed Cathal Brugha Barracks in 1952).

A gun crew from the Volunteer Force training under the watchful eye of a regular army NCO, with the officers' mess of McKee Barracks visible in the background. The gun crew are operating one of the 18-pdr field guns provided by the British Army in 1922 and used by the National Army during the Civil War, including during the bombardment of the Four Courts.

and £1.5m per annum, a sum even less significant than it appears, as the lion's share was eaten up by wages. Up to 10 per cent of the defence budget also went unspent every year.

The government's hands were, of course, somewhat tied by a difficult economic climate. The aftershocks of the 1929 Wall Street Crash were still reverberating around the globe, and in 1932 the Irish government became embroiled in an 'Economic War' with Britain, which lasted for six years and further constrained public finances. Investment in military equipment and other matériel, most of which ultimately came from Britain, remained at negligible levels. Personnel numbers reached a nadir in 1931 when less than 5,000 men were in uniform, and hovered just below 6,000 for most of the decade. In 1935, Aiken informed the Dáil that Ireland was spending less on military equipment than any other European nation, with the possible exceptions of Albania and Bulgaria. The Army's continued reliance on obsolete or outdated equipment is obvious from its transport budget for 1935/6: 25 per cent of the allocated £62,000 was earmarked for horse transport. Familiarization of troops with mechanised transport and armour remained at an experimental stage, despite longstanding requests from the General Staff for the funding necessary to integrate tanks, armoured fighting vehicles and mechanized artillery. Attempts to establish factories for manufacturing tanks and ammunition were shut down by the Department of Finance.

Uniform of the Volunteer Force, from the National Museum of Ireland's collection. The uniform differed from that of the regular Army, and was based on the Irish brigade recruited by Sir Roger Casement from among Irish prisoners of war held in Germany during the First World War. The civilian committees created to help run the Volunteer Force at a local level, known as Sluagh, were more popularly known as 'Aiken's Slugs', after the Minister for Defence.

Nonetheless, in 1934 two Swedish -made Landsverk L60 light tanks were acquired for the Cavalry Corps (formed in 1934), followed by eight Landsverk L180 armoured cars in 1938 and early 1939. Though far from sufficient to adequately defend the state, these purchases did provide opportunities for training personnel using modern equipment. Mechanization of the entire Artillery Corps was finally completed by 1940.

Two of the central elements of the defence policy adopted in the 1920s remained in place under Éamon de Valera's government: a commitment to neutrality and a guarantee that Ireland would not allow itself to be used as a base for attacking Britain. Tentative defence plans were nonetheless drawn up by G2 Branch (Intelligence) in 1934, recommending the adoption of a guerrilla-style defence plan, predicated on the assumption that Britain was the power most likely to invade Ireland in order to protect its western flank: 'There is a constant feeling that having fought the British on this basis before, with a certain measure of success, that it forms the obvious basis on which we should fight them again.'[5]

That plan was quickly dismissed in favour of the recommendations contained in 'Fundamental factors affecting Saorstát defence problem', a detailed examination of Ireland's defensive capabilities and a stark warning of their inadequacy. Drafted in early 1936 by Comdt Dan Bryan of G2 and intended as an internal document, 'Fundamental factors' became an unofficial memorandum on the status of the Defence Forces, forwarded by Brennan to Aiken in September 1936. It remains one of the most important statements of Irish defence policy.

111

TAR ASTEAĊ INS NA h-ÓSLAIŚ

This recruitment poster, encouraging enlistment in the Volunteer Force, was designed in 1934 by Seán Keating (1889–1977), a Limerick artist well known for his paintings of the War of Independence and the industrialisation of Ireland. The caption reads 'Tar asteach ins na h-Óglaigh' ('Join the Volunteers').

The simple truth it outlined was that the state's ability to mount a credible defence of its territory was non-existent. In September 1936 Brennan referred to 'Fundamental factors' in support of his request for an additional investment of at least £1.5m per annum for three years. That was the minimum sum required by the Defence Forces to enable mobilization of its existing 'paper strength' of four reinforced brigades (18,800 men, including all reserves):

The existing units are, with few exceptions, far from complete in either personnel, material or equipment. With few exceptions none of the Volunteer Units have even half their establishments

112

A trumpeter on horseback, dressed in the uniform of the Blue Hussars. The Blue Hussars were established in 1931 and more properly known as the Mounted Escort. They were typically used on ceremonial occasions, and are most well-known for their activities during the Eucharistic Congress in 1932. As their name suggests, the uniform was sapphire blue with gold frogging and lace, accompanied by a black busby (hat) with orange-yellow plumes (*see below*). The Blue Hussars were disbanded in 1948.

of personnel; in addition many units would if mobilized have practically no armament or equipment. For example only 9 out of the 24 Batteries of Artillery required are available. Military units without the necessary personnel and armament are of course useless.[6]

De Valera's public pronouncements on defence policy frequently caused some concern within GHQ, such as when he declared in June 1937 that 'we can have no real plan of defence for this country so long as there are parts of our territory which are capable of being occupied by the British at Britain's will … the proper foundation for national defence is the exclusive control of our own country'.[7] Noting the comments, Dan Bryan offered a subtle rebuke and

Dress uniform of the Blue Hussars as displayed in the National Museum of Ireland.

a reminder that time was a luxury the Defence Forces could ill afford: 'A European war may start while the undesirable conditions mentioned by the President continue'.[8] That was a chance the government were willing to take, on the assumption that, for its own safety, Britain would be obliged to come to Ireland's aid. Such reasoning formed the basis for the consistently trenchant opposition raised by the Minister for Finance, Seán MacEntee, to any proposed increase in defence spending.

Further analysis by the General Staff, presented to the government in late 1937, suggested that an adequate defence of the state would in fact require three divisions, alongside a wide array of specialist units including a coast guard, coastal defence units, a twelve squadron Air Corps (100+ aircraft) and a new naval force – more than 100,000 men in total. The outlay required was at least £4.5m. Military expenditure did in fact increase from 1937 onwards, though at a rate far below what was required to fulfil even the minimalist ambition to complete and equip four reinforced brigades.

Supplies of military equipment began to dry up, as Britain focused on strengthening its own forces. A military mission to America in 1939 had no success in procuring weapons or equipment. One positive element of the concessions gained by de Valera in ending the 'Economic War' with Britain in early 1938 was the return of the Treaty Ports, a crucial factor in allowing Ireland to maintain its neutrality when war broke out in September 1939.

Certificate awarded to Maj J.P.M. Cotter for coming third in the chess competition during the July 1932 Tailteann Games, the last year in which the games were held. Unlike in previous years, many of the top Irish and international athletes and competitors who had attended previous Tailteann Games were unable to do so, as the 1932 Olympics were held in Los Angeles in early August.

SUBJECT	Serial No.	Lecture	Conference	Map Problem	Tactical Walk & Terrain Ex.	Demonstrations and Practices	Total Hours	REMARKS
GROUP I:								
Combined Tactics	C.T.	14	39	2	18	10	101	34 days
Combat Orders	C.O.	5	5	--	--	1	11	
GROUP II:								
Infantry	Inf.	5	4	--	8	4	10	10 days
Artillery	Arty.	5	10	3	6	1	22	4 "
Cavalry	Cav.	3	12	1	3	2	15	2 "
Air Corps	Air.	2	8	2	--	--	10	½ "
Chemical Warfare	C.W.	1	17	--	--	1	18	1 "
Field Engineering	F.E.	13	1	2	5	1	18	2 "
Signal Communication.	Sigs.	2	2	1	--	1	4	1 "
Medical Services	M.S.	7	5	--	--	--	12	½ "
GROUP III:								
Command, Staff and Logistics	C.S.L.	5	14	13	3	1	32	10½ "
Methods of Training.	Trng.	32	1	1	--	1	23	½ "
Military Intelligence.	M.I.	5	8	--	--	--	17	
Military Organisation.	M.O.	9	2	--	--	--	11	
GROUP IV:								
Military History	M.H.	5	23	--	--	--	33	7 "
Leadership	L.S.	10	--	--	--	--	14	½ "
MISCELLANEOUS:								
Supervised Study	--	--	--	--	--	--	24	"
G. T. E's.	--	--	--	--	14	--	10	"
GRAND TOTAL	--	123	150	23	59	21	461	108½ days

Summary of the syllabus for the 1934–5 term at the Command and Staff School, a constituent school of the Military College. The Command and Staff School was established to train officers for higher field command and departmental and headquarters staff duty, and is the senior school in the Defence Forces. The first Command and Staff course commenced in February 1931.

'Only an adjunct of the field troops'

The years leading up to the Emergency were somewhat difficult for the Air Corps. In November 1931 the Council of Defence declared that the administration of the Corps was inadequate, unsurprisingly failing to consider the General Staff's culpability in appointing unsuitable commanding officers. The arrival in June 1935 of Col Patrick A. Mulcahy (younger brother of the former Minister for Defence) did little to improve the situation.

Mulcahy had made his name with the Artillery Corps and would later go on to serve as Chief of Staff, but had no aviation background. His brief

A souvenir programme for the Defence Forces Military Tattoo, held at the RDS in Ballsbridge, Dublin, from 17 to 21 September 1935. The cover image features a stylised Irish soldier presenting arms. His helmet is the distinctive German Stahlhelm pattern worn by the Defence Forces from the mid-1920s until 1940. The tattoo featured ceremonial parades, training demonstrations, a display by the School of Equitation and the re-enactment of historical episodes, including Patrick Sarsfield's famous raid on the army of William III at Ballyneety in 1690.

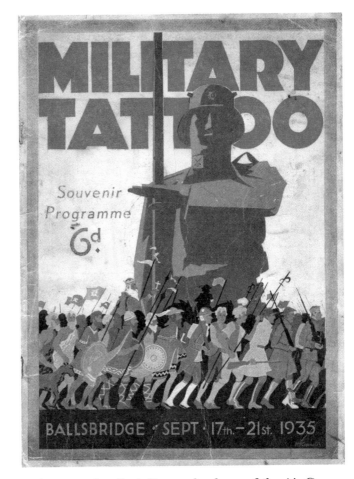

appears to have been to improve the discipline and culture of the Air Corps. Col Charles Russell, former OC of the Air Corps, publicly criticized the appointment: 'Flying personnel cannot be commanded and will have no real respect for anyone over them who is not an active flying officer. No greater mistake could have been made, therefore, than the appointment of a non-flying officer to command the Air Corps.'[9]

While problems with morale and mismanagement would eventually lead to an official investigation in 1941, the Air Corps continued to perform the few functions it was assigned. Its participation in the ceremonial elements of the Eucharistic Congress in 1932 included an escort of Vickers Vespas, in cruciform formation, for the mail steamer carrying the Papal Legate,

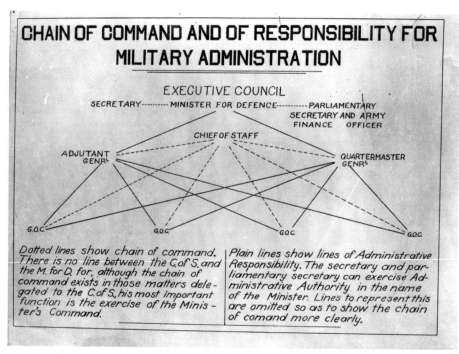

A diagram illustrating the convoluted chain of command for the Defence Forces, created by the Defence Forces (Temporary Provisions) Acts in conjunction with the Ministers and Secretaries Act of 1924. Note that administrative responsibility is differentiated from military chain of command. In the event of invasion during the Emergency, plans were in place to simplify the command structure by designating the Chief of Staff as General Officer Commanding the Forces. The chart can be dated to pre-1937 due to the reference to the Executive Council, but accurately displays the Defence Forces' command structure for the Emergency period, and beyond.

Cardinal Lauri, as it arrived in Dún Laoghaire. Aerial photography of the outdoor ceremonies was conducted throughout, with valuable opportunities for further practise in the techniques of aerial observation and reconnaissance photography provided during combined Defence Forces exercises in the Phoenix Park in September 1933. An air firing range was developed at Gormanston Camp in 1935, which continues to be used to this day.

Prior to 1936 the Air Corps was dogged by an inability to keep its planes airborne due to frequent manpower shortages of mechanics and technicians. Plans to recruit boy apprentices on nine- and twelve-year service terms had been approved by the Minister for Defence, Desmond FitzGerald, in March 1930, but it was not until March 1936 that arrangements were finalized and the first apprentices arrived at Baldonnel. Indeed, 1936 saw a flurry of activity around the Air Corps' main base. In May the state's new civil airline, Aer Lingus, began operating from Baldonnel, where it remained until transferred in 1940 to Collinstown (later renamed Dublin Airport).

The commencement of civil flights from Baldonnel provided the catalyst for professionalization of air traffic services, with specialist training provided for two Air Corps officers at London's Croydon Airport. 1936 also saw the opening of Rineanna Aerodrome – later renamed Shannon Airport – which would provide a home for an Air Corps reconnaissance and fighter detachment during the Emergency. In what amounted to a significant bucking of the overall trend of underinvestment in defence, more than twenty new aircraft were acquired between 1930 and 1938, including Vickers Vespas, an array of Avros and four Gloster Gladiators. As welcome as these new machines were, they were badly needed to replace existing aircraft that were obsolete or past their recommended life-span and merely allowed the Air Corps to maintain a token aerial capability.

By the outbreak of the Second World War the Air Corps had yet to be successfully woven into the general fabric of the Defence Forces and were regarded by Brennan as 'negligible … really only an adjunct of the Field Troops'.[10] As had been the case in the 1920s, there was little direction from government as to how the development of civil and military aviation might be co-ordinated. A share of the blame for the entropy that enveloped the Air Corps also lay, however, with the General Staff itself. Internal planning still

Minister for Defence, Frank Aiken (*third from the right*), inspects a Vickers Vespa. The first four Vespa IV entered service with the Air Corps in April 1930. Four Vespa V arrived a year later.

overwhelmingly focused on the infantry, with the Air Corps an afterthought, at best. Col Michael J. Costello would later recall how he had sought an indication, in the early 1930s, of the Air Corps' projected annual budget and a policy to guide expenditure: 'The net result of those discussions was that it could not be said in advance what sum of money would be available from time to time ... nor could anything definite be obtained on the question of policy [other] than a general decision that there would be an Air Corps.'[11]

'A relative freedom from outside interference'

As the outbreak of a major war grew increasingly inevitable following the Munich Conference of September 1938, it was abundantly clear to the General Staff that their forces were woefully ill-equipped, capable only of token resistance to any invasion. Repeated warnings to the government had failed to elicit an adequate response. Fianna Fáil had proved itself as unwilling as Cumann na nGaedheal to address glaring weaknesses in the state's defences. It had also failed to adequately prepare the public for the enormous national effort that would be required in the event of another major war. As observed by Dan Bryan in 1936, 'the Saorstát people are ... not prepared or educated to the stage at which they are prepared in practice to provide sufficient forces to guarantee even a relative freedom from outside interference.'[12]

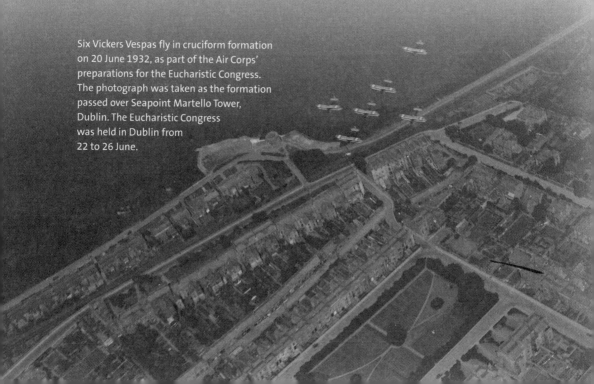

Six Vickers Vespas fly in cruciform formation on 20 June 1932, as part of the Air Corps' preparations for the Eucharistic Congress. The photograph was taken as the formation passed over Seapoint Martello Tower, Dublin. The Eucharistic Congress was held in Dublin from 22 to 26 June.

Three Avro Ansons at Baldonnel, photographed in June 1938. The Air Corps acquired nine in total between 1937 and 1939 and had seven more on order, which were never delivered due to the outbreak of the Second Word War. In the background can be seen the nose of a De Havilland DH.84 Dragon, acquired by the Air Corps in March 1937 to serve as a target tug for anti-aircraft and air-to-air target practise. It was the first twin-engined aircraft to enter service with the Air Corps. The nine Ansons and the Dragon formed No. 1 Reconnaissance and Medium Bomber Squadron.

When Germany invaded Poland on 1 September 1939, Ireland found itself with the barest outline of an air force, no navy, and an infantry hopelessly understrength and undertrained. The Artillery Corps possessed just eight anti-aircraft guns (four 3-inch guns acquired in 1928, and four Bofors L60 acquired in 1939). The Treaty Ports were well protected with BL 9.2-inch and 6-inch naval guns, while twenty 12-pounder naval guns were stationed at strategic points around the coast. Small quantities of modern infantry weapons had been purchased in the later 1930s, including Bren light machine guns and further quantities of .303 Lee Enfield rifles, but overall the weaponry and equipment necessary for a competent defence of the state on land, at sea, or in the air, were not in place.

The declaration of neutrality, explicitly communicated to the international community in the early days of September 1939, was an important affirmation of the state's independence, and a practical recognition that it

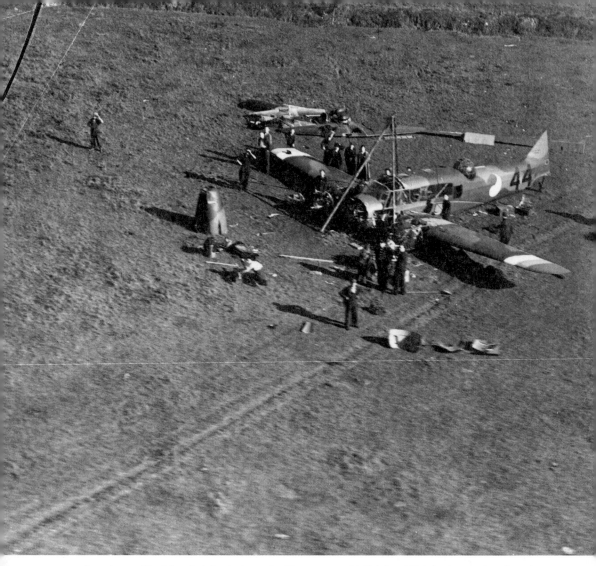

Avro Anson 44, pictured at Borrisokane, Co. Tipperary, on 10 October 1939, having made a forced landing. Though clearly badly damaged, it was repaired and returned to service before eventually being withdrawn in July 1946. Anson 44 was one of five delivered to the Air Corps in February 1939.

was economically and militarily incapable of joining hostilities. Politically, there was a very real danger that participation in a war alongside Britain would re-open the wounds of the Civil War, and reignite internal conflict in Ireland.

Despite the poor state of national defences, independent Ireland had a clear duty to defend itself, if necessary. The obligations placed on neutral states by the Hague Conventions of 1899 and 1907 included the prevention of belligerents using neutral territory (land, air and sea) to conduct military

122

Operation Order 1/1938, dated 5 July, issued to the Field Artillery Brigade, Plunkett Barracks, with details of the impending handover of Cork's harbour defences by the British as part of the return of the Treaty Ports.

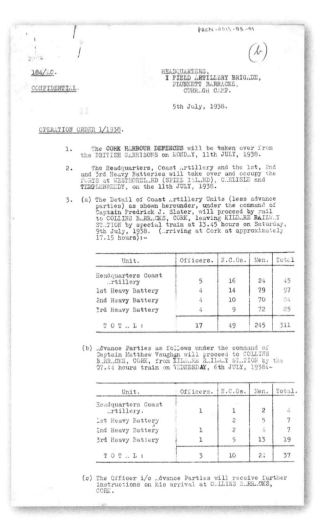

operations. There was no guarantee that the belligerent states would respect Irish neutrality, or indeed that of any other nation.

Even with the reserve and Volunteer Force, personnel numbers in September 1939 were just shy of 14,000, far short of what was required. A resource-poor organization for much of its existence, the Defence Forces were now starved of perhaps the most important resource of all: time. For the second time in less than two decades, it was about to be called upon to undertake a large scale, rapid expansion to meet what appeared to be an existential threat to the state it had been tasked to defend.

The first of the Treaty Ports to be returned was Spike Island, Cobh, Co. Cork. In a ceremony that took place on 11 July 1938, senior members of the government and officers of the Defence Forces watched on as the Irish flag was raised over the fort for the first time. Pictured here are Éamon de Valera (Taoiseach) and Frank Aiken (Minister for Defence), with de Valera's son Vivion in Defence Forces uniform, wearing glasses.

Left: One of the 9.2-inch BL coastal defence guns at Templebreedy Battery, Crosshaven, Co. Cork. Camouflaged against air attack, the gun is pictured being loaded by its crew. The gun had a potential range of almost 27 kilometres. It was handed over to the Defence Forces in 1938 along with the Treaty Ports, and was decommissioned at the end of the Emergency.
Opposite page: Record plan of Spike Island, drafted by Pte W.H. Rowe of the Army Engineers Corps and dated 31 October 1939.

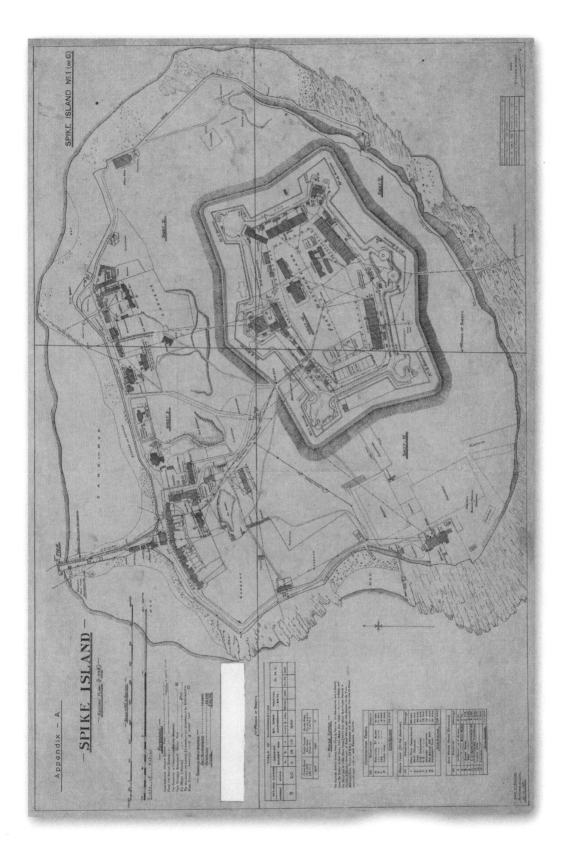

Below: A soldier demonstrating the correct method of throwing a grenade from a kneeling position. The photo dates from before the Emergency.

Opposite page: Undated publicity photograph, taken between 1928 and 1940. This infantry soldier is wearing British 1908 pattern webbing with respirator, tunic and breeches. He is armed with a Lee Enfield, No. 1 Mk III, .303 rifle, which remained standard issue in the Defence Forces until the early 1960s; by then it was long obsolete. The Stahlhelm-pattern helmet worn by this infantryman, used by Germany in the First World War, was selected by the Defence Forces following trials in the late 1920s. Due to a ban on Weimar Germany exporting steel helmets under the terms of the Treaty of Versailles, the helmet was actually manufactured by Vickers in Britain. Popularly known as the 'coal scuttle' helmet, it was replaced by the British Brodie Mark II in 1940, partly due to fears that the similarity of the Vickers to the German army's helmets would cause confusion in the event of an invasion. Many of the old Vickers helmets were painted white and redistributed to various emergency services. The 1908 pattern webbing worn here was replaced by 1937 pattern webbing during the Emergency.

126

BEGINNINGS: THE DEFENCE FORCES SCHOOL OF MUSIC

Army bands have long been considered essential to the creation of esprit de corps. When the first soldiers to wear the uniform of the National Army paraded through Dublin on 1 February 1922, on their way to occupy Beggars Bush Barracks, they were led by a hastily assembled band of pipers, freshly enlisted as members of the army. Pipe bands, recruited in ad hoc fashion, became attached to various units during the Civil War. Recognizing the need for a centralized approach to army band formation and a coherent policy to maintain standards, Richard Mulcahy was the driving force behind the establishment of the Army School of Music in January 1923.

Advised by John Larchet, Professor of Music at University College Dublin, Mulcahy envisaged a school that would play an important role in army and civilian life, with three main objectives: (1) the production of first-class military bands and bandsmen; (2) the training of highly skilled Irish bandmasters; and (3) the broader development of Irish music.

At all times, however, the role of the band in promoting esprit de corps was paramount. As Larchet would later write of the school's foundation: 'An Army without a band is in the same position as a performance of Hamlet without the Prince of Denmark; the central inspiration is lacking.' Among Larchet's recommendations was that the school's first

Col Fritz Brase (*left*) and Capt Friedrich Sauerzweig, respectively the first and second Directors of the School of Music, pictured at the Curragh Camp during the 1920s.

Members of Army Band Nos. 1, 2 and 3 pictured in 1929 in front of the old Military Hospital, Portobello Barracks. The building now houses Military Archives, which is located next door to the School of Music's rehearsal space. Sauerzweig and Brase are seated in the centre of the bottom row.

director should be drawn from the French or Prussian military traditions. Initial approaches to the French Republican Guard Band were unsuccessful, leading to the appointment of a German, Fritz Brase, as Director in January 1923. Friedrich Sauerzweig, a fellow German, was appointed as Assistant Director – both men were experienced military bandmasters and were later commissioned in the National Army, with the rank of Colonel and Captain, respectively. Even with the formal establishment of the School of Music, however, individual commands continued to maintain their own bands; in November 1923, for example, the Dublin Command could boast a fife and drum band with forty-eight members, which had its roots in the handover of Wellington Barracks on 12 April 1922.

Brase was the ideal candidate for the role of Director, having formerly been Director of the Kaiser Alexander First Grenadier Regiment's band. The Army No. 1 Band gave its first public performance on 14 October 1923, reviewed in the *Irish Times* two days later:

Col Sauerzweig and Lt James Doyle, pictured in 1937. Brase was succeeded as Director by Sauerzweig in 1940. Col James Doyle became the first Irishman to assume command of the School of Music when, in 1947, he in turn succeeded Sauerzweig.

The first of the bands turned out from the new Irish School of Military Music received an ovation at the Theatre Royal, Dublin, last night ... The scene in the Theatre Royal was a demonstration of the power of good music, and also a spontaneous tribute to the work accomplished by Colonel Fritz Brase, the head of the school, and his combination of forty instrumentalists.

Among the pieces debuted on the night was the 'General Mulcahy March', composed by Brase in honour of the Minister for Defence.

After brief stints at the Curragh and McKee Barracks, in 1924 the School of Music transferred to its current home in Portobello Barracks (renamed Cathal Brugha Barracks in 1952). By the end of the decade there were

The Army No. 1 Band regularly toured the country during the 1920s and 1930s, performing public concerts. This version of a piece composed by Fritz Brase, 'Spirit of the Irish Army (Irish Fantasia, No. 5)', was recorded at the Theatre Royal in Dublin on 14 November 1930 and released on His Master's Voice, a label of the Gramophone Company.

four Army Bands. No. 2 Band was formed in January 1924 by combining members of the Special Infantry Corps Band with a brass and reed band from Cork Command, while Army No. 3 Band was also formed later that year. Both were initially based at Portobello Barracks before being transferred to Cork and the Curragh, respectively, in 1926. The establishment of a Piping School at the Curragh in 1926 allowed for the more formal attachment of pipe bands to various units and corps, which had previously been done on an ad hoc basis. Pipers regularly serve abroad with units on peacekeeping duties and are a frequent feature of ceremonial events.

Originally a training group for the three main bands, Army No. 4 Band was formally constituted in 1936 and transferred to Custume Barracks, Athlone. Reorganization of the Defence Forces in the late 1990s and 2000s led to the demise of No. 3 Band, while No. 2 Band was renamed Band of the 1 Brigade, and No. 4 Band was renamed Band of the 2 Brigade.

CHAPTER 4

1939–45
THE EMERGENCY

On 2 September 1939, the day after the German invasion of Poland, the Irish government declared a state of emergency and introduced complementary legislation to the Dáil, including the Emergency Powers Bill. Debated and passed by the Oireachtas in one day, the resulting act granted sweeping powers to the government, including stringent censorship of the press and internment. The act also gave rise to the popular term by which the Second World War became known in Ireland: 'the Emergency'. On 3 September 1939 Britain and France declared war on Germany. Several European states responded by declaring their neutrality, including Denmark, Norway, Belgium, the Netherlands, Luxembourg and Ireland. On 12 September an Aide Mémoire was issued to the belligerent governments announcing the closure of Irish airspace and territorial waters.

Over the course of the Emergency the defensive plans of the Defence Forces adapted to changing circumstances, including its growing size, changes in the course of the war, and available matériel. GHQ remained at Parkgate Street, Dublin, while the Army and Air Corps were joined in September 1939 by a small Marine Service. The Army retained the administrative structure of the four commands established in the 1920s: Eastern, Southern, Western and the Curragh Camp, which was expanded to include much of south-east Ireland. That structure remained in place for the duration of the war, with some alterations in the geographical areas that fell under each command, and each command was strengthened by additional personnel as recruitment allowed.

Having spent more than seven years at the Department of Defence, in September 1939 Frank Aiken was appointed Minister for the Co-ordination of Defensive Measures. His replacement at the Department of Defence was Oscar Traynor. Addressing the Dáil shortly after his appointment, Traynor suggested that, despite the outbreak of war, little had changed regarding the government's policy for the Defence Forces:

> The Regular Army has been maintained mainly as a cadre for the Reserve and for reasons of economy its strength has been kept at the lowest possible figure. It is not therefore strong enough to take all the security measures necessitated by the emergency. Moreover the State has declared its neutrality and has thereby assumed the obligations imposed by international law and practice to equip itself to prevent violation of its neutrality by the belligerents.[1]

In late September 1939 the Chief of Staff, Michael Brennan, informed Traynor that two reinforced brigades had been mobilized, but were approximately 30 per cent under strength. Daunted by the cost of mobilization to the proposed war time establishment of 37,560, a strength previously approved, the government decreed that personnel would now be capped at 18,000.

A major international conflict involving Britain was one of the main defensive 'problems' which the Defence Forces had identified and planned for during the 1930s, though on the basis that a larger and better-equipped force would be available. Ireland's geopolitical importance as the western-most point of Europe, and its suitability as a staging post for an assault on Britain, meant that violation of its neutrality by either belligerent was a distinct possibility. Even so, the likelihood of any kind of invasion seemed remote in late 1939 and the early months of 1940.

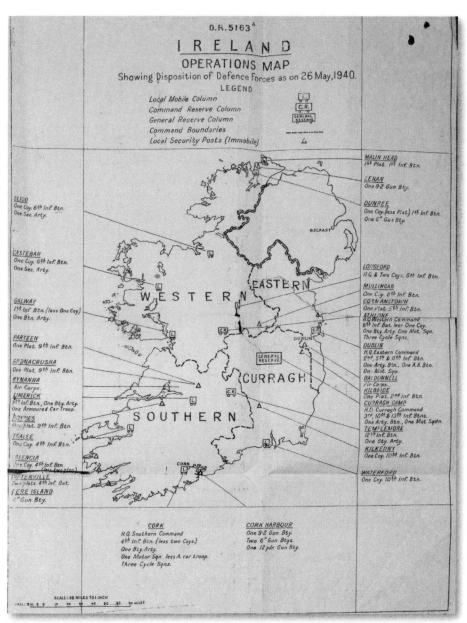

Map of Ireland prepared by the British War Office in May 1940, showing the disposition of the Defence Forces as the so-called 'Phoney War' drew to a close. The disposition shown on the map is not entirely accurate, as the information provided to the British at this time was intentionally obfuscated to disguise certain weaknesses in Ireland's defences.

Col Seán O'Sullivan inspects a Local Defence Force unit during the Emergency. The LDF wore a distinctive brown uniform, and its strength increased to more than 100,000. Though the units were of variable effectiveness, the LDF was an important element of Ireland's wartime defences.

Indeed, an IRA raid on the Magazine Fort in the Phoenix Park, on 23 December 1939, suggested that the greatest threat to the state lay within. More than thirteen tons of ammunition and some Thompson submachine guns were stolen, and though several of the raiders were soon apprehended and most of the stolen goods recovered, the incident was highly embarrassing for the government and the Defence Forces. Disciplinary action included the dismissal of two officers with another called upon to resign, while several other officers were subject to less severe sanctions. Acting under legislation introduced in 1939 and 1940, for the remainder of the Emergency the government implemented internment for IRA members. Seven IRA men were also executed for criminal activity, including the murder of three Gardaí, between September 1940 and December 1944.

Though not linked, Brennan's retirement as Chief of Staff soon followed the Magazine Fort raid. It was a disappointing endnote for an officer with a distinguished career dating from the 1916 Rising. He was replaced in January 1940 by Maj Gen Daniel McKenna, a somewhat surprising choice given he was promoted from the position of Deputy Quartermaster General. As with all his predecessors, McKenna had impeccable revolutionary credentials and, more importantly, was well-regarded by his contemporaries. He remained Chief of Staff for nine years, providing vital continuity in a time of crisis.

'Either of the belligerents may consider the violation of our neutrality'[2]

The joint German/Russian annexation of Poland in September 1939 was followed by eight months of sporadic activity, known as the 'Phoney War'. When those relatively peaceful conditions were shattered by the German annexation of Denmark and Norway, and its rapid advance through the Low Countries into France, the weaknesses of Ireland's defences were

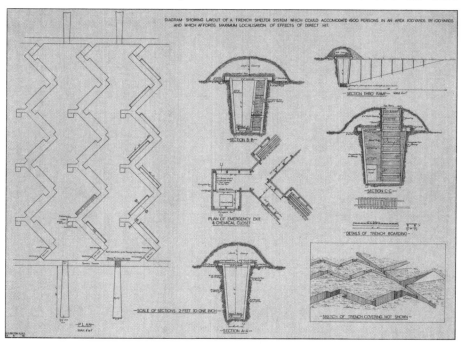

A diagram for a trench shelter system, dated 23 August 1940, capable of accommodating 1,500 people in an area measuring 100 yards by 100 yards. It was designed to 'afford maximum localisation' of the effects of a direct hit.

Hey, lads!
Give us
a hand

JOIN
THE CONSTRUCTION CORPS

As had been the case during the Civil War, a number of specialist units and corps were formed to meet specific tasks during the Emergency. Formed as a non-combatant element of the Defence Forces, the Construction Corps was created on 2 October 1940 and sought recruits aged between 18 and 25, largely from among the ranks of the unemployed. Planning for the Corps had been ongoing for much of 1940. The Department of Defence later referred to the Construction Corps as 'the greatest social experiment ever undertaken by the State ... a national unemployed youth movement'. That rhetoric was never quite fulfilled, with the thinly stretched resources of the Defence Forces preventing anything other than ad hoc and intermittent vocational training for recruits. Despite attempts to maintain the Corps after the Emergency, it was formally disbanded in 1948.

clearly highlighted. After the British Expeditionary Force was driven back to England, and France surrendered to the Germans on 22 June 1940, a simultaneous German invasion of Britain and Ireland seemed inevitable. The previous weeks had shown that neutrality offered no protection from German aggression. At the beginning of May 1940 the Defence Forces could call on just 13,346 all ranks, half of whom were reservists. Jolted into belated action, the government agreed to a new war establishment of 42,000 all ranks and ordered a general mobilization of the Defence Forces.

The first task was to bring the Defence Forces up to strength. A national recruitment drive improved personnel numbers to 37,310 by October – an increase largely facilitated by the introduction, on 5 June, of enlistment for the duration of the Emergency (such recruits were known as Durationists, or E-Men). Early training focused on rapid mobilization to meet any aerial

invasion, with exercises conducted to 'harden the men
and accustom them to
long marches and arduous
service'.[3] A quantity of arms
confiscated during the Civil
War and stored at Island-
bridge, Dublin, was dis-
tributed to new recruits.
Twenty thousand .300 rifles
were received from the US in
September 1940.

General mobilization also
led to the first restructuring
of the Emergency era, with
GHQ separated into forward
and rear echelons. In the
event of invasion, the Chief
of Staff would command
the forward echelon, while
the rear echelon would be
commanded by the assistant
Chief of Staff, a position
successively held by Col

A Defence Forces recruitment poster designed by the artist
Jack MacManus, c.1941.

Michael Costello (until November 1939), Maj Gen Hugo MacNeill (August
1940–June 1941) and Col Liam Archer (June 1941–January 1949). Invasion would
also see the Chief of Staff appointed General Officer Commanding the Forces,
an unorthodox decision that would have delayed unification of command
until *after* an invasion, and one that highlighted the ongoing challenges of the
command structure imposed on the Defence Forces by its founding legislation.

By April 1941 McKenna was able to report a strength of 40,607 all ranks.
Such whirlwind growth in less than a year inevitably created challenges,
mirroring those encountered by the expansion of the National Army during
the Civil War. Well established administrative structures allowed some of the
mistakes of that era, such as haphazard and uncontrolled recruitment, to be
avoided. Other challenges required prudent management:

Great care was taken to ensure that new units were provided with an adequate leavening of experienced leaders and administrative personnel to ensure proper formation, development, training and discipline of the new units. At the same time effective steps were taken to avoid the danger of impairing the efficiency of our older units and of the military machine, generally, through over-expansion and too great a decentralization of trained personnel.[4]

The possibility of invasion either by Germany or Britain continued to inform defence planning in 1940 and 1941. Detailed German invasion plans (codenamed Operation Green) were in the hands of the Defence Forces' Intelligence Branch, G2, by 1942. Preparations to meet either contingency had two main elements: garrisoning troops at locations most likely to be used as an entry point by invading forces, and developing 'fast moving, well trained strike forces' capable of swiftly engaging and harassing the enemy.[5]

By the summer of 1941 the Defence Forces had re-organized its field forces into two divisions of three brigades and supporting units each, with a further brigade remaining independent. Regarded as the most effective officers available to the Defence Forces, Maj Gen Michael Costello was appointed

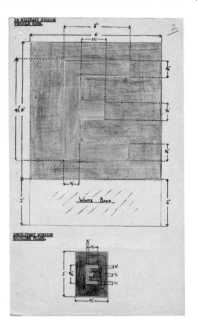

officer commanding 1 (Thunderbolt) Division, with Maj Gen Hugo MacNeill taking charge of 2 (Spearhead) Division. MacNeill's division was tasked with defending the Border against invasion by the British, while Costello's division protected the southern ports and coastline – the areas under most threat of German invasion. An independent brigade was kept in reserve as a mobile strike force, capable of deployment as needed. Divisional exercises conducted during the summer and autumn of 1941 simulated both scenarios, allowing

Suggested design for shoulder flashes and vehicle signs to be displayed by British personnel appointed as liaisons with the Defence Forces and stationed in Ireland as part of 18 Military Mission, in the event of a German invasion.

S E C R E T.

Ref. 10/2.

12 July, 1941.

To : Col. L. Archer,
      Asst. Chief of Staff.

Dear Archer,

        INTERCOMMUNICATION.

        You may remember that it was considered desirable
that you should have a wireless set which would be able
to listen in to news of an approaching invasion of EIRE
collected by our Naval and Air Forces and broadcast in
clear in Northern Ireland for your benefit, and by means
of which urgent messages could be sent to the North
in an emergency.

2.   Such a set is now probably available and I should
be glad if you will let me know whether you would like
arrangements put in hand for letting you have the set
on loan.   It would have to come South in its 3-ton
lorry.

3.   I understand that the set is a new one and that
our people themselves have to train and practise with
it before getting satisfactory results, and that
therefore it is desirable that some of your signal
personnel should go North for about 2 weeks' instruction
and practice before bringing the set South.

        Will you let me know whether this is agreed to ?

                                Yours sincerely,

                                M. H. Pryce.

British Military Attaché to Ireland, Col Meyrick H. Pryce, to Col Liam Archer, Assistant Chief of Staff, 12 July 1941, offering a wireless set to the Defence Forces to enable them to listen to broadcasts 'in clear' from Northern Ireland, which would contain details of an approaching German invasion force.

officers and soldiers to familiarize themselves with the terrain in which they would operate.

'To ensure that proper co-operation exists between British and Éire forces'[6]

On the day that war broke out, Michael Rynne, legal adviser at the Department of External Affairs, observed that in addition to preserving its territorial integrity, it was imperative that Ireland maintain 'complete impartiality in our relations with the two belligerents, abstaining from any action which might amount to *auxiliary aid* to one of the combatants.'[7] Ireland's geopolitical importance meant that Rynne's analysis, while perfectly correct, was one to which the government was neither inclined or capable of adhering as the war progressed. The role of Ireland's foreign service in assiduously managing intermittently fraught relations with the British, German and American administrations is well known; the deft management by the Irish General Staff, which numbered just a handful of officers, of the relationship with its British and American counterparts was no less important.

Diplomatic relations with Britain teetered on a knife edge in the early stages of the war, particularly prior to America's decision to enter the war in

Defence Forces personnel, well wrapped up against the cold, watch a demonstration of the manoeuverability of a Universal 'Bren' Carrier.

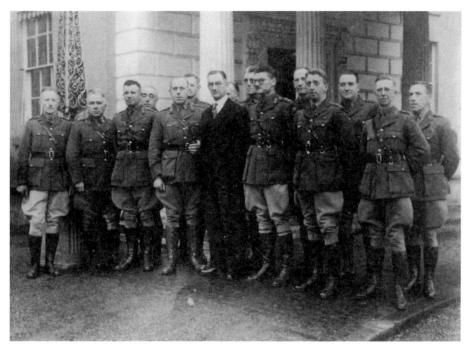

A group of senior officers pictured outside Áras an Uachtaráin during the Emergency. Oscar Traynor, Minister for Defence, stands in the centre. Chief of Staff Lt Gen Dan McKenna stands to Traynor's right, with his left hand tucked into his Sam Browne belt. Maj Gen Michael J. Costello stands to the right of McKenna. Maj Gen Hugo MacNeill, wearing glasses, stands to Traynor's left. To MacNeill's left is Maj Gen Liam Archer, Assistant Chief of Staff. Col Dan Bryan, head of the Defence Forces' Intelligence Branch (G2), is almost obscured behind Traynor.

December 1941. While Neville Chamberlain remained Prime Minister, the British government employed gentle persuasion in its efforts to have Ireland join the war effort, or at a minimum allow the Royal Navy to use the Treaty Ports to aid its operations on the Atlantic Ocean. Relations plummeted in May 1940 when Chamberlain was replaced by Winston Churchill, who regarded as betrayal Ireland's neutrality and stance on the ports. The position outlined by de Valera to the British government was that Ireland would fight if attacked by Germany, and would call on the assistance of Britain 'the moment it became necessary'.[8] De Valera's message, repeatedly amplified by the diplomatic corps and General Staff, was that the timing of any British military assistance would be crucial – public opinion would swing behind British troops if fighting was already underway. If, on the other hand, British

Judith Brereton of Old Court, Nenagh (*second from left*), with fellow members of the Army Nursing Service. The photo is undated but possibly shows the new 'walking out uniform' introduced in 1942. The Army Nursing Service was set up on an ad hoc basis in 1922, and formally established during the 1924 reorganisation.

troops arrived on Irish territory before the Defence Forces had first engaged the Germans, the political consequences were likely to be catastrophic.

Meetings between the British and Irish General Staffs in May 1940 focused on potential areas of mutual co-operation. The establishment of the 18th Military Mission (18MM) in summer 1940 provided a vital conduit between both General Staffs. One of several missions created by Britain to liaise with friendly forces during the war, 18MM's primary goal was to foster and protect 'proper co-operation' with the Defence Forces.[9] 18MM was headquartered in Belfast and its records reveal just how closely both staffs co-operated from late summer of 1940 through to the end of the war. These contacts played a crucial role in easing the likelihood of a British invasion of Ireland – a very real threat prior to the German invasion of the Soviet Union in June 1941.

Observations prepared in January 1941 by Col James Flynn, GHQ Plans and Operations Branch, highlighted the contradictions now inherent in British–Irish relations. Despite the work of 18MM, at that time Britain

Following the crash landing in Co. Kerry of a German Luftwaffe Focke Wulf 200 with a crew of six in August 1940, the government decided to intern belligerent airmen who became stranded in Ireland during the war. In August 1940 the Army Corps of Engineers built Internment Camp No. 2 (more popularly known as K-Lines) on the east side of the Curragh Camp, situated about a mile from Camp No. 1, which housed interned IRA members. K-Lines was divided into two sections: B for British and G for Germans, and conditions within were comfortable. Beginning in 1943, most of the British internees were discreetly repatriated. Restrictions on the movement of the German internees were also gradually relaxed. Twenty-one were allowed to attend university classes in Dublin, while a liberal parole system was put in place. By the end of the war 54 Luftwaffe personnel and 210 German sailors had been interned at the Curragh, with the majority repatriated to Germany by the end of 1945. A group of German officers are pictured here in K-Lines.

remained the most likely aggressor against Irish neutrality. Preparations for such an eventuality, however, risked further alienating the British government, already notably bellicose in its pronouncements on Ireland's position. Yet while the Defence Forces were planning to resist British invasion, they were simultaneously attempting to purchase British arms, equipment, aircraft and petrol, and to improve trading. In Flynn's view an easing of tensions and of the threat of invasion by Britain was highly desirable:

Our Forces are so small, even at their present strength, that we cannot afford to have their attention focused one week on the

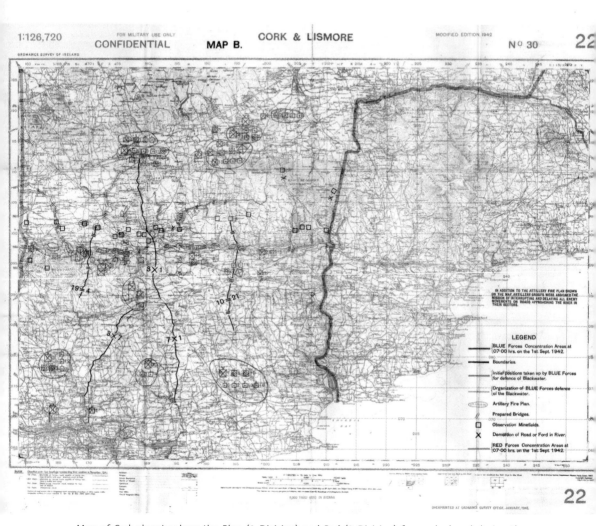

Map of Cork showing how the Blue (1 Division) and Red (2 Division) forces deployed during the Blackwater Manoeuvres, September 1942.

German move and the following week on the British … from the British point of view it would be desirable that we should make our best endeavour to meet the German menace. It would be to Britain's advantage that we should do so. That we cannot do so is Britain's fault. From the military point of view the removal of the possibility of British aggression, would, if it could be accomplished diplomatically, considerably strengthen our position vis-a-vis

Germany and I believe materially increase our chances of having our neutrality respected.[10]

Regardless of diplomatic tensions, information continued to be exchanged in a variety of ways, albeit warily on occasion. The British submitted highly detailed questionnaires seeking clarity and detail on virtually every aspect of Irish defence planning, military preparedness, and other operational matters, including communication networks in Dublin and plans for large-scale civilian evacuations. Eight lengthy questionnaires were submitted between May 1940 and January 1942, along with dozens of ad hoc requests for other details as the war progressed and operational planning was adjusted. Col Seán Collins-Powell served as unofficial chief liaison officer with 18MM, frequently travelling to Northern Ireland for meetings and to observe training exercises.

Engagement by the Defence Forces with these questionnaires varied. Occasionally, the information requested was unavailable and required specialized research, as in the case of a request for suitable coastal locations for the landing of armoured fighting vehicles and other arms. In at least one instance, when the British inquired as to the numerical strength of each battalion in August 1940, the information supplied was deliberately altered to conceal weaknesses.

Logistical assistance included the facilitation of troop movements on flights by Pan American Airways and the British Overseas Airway Corporation (BOAC) at Foynes Airport, Limerick. Belligerent nations were expressly forbidden, by the terms of agreements signed with the Department of Industry and Commerce, to transport members of armed forces on active duty; that restriction was increasingly flouted as the war progressed. Inspecting arrangements at the airport in May 1942, Capt Norman Hewett of the Air Corps reported that the main issue with arrangements at Foynes was a tendency among BOAC officials to regard it as under British control: 'If this BOAC attitude persists it may be advisable to give the Company a display of the powers of the Emergency Act'.[11]

McKenna was given considerable latitude in his management of information exchanges. During a meeting with Traynor in May 1941, at which McKenna mentioned a delay in providing the British with strategic information, the minister advised McKenna to 'go slow'. McKenna noted that Traynor was, however, ultimately willing to defer to his Chief of Staff's discretion: 'If we felt that by giving information we could get supplies then we should sympathetically consider giving further information.'[12]

Beginning in July 1940, 18MM supplied the Defence Forces with nearly all training instructions issued to the British Troops in Northern Ireland (BTNI). These manuals were never circulated, but were studied by the General Staff in order to abstract 'such ideas on training as might be useful to us.'[13] 18MM also prepared special intelligence reports for GHQ, based on weekly briefings from the British War Office. From November 1941 until August 1943, 18MM simply forwarded the original War Office briefings. These in turn were summarized by G2 Branch for distribution to Irish commands.

From January 1942 the level of co-operation accelerated. Reciprocal visits by commanding officers between Dublin, Belfast and London increased in frequency. Agreement was reached to allow the British to establish coal and fuel dumps in Ireland. By October 224,000 gallons of petrol were in store at Carton House, Co. Kildare. Planned locations for the destruction of transport infrastructure in the event of a German invasion were provided to the British to ease their arrival in Ireland. Co-operation also improved British willingness to supply material and equipment, if only marginally and in cases where it was of benefit to their own interests, such as guns and searchlights to strengthen anti-aircraft defences in the Shannon area.

Infantry crossing the River Blackwater during the Blackwater Manoeuvres, September 1942.

The arrival of American troops to Northern Ireland in January 1942 was a blow to the Irish government, which regarded it as a tacit acceptance of Partition by the American administration. Contact between the Defence Forces and their American counterparts was quite sporadic, as American troops in Northern Ireland came under the command of BTNI. The difficult relationship between the Irish government and David Gray, the splenetic American Minister Plenipotentiary to Ireland, also complicated matters. The Americans never established anything similar to 18MM, and its military attachés displayed little interest in liaising with the Defence Forces. More junior ranking US diplomats, such as the Consul General in Cork, did however maintain contact with senior Defence Forces officers, including Costello.

A note on relations between the two militaries, compiled by the General Staff after the war, observed that McKenna enjoyed a good relationship with Brig Gen Edmund Hill, commanding officer of the US Air Force in Northern Ireland. That relationship proved crucial in alleviating the problem most likely to cause friction in Irish–American relations – repatriating American pilots who landed in Ireland because they had lost their bearings. The Irish government made clear that it was perfectly happy to allow Americans slip over the Border, if they could be briefed to employ a little subterfuge if they should be forced to land in Ireland. All they were required to do was to state that the flight was for non-operational purposes, no matter what its actual circumstances. To aid pilots as they flew over unfamiliar terrain, the word 'Éire' and a code number were placed beside each of the 83 Look Out Posts maintained by the Coast Watching Service. A list of the code numbers, together with map references, were given to the US and British authorities. 18MM was effectively dismantled by August 1943, when most US and British troops were relocated to England.

'The Army is now an effective and mobile field force'

In the late summer of 1942 the Defence Forces carried out the largest combined training manoeuvres in its history, a high point of organizational accomplishment and a major step in the maturation of the rapidly expanded Emergency forces. Staged along the River Blackwater, Co. Cork, 1 and 2 Divisions carried out three different exercises between 1 and 13 September, designed to simulate reaction to an invasion along the south coast. Two further exercises, incorporating 2 Division, Cavalry units and the LDF, were carried out in Wicklow and Dublin between 19 and 26 September.

At the conclusion of the exercises, McKenna offered a positive assessment of the speed of the development of the Defence Forces' capabilities, particularly the Army:

> The training carried out ... has been much more arduous, more extensive and more progressive than anything attempted since the establishment of the Army. While it has performed the vital function of revealing faults and weaknesses, it has also proved conclusively that the troops have passed from the stage of barrack square training and that the Army is now an effective and mobile field force, whose further training must be of an advanced and intensely practical nature.[14]

The Blackwater Manoeuvres were particularly valuable to officers whose previous experience of commanding units on this scale had been restricted to sand table exercises. Among the weaknesses identified was a general inability among platoon commanders to maintain effective control of their units after contact with the enemy; a special course of instruction at the Military College was developed to help improve tactical training. Selected officers were also sent to Northern Ireland for specialized training, particularly in commando tactics, another positive outcome of 18MM.

Despite McKenna's hopes that future training would be of an advanced and practical nature, the heights of the Blackwater Manoeuvres were never again attained. Recruitment began to tail off in 1942, despite an increase of up to 50 per cent in the basic rate of pay for privates. The receding likelihood of an invasion, as perceived by the general populace, sapped the urgency of recruitment campaigns. In April 1943 McKenna noted that the burst of enthusiasm that had characterized enlistment in the summer of 1940 had all but disappeared, 'while those who have a taste for military life are more inclined to join the British Services, where a more exciting career is expected'.[15] The allure of service with the British forces also contributed to the problem of desertion. Between 1 April 1941 and 31 March 1945 there were 6,602 desertions, with the problem particularly pronounced in 1941 and 1942 among units stationed close to the Border. Liaison with BTNI saw the military authorities in Northern Ireland begin to refuse to enlist men known to have

A Defence Forces Cyclist Squadron, accompanied by an ambulance and four armoured fighting vehicles. The two to the rear are Landsverk L180 model, with registration numbers ZC 757 and ZC 758, ordered from Sweden in 1937 and delivered in 1938. Six more were subsequently ordered and delivered in 1939; further orders were disrupted by the outbreak of the Second World War. Formed during the Emergency, Cyclist Squadrons typically consisted of 120 men, with their rifles mounted on the bicycle frame.

deserted from the Defence Forces. At the end of the war, approximately 5,000 soldiers still listed as 'absent without leave' were dismissed from the Defence Forces and stripped of any pension or financial entitlements they might have accrued. More punitively, they were also excluded from employment in any branch of the public sector for seven years.[16]

Morale suffered in 1943 and 1944 as the Defence Forces were increasingly deployed to aid the civil authority, largely in the tedious and difficult work of cutting turf. Those who had enlisted in the early days of the Emergency had, by summer 1944, spent four long years in training for an invasion that was now increasingly remote: 'many of the troops feel that they were wasting their time ... that their sacrifice was unnecessary and unappreciated by the people as a whole'.[17]

151

Three years of close co-operation with British (and to a lesser extent American) General Staffs allowed for defence planning to concentrate more fully on any potential Axis advance – though even that threat was increasingly remote given German setbacks on the Eastern Front. Nonetheless, the 'American Note' incident of February 1944 once more saw Irish soldiers mobilized and deployed in anticipation of Allied invasion from Northern Ireland. The diplomatic incident was sparked by David Gray, who insisted that de Valera expel all German, Italian and Japanese diplomats. Gray had never been able to shake the incorrect suspicion that Ireland was riddled with German spies, and he rather needlessly feared that details of Operation Overlord, the Allies' plan to invade Normandy later that summer, would make their way to the Axis powers via a leak from neutral Ireland.

Relations between the Irish and Allied governments survived the scare. Indeed, one of the most important demonstrations of the favourable neutrality shown by Ireland to the Allies was in intelligence co-operation. Weather forecasts from Blacksod Lighthouse, situated on the Belmullet Peninsula in Co. Mayo, were transmitted to the Supreme Headquarters of the Allied Expeditionary Force. The successful launch of Operation Overlord was heavily dependent on favourable weather conditions. Regular reports from Blacksod between 4 and 6 June 1944 enabled Allied planners to make last-minute adjustments and to postpone the invasion of Europe until

This radio set was one of several smuggled into Ireland by German spies and captured by G2, the Defence Forces' Intelligence Branch. Under the leadership of Col Liam Archer, and of Col Dan Bryan from July 1941, G2 had notable success in thwarting German espionage during the Emergency, and co-operated closely with British and American intelligence services in a number of areas.

6 June, when data from Blacksod – which remained unseen by Wehrmacht forecasters – indicated a favourable break in the weather. Nor was this an isolated incident, as noted in a memorandum presented to Éamon de Valera in 1944, briefing him on the sharing of weather data with the British Meteorological Service throughout the war: 'These are not being supplied to any other country. They are of course extremely important as a basis for weather forecasts.'[18]

Intelligence was an area in which the Defence Forces excelled during the Emergency, both in collaboration with British and American intelligence services and in its own operations. G2 Branch repeatedly proved its effectiveness, particularly after Col Dan Bryan's appointment as director in July 1941. Attempts by the German Abwehr, the military-intelligence service of the Wehrmacht, to establish a network of spies in Ireland were rapidly thwarted by G2's counter-intelligence operations; all twelve Abwehr spies sent to Ireland during the war were identified and captured, most shortly after their arrival. Dr Richard Hayes, director of the National Library of Ireland and an amateur cryptographer, worked on signals intelligence with G2. His success decrypting German ciphers was shared with British intelligence, which used the information to aid its own operations.

'To control our territorial waters'

Almost sixteen years after the Coastal and Marine Service was disbanded, a new Marine and Coast Watching Service was established in August and September 1939, a belated acknowledgment that neutrality would require Ireland to prevent use of its territorial waters by any belligerent forces. The naval element of the Service's role was defined by the Hague Convention of 1909, summarized by McKenna as:

> to control our territorial waters and to fulfil the obligations of a neutral state so that belligerents had no cause for complaints ... This duty was mainly the policing of our territorial waters. As the war progressed and the battles drew nearer to our shores bringing with them the grave danger of invasion, we found it necessary to allot further tasks that required more active steps of this service in preparing for the defence of the state.[19]

Despite years of relative neglect, the old Royal Navy shipyard and hospital on Haulbowline Island in Cork Harbour was adopted as the Service's headquarters in the summer of 1940. Acquisition of vessels, personnel and uniforms initially proved difficult. For the second time in its service history, *Muirchú* underwent conversion for deployment with the Defence Forces, where it was soon joined by *Fort Rannoch*. Both vessels were commissioned as armed patrol boats in January 1940 and underwent a refit to allow installation of 12-pounder guns, Vickers machine guns and extra accommodation.

The 'fleet' was augmented in 1940 by the acquisition of three Motor Torpedo Boats (MTBs) from Thornycroft & Co. shipbuilders, which had 20mm Madsen guns fitted. Ignoring advice that MTBs were unsuited to the conditions found off the Irish coast, three more were ordered in February 1940 but not delivered until December 1942/January 1943. Apart from sundry other vessels that fulfilled a variety of roles, including inspection vessels for port control and a training ship, the Marine Service's fleet was completed by *Shark*, which was commissioned in December 1940 as a minelayer.

Two MTBs on manoeuvres, close to the shoreline in the kind of calm waters best suited to their capabilities. The 18-inch torpedo tubes are clearly visible.

The newly formed Marine Service operated six Motor Torpedo Boats (MTBs 1–6) during the Emergency, which were acquired between 1940 and 1943. Here MTB M1 is seen operating at speed, with torpedo tube visible to the rear.

Uniforms were not available until April 1941 and recruiting was undertaken through special appointment boards. Until officers of the Marine Service could be adequately trained, basic weapons and military training were provided by Army NCOs. A marine reserve, known as the Maritime Inscription, was founded in Dublin in September 1940, followed by a Cork unit in October. The Inscription was open to any man who passed a medical, with no seagoing experience required.

As the war intensified the Marine Service's role expanded to include coast watching duties (in tandem with the 83 Lookout Posts manned by the Coast Watching Service), patrolling of territorial waters, defence by sea, control of ports and harbours, mine laying and destruction, and examination and searching of shipping entering Irish ports. Apart from port control, the Service was largely unable to fulfil these functions with any real effectiveness. Better suited to calm waters, the MTBs frequently ran into trouble in heavy swells and were unsuitable for coastal patrols. GHQ estimated that at least ten ships were required to adequately patrol the coastline; with only two suitable vessels available to the Marine Service, the reality was that the Irish coast was defended by the Royal Navy from beyond Ireland's territorial

Pictured here during the Emergency, the *Muirchú* was the main vessel of the Marine Service during this period. Better known to history as the *Helga*, the British ship that shelled Dublin city during the Easter Rising, the *Muirchú* first entered service for the Coastal and Marine Service in 1922, before being transferred to the Department of Agriculture in 1923. It was recommissioned in the Defence Forces in January 1940. Its 12-pdr gun is visible on the foredeck.

waters. In April 1942 the Service was reportedly so short of equipment 'it is almost impossible for it to reach any degree of effectiveness ... the Service is still in a very backward condition'.[20]

Though McKenna had been pleased by improvements in training and administrative standards after 1943, those improvements were limited and as the Emergency drew to a close, he offered a downbeat assessment of the Service's future:

> I have now to say that the Marine Service is not in a satisfactory condition. It has failed to develop properly either along military or naval lines. A general looseness of control and lack of responsibility among the officers, and particularly among the senior officers, has resulted in the whole service being unreliable. The internal organization and training are of a low standard. To what extent these weaknesses are caused by factors outside the control of the Marine Service it is hard to say. Probably the underlying cause of all the trouble is that we were unable to pick officers of the best type ... The unsatisfactory state of affairs mentioned above, coupled

with the general uncertainty as to the future of the Marine Service led to a decision to suspend recruiting for it. If the service is to be maintained as an arm of the Defence Forces, then it will be necessary to make some very drastic changes in personnel. I certainly could not recommend that it continue as at present.[21]

'German squadrons droned by Dublin on bombing raids over Britain'

Entering the Emergency, Ireland was virtually defenceless against aerial attack. The capability of electronically detecting any encroachment on Irish airspace was limited and ineffective, and there were initially no light anti-aircraft guns available for troops to engage low flying aircraft. By March 1941 anti-aircraft defences had been enhanced to include eight searchlights and fourteen AA guns, including four modern 40mm Bofors. Further acquisitions brought the number of anti-aircraft guns to twenty-eight by the end of the war.

Entering the war the Air Corps was in a state of disarray. With no strategic plan in place to guide aircraft acquisitions during the 1930s, the result was a disjointed fleet of ten different aircraft types:

> Our Air Force does not include one single homogenous unit. It has no reserves of men or material worth taking into consideration. It cannot either patrol our coast or provide an effective unit to participate in the defence of the capital.[22]

The Air Corps was soon further hampered by a major investigation into all aspects of its operations, following complaints from junior officers about the aircraft available to the Air Corps, and its administration under its OC, Col Patrick Mulcahy. The consequences of the government's refusal to properly define military aviation policy between 1924 and 1939, and the General Staff's error in appointing a commanding officer with no aviation experience, had been brought into sharp relief by the onset of the war.

In September 1940 the German Luftwaffe initiated an intense bombing campaign of Britain, concentrated largely on London. An invasion of the British mainland was also widely anticipated that month. Air Defence Command presented a bleak outlook for Ireland's future air defence position: 'The longer the war lasts, the more intense the air effort is likely to become;

(*Left to right*) Volunteers Paddy Green, Aby Goodall and Jim Bishop, manning Greenore LOP during the Emergency. The Volunteers at Greenore LOP identified the aircraft responsible for dropping bombs on Campile Creamery, Wexford, on 26 August 1940, during which three women working at the creamery were killed. This identification was one of the pieces of evidence that enabled the Irish government to establish responsibility and claim compensation of £12,000 from the German government. Paddy Green, said to be the biggest man in the Defence Forces, is not in uniform here because a special one being made to measure had yet to arrive.

and the harder pressed either of the belligerents become, the less regard will be paid to our neutrality.'[23]

Soldiers stationed at Look Out Posts and anti-aircraft artillery posts on the east coast were able to track the intensity of the Luftwaffe's actions throughout the later months of 1940, with German planes flying through Irish airspace above Waterford and Wexford and up the east coast. Brian Maguire, stationed with anti-aircraft artillery in Dublin, later recalled the intensity of those early months of the war: 'Nightly, from midnight, German squadrons droned by Dublin on bombing raids over Britain. These were so regular, in fact, that time-pieces could be set and checked by them.'[24]

When the Luftwaffe commenced its bombing campaign of Britain, the Air Corps had a paper strength of 54 planes – 22 service craft and 32 training craft. Nineteen of these (5 service, 14 training) were unserviceable, however, due to lack of parts. No. 1 Fighter Squadron, formed in March 1939 to replace

Aerial photo of Hook Lighthouse, with its Eire 16 sign denoting an Emergency-era Look Out Post – these signs were created as navigational aids for American and British pilots.

the Army Co-operation Squadron, relied on just three Gloster Gladiators and the Westland Lysander. The Lysander – a baffling purchase in 1939 – was developed for reconnaissance rather than as a fighter plane. The Gladiator, a biplane, had already been rendered obsolete by the more advanced fighters flown by the British and German air forces, though its capability was shown by its service in the Mediterranean and Middle East.

Air Corps participation in the Blackwater Manoeuvres highlighted some of the deficiencies in the aircraft available. Lacking radio, pilots on reconnaissance duty in Miles Magisters aircraft were forced to communicate with ground troops by dropping hand written messages. Nonetheless, their participation was well received by Michael Costello, OC of 1 Division: 'I am more than pleased with the work of the air component ... They supplied a stream of information which was in the main much more accurate than that supplied by the ground forces.'[25]

Acting on the recommendations of the investigation committee, which concluded its work in 1942, McKenna ordered a significant reorganization of the Air Corps. Mulcahy was replaced as OC by Maj Walter Delamere, a former RAF pilot. Bomber and reconnaissance squadrons were discontinued in favour of developing a second fighter squadron; an ambition that was, however, never realized. Between 1939 and 1943 efforts to procure additional first line fighter aircraft were unsuccessful, with the exception of three Hurricanes that made forced landings in Ireland, while four more were subsequently purchased from the British Air Ministry. The fleet's complement of Hurricanes was eventually raised to eleven by the end of the Emergency. Even so, the Air Corps' operational capacity was 'largely notional'.[26] Though aircraft were scrambled on reports of hostile aircraft entering Irish airspace, the Air Corps' ability to intercept aircraft flying over Irish territory was virtually nil. Had it been called upon to do so, it would have been incapable of offering even a token resistance to any aerial or seaborne invasion.

'Probably the finest achievement yet attained'

The success of the Allied advance through Europe from June 1944 meant that McKenna could, in April 1945, recommend a return to peacetime conditions and begin preparations for demobilization. His task was considerably eased by the fact that strength then stood at 32,115, well below establishment. Notwithstanding the difficulties experienced in maintaining morale and enticing new recruits in 1943 and 1944, McKenna reflected on the enormity of the task that had faced the Defence Forces in the summer of 1940, and the singular effort required to create a force capable of defending the state from invasion: 'The Army as it stands today is probably the finest achievement yet attained since this country won its freedom and is the most hopeful sign of the country's ability to overcome the new trials which it must face in the coming years.'[27]

The secrecy surrounding 18MM and other covert assistance rendered to the Allied forces, particularly Britain, has obscured the extent to which Irish neutrality moved far beyond the 'complete impartiality' envisaged by Rynne in September 1939. The declaration of an emergency in Ireland in September 1939 had been intended as the final step in preparations for war. That Ireland never entered the war and escaped its full horrors, when coupled with the passage of time, has dulled popular memory of the very real threats to Ireland's security, especially between May 1940 and mid-1943. Lives were nonetheless lost during the Emergency. Bombings by the Luftwaffe,

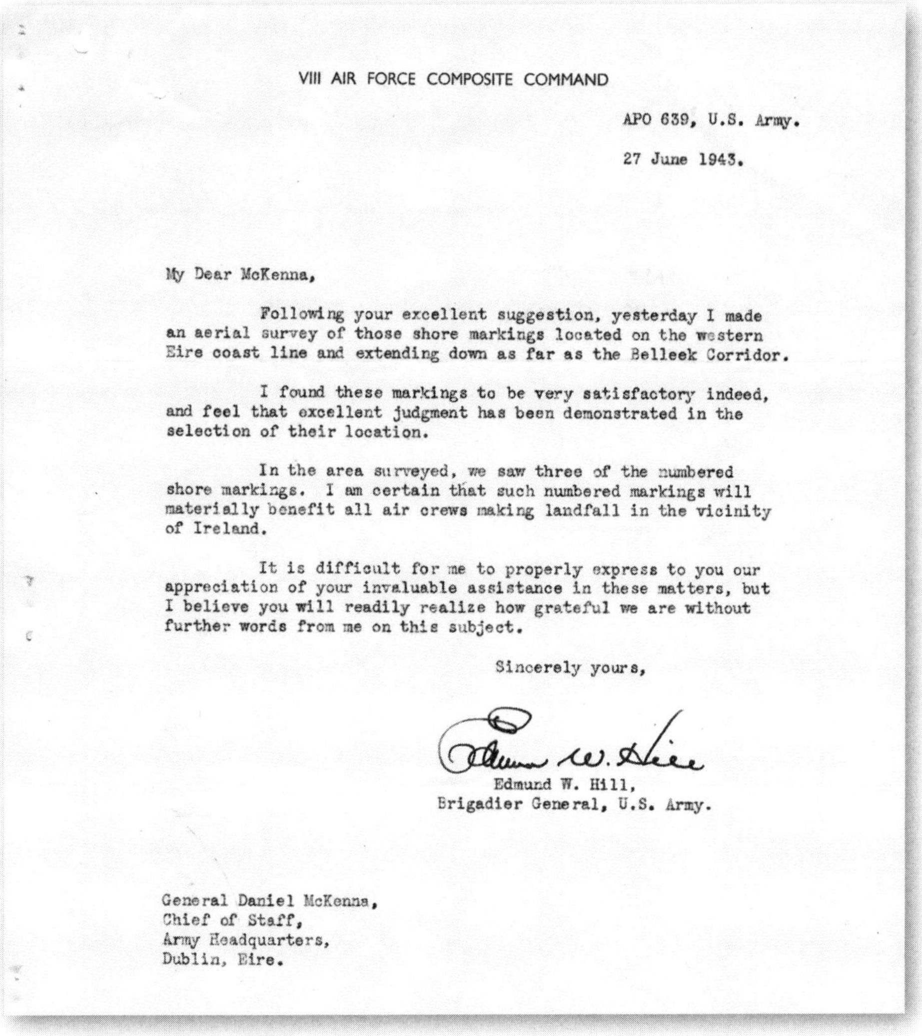

VIII AIR FORCE COMPOSITE COMMAND

APO 639, U.S. Army.

27 June 1943.

My Dear McKenna,

Following your excellent suggestion, yesterday I made an aerial survey of those shore markings located on the western Eire coast line and extending down as far as the Belleek Corridor.

I found these markings to be very satisfactory indeed, and feel that excellent judgment has been demonstrated in the selection of their location.

In the area surveyed, we saw three of the numbered shore markings. I am certain that such numbered markings will materially benefit all air crews making landfall in the vicinity of Ireland.

It is difficult for me to properly express to you our appreciation of your invaluable assistance in these matters, but I believe you will readily realize how grateful we are without further words from me on this subject.

Sincerely yours,

Edmund W. Hill,
Brigadier General, U.S. Army.

General Daniel McKenna,
Chief of Staff,
Army Headquarters,
Dublin, Eire.

On 27 June 1943, Brig Gen Edmund Hill, Commander of the US Air Force in Northern Ireland, wrote to Lt Gen Dan McKenna expressing his gratitude for the numbered Éire signs attached to Look Out Posts.

though infrequent and likely accidental, led to several civilian deaths, most disastrously when the bombing of Dublin's North Strand on the night of 30/31 May 1941 resulted in twenty-eight deaths.

Casualties were also suffered by Defence Forces personnel while performing their duties, and while undertaking intense training. On 16 September 1941 the Defence Forces suffered its greatest loss of life in a single incident since the

Civil War. During an anti-tank mine demonstration at the Glen of Imaal in the Wicklow Mountains, an accidental explosion killed sixteen soldiers. On 6 September 1942, during the Blackwater Manoeuvres, Lt Thomas Ryan and Sgt Michael McElligott drowned while trying to cross the river at Thomas Ashe Quay in Fermoy. Three months later four hands were lost when a Marine Service examination vessel collided with another ship at Cobh, Co. Cork.

Nearly two decades of continual neglect and underinvestment had drastically reduced the state's military capabilities on the eve of the war. Yet within two years the Defence Forces were able to field two divisions, a force capable of mounting a defence of Irish independence. For all of the deficiencies that yet remained, it was a remarkable achievement and planning for the post-war organization of the Defence Forces had begun even before the end of the war. Throughout 1944 the General Staff conducted a detailed study of its present and future needs, presented to the government in August 1944 as the 'Memorandum on the Defence Forces'. De Valera's initial reaction was positive, though he warned that its recommendations would require substantial investment, and therefore considerable advocacy. It was, he intimated, up to the Defence Forces to convince cabinet ministers to divert scarce public funds to military spending – a historically difficult task that would once more prove impossible to achieve. McKenna's wartime achievements, and those of the thousands under his command, were soon forgotten.

A publicity photograph, taken at Baldonnel by G2 (Intelligence Branch) on 4 March 1941, of the Air Corps' Miles Magister training aircraft.

In this publicity photo, Air Corps airgunners are pictured at Baldonnel on 4 March 1941. In the background is a Gloster Gladiator, serial No. 26. The Gladiator, a biplane, was largely obsolete by the time of the Second World War, superseded by more modern aircraft such as the Vickers Spitfire and Hawker Hurricane. The Air Corps acquired four Gladiators in March 1938 and had four more on order, which were not delivered due to the outbreak of war. Gladiator No. 26 was damaged in a landing accident in June 1938, but was repaired and returned to service by July 1940.

For much of the Emergency the Air Corps lacked modern fighter aircraft, with the exception of three Hawker Hurricanes which made forced landings in Ireland. Four more were purchased from the British in 1943, each of which had seen extensive operational service with the RAF. The three Hurricane Mk IIc pictured here were among six acquired in March 1945, and entered service with No. 1 Fighter Squadron. All of the Hurricanes acquired during the Emergency had been withdrawn from service by November 1947.

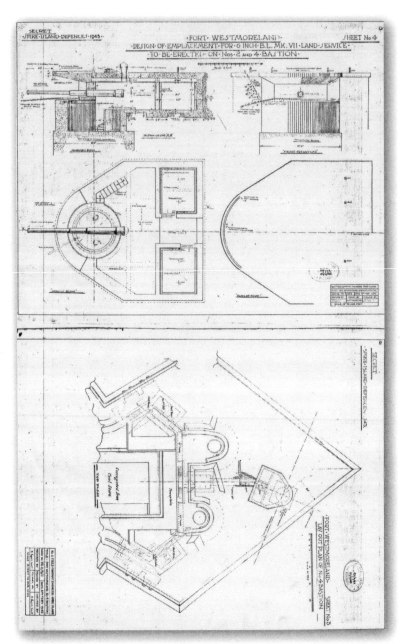

Design for an emplacement for a 6-inch BL Mark VII naval gun, drawn up in February 1943. The design was for the improvement of the coastal defences at Fort Westmoreland (later renamed Fort Mitchel) on Spike Island, Cork Harbour – one of the Treaty Port defences returned to the Irish government in 1938.

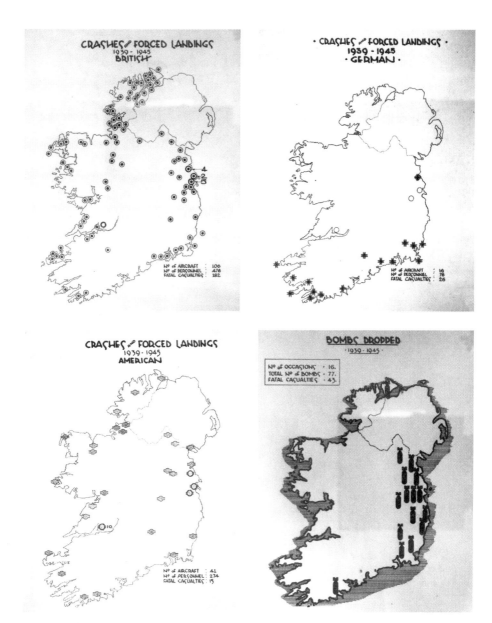

Four maps showing the locations and statistics for crashes and forced landings of British, German and American aircraft during the Emergency. The fourth map shows the locations where German bombs were dropped on Irish territory. The most infamous bombings took place at the Shelbourne Creamery Co-op in Campile, Co. Wexford, killing three people (26 August 1940), Boris, Co. Carlow, killing three people (2 January 1941) and Dublin's North Strand, killing 28 people (30/31 May 1941).

BEGINNINGS: THE EQUITATION SCHOOL

Given the perilous state of the nation's finances and the difficulty in securing funding for even the most insignificant Defence Forces' expenditure, the establishment of the Army Equitation School was a significant achievement. Initial impetus came from Judge William Wylie of the Royal Dublin Society, which was eager to add Dublin to the list of host cities for the relatively new Nations Cup show jumping competition, in which military teams of three from Europe and the Americas competed. Military team jumping competitions had been growing in popularity since the 1910s, and had been included in the 1912, 1920 and 1924 Olympic Games. Irish-bred horses featured heavily in these competitions for teams from other nations, often sourced at the RDS Annual Horse Show. As the advocates of an Irish military jumping team argued, not only would such a team be flying the flag of the new state at international competitions, they would be further promoting the Irish horse.

Formal sanction for an Army jumping team was granted in April 1926. That the Minister for Agriculture was the brother of Col Michael Hogan, one of the principal supporters of the proposal, was of no little help. Maj Liam Hoolan was named officer commanding of the new Army Equitation School, based at McKee Barracks where the Army's horse transport unit was housed. The team's first recruits were Capt Ged O'Dwyer, Capt Dan Corry, Capt Cyril Harty, and Comdt Tom Mason. In May and June six horses were acquired, and just three months after coming together the team competed for the newly created Aga Khan trophy, in front of a record attendance at the Royal Dublin Society's inaugural Nations Cup event. In what was an extraordinary achievement the Irish team placed second, behind the Swiss.

Following that initial success proved difficult for the Irish team, which struggled to adapt to the demands of competing abroad in 1927. Col Hogan, then Assistant Quartermaster General, arranged for the Equitation School's separation from the Army Transport Service and reconstituted it as a separate unit reporting directly to the Quartermaster General. Hogan also convinced Col Paul Rodzianko, a Russian riding expert, to come to Dublin to train the

The horses and riders of the Army jumping team that competed at Ballsbridge in August 1927, during the second Annual Aga Khan competition, photographed at McKee Barracks on 17 September 1927. (*Left to right*): Capt Cyril Harty, riding Cúchulain; Capt Dan Corry, riding Finghin; and Capt Ged O'Dwyer, riding Craobh Rua. Though the Irish team placed last that year, Capt Harty won the prize for best individual round.

jumping team. Rodzianko accepted the challenge, and would later recall that

> The Irish show jumping team had splendid horses, great courage and a certain amount of experience but no technical knowledge ... what grand material they were! With Irish horses and Irish hearts I knew I ought to win around the world.[1]

Rodzianko's tenure was brief, ending in 1931, but his influence was profound. He introduced modern techniques and equipment, and through intense training fine-tuned the skill sets of riders more accustomed to the hunt than show jumping. It was no coincidence that the Irish team of Harty, Corry and O'Dwyer won the Aga Khan trophy for the first time in 1928.

Postcard advertising the 1929 Dublin Horse Show, depicting the Irish Army jumping team competing for the Aga Khan trophy in the RDS Arena.

Rodzianko was succeeded as trainer and team leader by O'Dwyer, and the Irish team continued its rapid rise to the foremost ranks of international jumping. Between 1929 and 1939 the Equitation School's team won twenty-one Nations Cup events, in Lucerne, Amsterdam, Nice, Aachen, Boston, New York, Toronto. Dublin was the scene of its greatest triumphs in this period, with four victories in a row at the Aga Khan (1935–8).

The Equitation School was closed during the Emergency and struggled to adapt to a much-changed international jumping environment in the

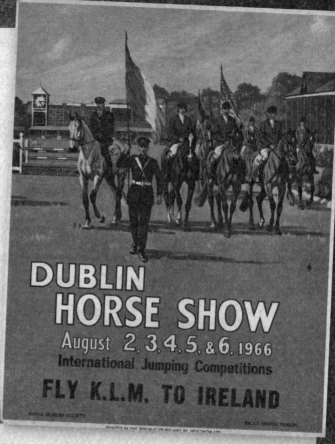

The official poster for the 1966 Dublin Horse Show, designed by Violet Skinner and depicting a flag-bearing Irish soldier leading the 1963 Aga Khan winning Irish team in the RDS Arena. They were the first combined Army-civilian team to win the Aga Khan: (*left to right*) Capt Billy Ringrose, Diana Connolly-Carew, Seamus Hayes, and Tommy Wade.

years that followed. Starved of funding, and employing outdated methods, between 1949 and 1959 the Equitation School won just seven events, a sharp contrast to the success of the 1930s.

Teams competing in the Nations Cup in Dublin have the added incentive of keeping the Aga Khan trophy for sustained excellence. The trophy is replaced on each occasion. First achieved by the Swiss in 1930, who kept the inaugural trophy in recognition of their third victory in just five years, the rules were changed that year so that the new trophy would be kept by any nation that won three years in a row. The distinction has only been achieved on four occasions, twice by Irish teams: 1935–8 and 1977–9. That latter success signalled the re-emergence of the Equitation School from a difficult period, allowing it to resume its mission of promoting the Irish horse on the international stage.

CHAPTER 5

1946–69
STAGNATION AND REVITALIZATION

In August 1944 the 'Memorandum on the Defence Forces', prepared by the General Staff, requested several policy decisions and directions from the government, to help guide the future development of Ireland's military. Chief among its objectives was prevention of a post-war regression to the dilapidated and ineffective state that had characterized the Defence Forces in the early 1930s, when the drudgery of guard and fatigue duty dominated daily routine. At a September 1944 meeting between the Chief of Staff, Lt Gen Dan McKenna, and the Taoiseach to discuss the Memorandum, de Valera vowed: 'We must never allow that to happen again'.[1]

Initial indications were that the government would heed the lessons of the Emergency by refusing to allow the Defence Forces to regress to the status quo ante of the 1930s. Guided by the 'Memorandum on the Defence Forces', in April 1945 a peacetime establishment of 15,800 men was approved, to be gradually reduced to 12,500 men. Those figures proved almost entirely aspirational.

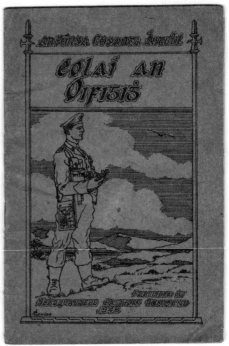

Covers of soldiers' and officers' information booklets, produced by Eastern Command HQ in 1948, for members of An Fórsa Cosanta Áitiúil.

A change of government in February 1948, which saw Fianna Fáil replaced by the first inter-party coalition, led by Fine Gael, was followed in January 1949 by McKenna's retirement. His successor was Maj Gen Liam Archer. Another veteran of the Irish Revolution who had been active with the Volunteers during the Easter Rising, Archer had served as Assistant Chief of Staff since the summer of 1941.

De Valera's 1944 vow soon rang hollow. Between the end of the Emergency and the deployment of troops on a UN-mandated mission in Congo in 1960, the Defence Forces were once more allowed to stagnate. It was a period one future Chief of Staff would later recall as 'the terrible 40s and 50s, [when] the Defence Forces were allowed to just wither on the vine'.[2]

A series of ambitious plans, based on an establishment of 12,500, were drafted by GHQ in the late 1940s and early 1950s. After post-Emergency demobilization concluded in October 1946, the Defence Forces' strength stood at 9,942, well below establishment. That figure remained largely

Front page of *Flash* (April 1954). *Flash* was an FCÁ newspaper carrying 'news and views', published from Portobello Barracks in the early 1950s.

unchanged until the launch of a major recruitment campaign in the Autumn of 1952, which briefly raised personnel numbers to just over 10,000. However, the natural 'wastage' of soldiers who left the Defence Forces every year at the end of their initial period of enlistment meant that a constant stream of new recruits was required merely to maintain a steady strength. Tentative proposals from GHQ for the introduction of some form of compulsory national service, first raised during the Emergency, were firmly rejected from the late 1940s. Mass emigration in the two decades after the Emergency became one of the principal factors inhibiting recruitment, as were poor pay and conditions. According to an analysis conducted in 1955, the Defence Forces were unable to compete with better rates of pay in both the British forces and in British industry.

Between 1954 and the outbreak of the Troubles in 1969, personnel numbers rose above 9,000 in just two years, in 1955 and 1959. The introduction of cinema

Col Justin MacCarthy (1914–60) was among the first Irish officers despatched for service with UNOGIL in 1958 where he served as Deputy Chief of Staff. MacCarthy was transferred to the United Nations Truce Supervision Organisation (UNTSO), and later to ONUC. He died in a car crash in Leopoldville on the night of 27 October 1960.

advertising seeking recruits in the mid-1950s proved to be a disappointment. Peacetime establishments were gradually revised downwards in the 1960s, a reflection of reduced government funding and continuing problems with recruitment and retention.

'Some people joined for the boots'[3]

In the aftermath of the Emergency, second line reserve forces were once more reimagined. From a strength of more than 100,000 men in late 1943, the Local Defence Force had begun to dwindle as the perceived threat of invasion receded. Demobilization and a post-war reorganization saw the LDF reconstituted in February 1946 as An Fórsa Cosanta Áitiúil (FCÁ). Organized into ninety-nine battalions across twenty-four territorial areas, its strength stood at just over 37,000 when formed. Projections for a force of 60,000 proved wildly optimistic. Largely held together in its early years by the determination of its NCOs and the willingness of reservists to remain with their units despite less than ideal conditions, between 1954 and 1969 the paper strength of the FCÁ hovered between 18,000 and 20,500.

The FCÁ suffered from the same problems as all previous reserve forces: lack of equipment, a shortage of qualified officers and insufficient time for training. Reporting to the Minister for Defence, Thomas O'Higgins, in April 1950, Archer was notably pessimistic regarding the new reserve force:

> The FCÁ, as it stands, cannot be regarded as anything but an untrained force with little or no arms and equipment and unsuitably organized for immediate absorption into the Permanent Force. It is impossible to estimate with any certainty what percentage of its effective strength of approximately 26,000 men would offer for permanent service in an emergency ... Consequently what would only take weeks, in the expansion of the Forces with a trained Reserve available, will take months, and the use of valuable time in recruiting and training during a critical period when both the men and the time are required for other urgent tasks.[4]

Archer was clearly influenced by his direct experience of the length of time required to first recruit and then train the Emergency forces, and was desperate to avoid a repeat of that situation in the uncertain international climate of the Cold War. Within a decade, however, the virtual disappearance of the first line reserve and need for rationalization of the FCÁ prompted a reorganization of the Defence Forces. Perceptions of the FCÁ had vastly improved by the end of the decade, with a memorandum prepared for the Council of Defence in July 1958 noting that it had 'reached a standard of training which permits of the expectation that it can be given the further training to enable it to assume the role hitherto visualized for the First Line Reserve'.[5] In 1959 the FCÁ was allotted the role of first line reserve and integrated with the Permanent Defence Forces (PDF) to create six mixed brigades, with PDF officers and training staff attached to FCÁ units.

The reorganization was the latest iteration of the concept of a small, well-trained standing army that would provide a core around which a projected force of 47,000 men could swiftly mobilize. Integration of the FCÁ with the PDF was a recognition that, in the event of a new world conflict, there would be little time to organize and train new recruits. Completed during Maj Gen Patrick Mulcahy's tenure as Chief of Staff (1955–9), the reorganization was viewed by GHQ as an exercise in cutting its cloth to suit its measure, an adaptation to the personnel and equipment then available, but far short of what it advised was necessary 'to sustain successfully a policy of neutrality'.[6]

The following year the Defence Forces warned that it had insufficient personnel to allow both for garrison duty and adequate training, a situation exacerbated by the reopening of an internment camp at the Curragh for dissident republicans during the IRA's Border campaign (1957–62). The Naval Service stood at 'rockbottom strength in seamen and is seriously short of NCOs and officers' and was struggling to fulfil its core duty of fisheries protection. Its manpower problems were replicated across the Defence Forces, carrying strong echoes of the 1930s:

> If our peace-time strength is to be further reduced … serious consideration may have to be given to a complete review of our peace-time military organization. If the State cannot afford the numbers asked for then it may be necessary to disband units and close some posts and stations, in order to allow remaining units to function in anything approaching an efficient manner. The effect of such a step would be so serious that it can hardly be contemplated. It would disrupt the organization that has only recently been effected and is still getting underway.[7]

There seemed little chance of an improvement in resource allocation. When measured in the late 1950s, Ireland's expenditure on defence accounted for approximately 5 per cent of its overall national expenditure, substantially less not only than that of NATO member states, but also the other neutral countries of Western Europe. The next lowest were NATO members Belgium and Italy, at 16 per cent, with neutral Sweden at 17 per cent.[8]

The effects of such a low level of investment were stark. Manoeuvres were a rare occurrence, and when held limited to skeleton battalion exercises. Shortages of ammunition meant that artillery shoots had virtually ceased by the early 1950s. As early as 1955 it was estimated that a mobilization on the scale of the Emergency would result in a shortage of $c.63,000$ rifles, almost 100 million rounds of ammunition, and more than 3,000 light machine guns. Moreover, much of the stock of weaponry on hand was either obsolete or unserviceable and suitable only for drill instruction. Obsolescence was an especially acute problem in the areas of armoured cars, tanks and aircraft.

Four Churchill Mk VI tanks were rented from the British in 1948 and 1949 as replacements for the ageing Landsverk L60, and eventually purchased

(*Left to right*): Capt Patrick Keogh, Capt James Liddy, Comdt Patrick Hogan and Capt Thomas Furlong pictured at Geneva Airport, on their way to serve with UNOGIL in Beirut, 28/29 August 1958.

outright in 1954 despite being already obsolete; these in turn were replaced in 1958 by four Comet A34 tanks, with another four acquired in 1960. On 1 August 1961 the Minister for Defence, Kevin Boland, was informed that the Defence Forces were:

> Completely and totally unprepared to resist invasion or indeed to pose anything other than an insignificant threat to a would be aggressor. We are deficient in manpower, we are short of, or entirely deficient in, certain types of weapons and equipment and the standard of training, particularly that of the FCÁ (who will form a large part of our forces on mobilization) is extremely low.[9]

It was a stark assessment, all the more so given that, despite such evident shortcomings in resources and personnel, the Defence Forces had risen to the challenge presented by the government's commitment to the United Nations and had deployed more than 1,000 troops to Congo, the first Defence Forces batallions on active service since the Civil War.

'Ireland has refused to consider association with the Pact while Partition continues'[20]

Ireland found itself on the margins of the emerging Cold War world order, dominated by tensions between the US and USSR, two global superpowers with nuclear arsenals. After 1955 Irish foreign policy adapted to embrace multilateralism and engagement via the United Nations, established in 1945, which offered a chance for the Defence Forces to find new purpose under the umbrella of UN peacekeeping missions. Cold War politics intervened, however, when Ireland's application for membership was blocked by the USSR in 1946; it was not until 1955 that Ireland was finally admitted.

Yet the adaptation to multilateralism had its limits. Invited to join what would become the North Atlantic Treaty Organization (NATO), in January 1949 the government had formally declined; not, however, on the basis of 'neutrality or non-alliance as a principle'.[11] Rather, the possibility of joint military action with Britain while the island of Ireland remained partitioned was deemed too unpalatable: 'It is impossible for Ireland, as long as Partition lasts, to participate in a joint security treaty with the state responsible for the unnatural division of this country.'[12]

When coupled with neutrality during the Second World War – however partial that neutrality might have been – the decision not to join NATO was one that contributed to the retrenchment of the Defence Forces and hampered its development in the 1950s. Supplies of military equipment from Britain and America were virtually non-existent in the 1950s, as both nations largely concentrated on maintaining their own forces and supplying their partners in NATO. There were also suspicions that the British were intentionally withholding equipment:

> For years past we have asked the British each year in our annual forecast to supply a few modern tanks. Our requests have never been met and it appears evident that the British are not prepared to sell us modern vehicles, even though they have sold them to non-NATO countries such as Sweden and Switzerland.[13]

Those suspicions were not without foundation. A report to the British Dominions Office from the British military attaché in Dublin observed

Duffle bag belonging to Sgt Keane, No. 1 Platoon, 32 Infantry Battalion, photographed prior to the battalion's departure for Congo on 27 July 1960.

that there were three reasons for Britain's reluctance to supply equipment: rearmament of Commonwealth countries, rearmament of NATO countries, and the 'refusal of the Irish Republic to take part in any form of collective defence'.[14]

Forced to look beyond its traditional suppliers, the Defence Forces secured permission from Oscar Traynor, serving his second term as Minister for Defence, to explore alternative sources. A military mission to Sweden in 1952 procured 4,000 Gustav submachine guns and eighteen Bofors light anti-aircraft guns, while mortars and Energa anti-tank rifle grenades were purchased from France and Belgium.

Exclusion from the United Nations for the first decade of its existence was a further blow, removing an early opportunity of participating in the first multilateral peacekeeping missions, a stated ambition of the United Nations and a commitment which the Defence Forces had in view from a very early

179

stage. In January 1946 the British commanding officer in Northern Ireland, G.C. Bucknall, reported that Chief of Staff, Dan McKenna, envisaged that when the Defence Forces were 'trained and equipped to modern standards, they would be prepared, within their small capacity, to undertake international obligations.'[15]

The post-war years have been characterized as a period of 'unfruitful repetitious representations' for the Defence Forces, a description particularly apt for the years between the end of the war and the first Irish deployment with the United Nations in 1958.[16] Those thirteen years saw a string of memoranda from GHQ to successive Ministers for Defence, presenting up-to-date and professional analyses of international military trends, the potential threats those trends presented to Ireland, and the steps required to enable the Defence Forces to defend the state from external aggression.

In presenting these analyses the Defence Forces were placed in a Catch-22 situation. Professionalism demanded an honest and rigorous appraisal of the weaknesses in Ireland's defensive systems at a time when the prospect of another global war, incorporating nuclear weaponry, was very real. Yet the financial investment needed to rectify those weaknesses and to allow the Defence Forces to act as a credible deterrent to belligerent forces was enormous, and GHQ's recommendations easily dismissed as outlandish and quietly shelved.

'Ireland's participation in a joint UN team has been requested'

The practicalities of participation in the developing concept of UN observer or emergency peacekeeping missions came under consideration at the Department of Defence from at least January 1954. At the Departments of the Taoiseach and External Affairs, however, staff shortages and more pressing priorities that arose during Ireland's initial engagements at the UN ensured that those initial preparations fell into abeyance.

In November 1956 Peadar MacMahon, long-serving Secretary of the Department of Defence (1927–57) and a former Chief of Staff, reminded his minister, Seán Mac Eoin (another former Chief of Staff), that 'legislative and other action would be necessary before the Defence Forces or any part thereof could participate in an International Police Force'. MacMahon also drew his minister's attention to a memo submitted by Lt Gen Liam Egan, warning that extensive study was needed to prepare and provide adequate training, organization, and tactical doctrines for any troops sent overseas. The perennial problem of acquiring matériel would also have to be addressed, perhaps even exacerbated, by the need for gathering stores of equipment suitable for different climates.[17]

MacMahon's efforts did prompt some initial study of the requirements for UN service. The decisions to investigate the possibility and subsequently to proceed with putting in place the structures for Irish participation straddled the general election of March 1957 and change from the second inter-party government to a Fianna Fáil administration. Seán Mac Eoin was replaced as Minister for Defence by Kevin Boland, who remained in office until October 1961.

When canvassed in the summer of 1957, the Defence Forces were hesitant to support overseas deployment (then most likely with the UN Emergency Force in Egypt), citing low strength and the lack of enabling legislation. Nonetheless, instructions were issued by government in September 1957 to prepare the required legislation, a formal endorsement of the principle of the Defence Forces serving overseas with the United Nations.

Preceded by their colour party, soldiers from 32 Infantry Battalion march down O'Connell Street on 27 July 1960, prior to their departure for Congo. Standing on the raised platform in front of the General Post Office, alongside the senior officers of the Defence Forces, are Taoiseach Seán Lemass and Minister for External Affairs, Frank Aiken.

In June 1958 a telegram from Ireland's Permanent Mission to the UN, New York, landed in Iveagh House, home of the Department of External Affairs. Labelled 'most urgent', it conveyed a request from the UN Secretary-General, Dag Hammarskjöld, for five officers of Major or Captain rank, to join the UN Observer Group in Lebanon (UNOGIL). The advice from New York was to grasp this opportunity:

> We, for our part, would like to express the hope that this opportunity to participate in a useful and practical task of the United Nations in a vital area for world peace will not be missed. This is the first time that Ireland's participation in a joint UN team has been requested ... our successful participation would open the door to sharing in further efforts of this kind for which our position in the Organization is admirably suited.[18]

The government's response was immediate: 'Please inform Secretary-General agreeable in principle. Details being settled and will wire later. Request no publicity until details settled.'[19] Four days later five officers, led by Lt Col Justin McCarthy, departed Dublin Airport for Lebanon. At Hammarskjöld's request they were joined by another forty-five officers across August, September, and October. The contention that the officers deployed with UNOGIL were military observers in a non-combat role, along with a relatively liberal interpretation of the 1954 Defence Act, meant that the ongoing lack of legislation empowering the government to send Irish soldiers abroad was not deemed a stumbling block. When UNOGIL's operations were wound up at the end of the year, forty-eight Irish officers returned home, while McCarthy and Capt Pat Jordan were redeployed to the UN Truce Supervision Organization (UNTSO).

Ireland's participation in UNOGIL marked not just its entry to international peacekeeping, but the beginning of an unbroken period of service with UN-mandated missions that has lasted more than six decades. In practical terms it enhanced the state's reputation at the UN, and provided a valuable opportunity for the Defence Forces to adjust to the command and control structures of UN missions, which maintained operational independence from constituent military forces. Public reaction to Irish involvement with UNOGIL was extremely positive, perhaps most noticeably in the successful recruitment campaign of 1958, which briefly raised the Defence Forces' strength above 9,000. Hand-picked by the General Staff for deployment to Lebanon, the performance of the fifty officers who served with UNOGIL bolstered the reputation of the Defence Forces among its international peers.

That burgeoning reputation, in addition to Ireland's lack of a colonial history on the African continent, marked the Defence Forces as ideal candidates to participate in a UN-mandated mission in Congo (ONUC) in July 1960. Internal strife and interference from Belgian troops had brought newly independent Congo to the brink of disintegration. When its government sought UN assistance, Hammarskjöld once more requested Irish participation, this time in the form of a battalion 'with light arms and supporting services'.[20] Enabling legislation was swiftly passed by the Oireachtas and Taoiseach Seán Lemass assured the legislature that Irish troops were being deployed purely for peacekeeping purposes.

32 Infantry Battalion was activated on 2 July 1960 with a strength of 685 all ranks. A, B and C Companies were drawn from Eastern, Southern and Western Commands respectively, with the Curragh Training Camp providing HQ Company. The main body of troops deployed from Baldonnel to Congo on 27 July, airlifted by the US Air Force.

Maj Gen Seán Mac Eoin, appointed Chief of Staff in January 1960, later recalled that the speed with which the Defence Forces were required to deploy caught the General Staff somewhat off guard. But the opportunity to revitalize the Defence Forces after the crippling inertia of the preceding decade could not be turned down:

> The request for a battalion was quite staggering, and I must confess ... I was prompted entirely by the state of affairs in the Army at the time ... We said to hell whether they were well prepared or not, it was worth it to give 700 men an opportunity of this experience.[21]

When the UN requested a second battalion just a month later there was little hesitation on the government's part, though there were reservations at GHQ:

> The meeting of this challenge – the participation of a country with an unprepared army in the tropics – was magnificent, and in fact it

was that very response that resulted in what a good many people, including myself [Mac Eoin], thought a bit rash. This was the sending of a second battalion off a few weeks later.[22]

Within the space of five weeks there were just under 1,400 Irish troops in Congo, a staggering 16 per cent of the Permanent Defence Forces. Lt Col Richard Bunworth, OC of 33 Infantry Battalion, would later recall the adjustments required for UN service:

> We lacked experience, and consequently it was difficult for all of us to visualize what a UN Peacekeeping Mission entailed. To be equipped with and trained in the traditional infantry weapons, yet circumscribed in their use by the well-known and accepted UN policy of avoiding the use of force, if at all possible, in solving the many operational problems, was a situation difficult to understand in its finer points.[23]

Mac Eoin was seconded to Congo as ONUC Force Commander in January 1961, where he remained for fifteen months. Maj Gen Seán Collins-Powell was appointed Chief of Staff in Mac Eoin's absence.

'I came of age as a soldier in Jadotville'[24]

ONUC was on the ground in Congo from July 1960 until June 1964. The Irish troops of the twelve battalions, infantry groups and armoured units deployed to Congo across those four years entered a volatile and often dangerous situation, especially in the first eighteen months of the mission. Acclimatization to a new continent was hindered not just by hostility, but also cultural differences and an inability to communicate effectively with members of the different Congolese tribes.

The first Irish battalions deployed without anyone in their ranks who could speak French, Swahili, or Lingala. Peadar MacMahon's warnings about the need for climate-appropriate equipment had effectively been ignored. 32 Infantry Battalion deployed in 'bulls wool' uniforms entirely unsuited to a tropical climate. A promise from the UN of more suitable attire for the battalion never materialized, a symptom of the UN's broader failure

Pte P. Fennessy of 32 Infantry Battalion enjoying a can of Guinness Extra Stout while relaxing in Albertville, 1 August 1960.

to adequately prepare for troops on the ground in Congo. Though also supplied with Gustav submachine guns, 32 and 33 Infantry Battalions were mostly armed with obsolete Lee Enfield rifles.

Procedures for the command and control of UN-mandated forces were in their infancy, with a frequent disconnect between HQ ONUC and the UN Secretariat in New York. As a result, ONUC's operational objectives were not always clearly defined, and armed clashes with different factions on the ground in the Congo were frequent. For the first time since the Civil War, Irish soldiers found themselves in combat operations. Of the twenty-six Irish soldiers who died in Congo, sixteen were killed in action.

Eight of those casualties occurred when a patrol from A Coy, 33 Infantry Battalion, was ambushed by Baluba tribesmen at Niemba, on 8 November 1960. During Operation Morthor, an ONUC offensive launched on 13 September 1961 to force the secessionist Congolese province of Katanga to reunite with the Republic of the Congo, B Coy and C Coy of 35 Infantry Battalion, along with the Battalion's Armoured Car Group, were engaged in heavy fighting for control of the city of Elisabethville, the Katangese capital. Three Irish soldiers died during the operation. 36 Infantry Battalion, which arrived in Elisabethville between 5 and 24 December 1961, has the distinction of being the only unit in Defence Forces history to land in an active combat zone and immediately engage in fighting. On 7 December one of the battalion's troop transports was hit by enemy fire during its landing at Elisabethville, while two members of the battalion were killed during the Battle of the Tunnel on 16 December 1961; a third died the same day from wounds received on 12 December.

A Coy, 35 Infantry Battalion, had been despatched on 3 September to protect the white population in Jadotville, a town in the southern region of Katanga. On the day that Operation Morthor commenced, the Katangese Gendarmerie launched an attack against A Coy. 156 Irish soldiers engaged in a fierce battle against a much larger force of Katangese Gendarmerie. Led by Comdt Patrick Quinlan and vastly outnumbered, A Coy suffered casualties of just five wounded men. After four days of heavy fighting, having run out of water and other vital supplies, and with attempts to relieve A Coy

Soldiers from B Coy, 33 Infantry Battalion, on board a train about to depart Kamina for Albertville. August 1960.

Seated in the car, *Time-Life* photographer Terry Spencer is stopped by a roadblock manned by Baluba tribesmen on the outskirts of Manono, a few days after the Baluba uprising of 14 September 1960. The tribesmen are armed with a variety of weapons, including a bow and arrow and what appears to be a shotgun.

unsuccessful, Comdt Quinlan took the difficult decision to surrender. A Coy were taken into captivity on 18 September and were not released until the end of the following month.

Misunderstandings of the nature of the fighting at Jadotville, and of the reasons for A Coy's surrender, contributed to tensions following A Coy's return to Ireland. The 'Jadotville Jacks', as they were sometimes known, initially arrived home to a warm welcome and to sympathetic press reports about the fighting at Jadotville. Their surrender was, however, poorly received by GHQ and some fellow soldiers and led to a decades-long tarnishing of the reputation of the men who fought at Jadotville. It was not until the completion in 2004 of a review that the Defence Forces accepted the view that surrender had been the only option available to Comdt Quinlan.

However urgent the chance to revitalize the Defence Forces via UN peacekeeping missions may have been, the casualties at Niemba highlighted the grave risks taken in deploying soldiers untrained in jungle warfare,

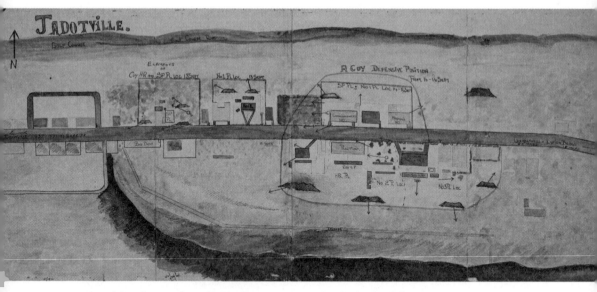

Lt Noel Carey's map of A Coy's area of operations in Jadotville during the battle, drawn while Carey and the other members of A Coy were held in captivity in September and October 1961.

equipped with obsolete, bolt action rifles, and no armoured cars. It was no coincidence that an armoured car group of eight Ford Mk VI was sent to Congo in January 1961. A second armoured car squadron deployed to Congo in October 1962, and in November received UN-supplied Daimler Ferret Mk II armoured cars. From 1961 Irish troops were equipped with the modern FN FAL automatic assault rifle. The benefits of such equipment, and of greater tactical awareness of the demands of ONUC operations, were amply demonstrated at Jadotville and in the various battles in and around Elisabethville in late 1961.

From a highpoint of two battalions in late 1960/early 1961, thereafter Ireland's commitment to ONUC was slightly reduced, though the Defence Forces frequently maintained as many as 1,000 troops on the ground at any one time. Twelve Defence Forces units served in Congo during the four years of ONUC's presence, comprising 6,191 cumulative missions.

As the end of ONUC's mission approached, rising tensions between the Greek and Turkish communities in Cyprus led to the deployment of a United Nations peacekeeping force (UNFICYP) in April 1964. Irish participation in UNFICYP was a specific request of the country's president, Archbishop

Makarios. Yet when first approached in January 1964, the Irish government expressed serious reservations, many of which arose out of Ireland's experiences dealing with the UN Secretariat during the Congo operation. International pressure on Ireland to contribute troops to UNFICYP came from within the halls of the UN building in New York, as well as directly from the American administration.

On 24 March the Minister for External Affairs, Frank Aiken, informed U Thant, UN Secretary-General, that Ireland was prepared to send a battalion of 600 men. Under the command of Lt Col Patrick Pearse Barry, 40 Infantry Battalion deployed to Wolfe Tone Camp, Famagusta, in April. It was joined by 4 Infantry Group in July, bringing the Irish contingent in Cyprus to more than 1,000 men. Nine Irish soldiers died while serving with UNFICYP, though none were as a result of combat operations.

Between July 1960 and July 1964, beginning with 32 Infantry Battalion's deployment to Congo and including initial deployment to Cyprus, the Defence Forces' contribution to UN missions had amounted to nine infantry battalions, seven armoured car groups, three infantry groups and two armoured car squadrons.

Fr C.P. Crean, HCF, presides over Mass at Albertville Airport on 19 November 1960, prior to the repatriation of the bodies of Irish soldiers killed at Niemba.

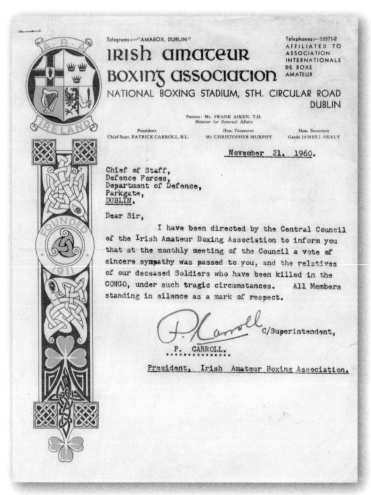

News of the killing of Irish troops at Niemba caused widespread shock at home. Expressions of sympathy flooded in from across the country and abroad, including this letter from the Irish Amateur Boxing Association to Chief of Staff, Lt Gen Seán Mac Eoin, 21 November 1960.

'You can regard all our army as a stand-by force, trained and ready'[25]

While policy regarding Irish participation in peacekeeping missions was being fashioned in the corridors of Iveagh House, Leinster House and UN Headquarters in New York, actual implementation fell to the civil and military branches of the Department of Defence. For the military branch, the lack of warning prior to overseas deployment, especially to Congo, had not proven to be an insurmountable burden, though the first battalions sent to Congo were poorly equipped, had received no specialist training and virtually no briefings on the situation on the ground.

One possibility, raised on several occasions, was that the Defence Forces could adopt the Nordic model of preparing standing units for UN deployment, on peacekeeping duties of a police character. Hard won experience in Congo had, however, shown that peacekeeping missions could involve engagements that escalated to full combat situations. Responding to a proposal to attend a conference arranged by the Canadian government to discuss the formation of stand-by units, the Department of Finance opposed both the concept and any additional expenditure on training and equipment for troops earmarked for UN service. In Finance's view, expenditure incurred during UN operations 'should be recoverable from UN funds'.[26] ONUC and UNFICYP had shown that the Defence Forces could supply units for peacekeeping missions at very short notice. Nonetheless, Ireland's availability to participate in future missions would ultimately be dictated by political and financial considerations.

Lt Gen Seán Mac Eoin, Force Commander of ONUC from January 1961 to March 1962, pictured at a press conference on 1 June 1961 discussing security arrangements for the convening of the national parliament at Lovanium University in Leopoldville. Dr Sture Linner, Officer in Charge and Chief of UN Civilian Operations in the Congo, is seated on Mac Eoin's left. To his right is Oscar Faura, UN Information Officer. A map showing the provinces of Congo is visible in the background.

Handwritten list of English phrases and their Kiswahili counterparts, compiled by RSM Greensmyth prior to his deployment to the Congo.

Despite the importance of the Defence Forces in enhancing Ireland's reputation at the United Nations, the issue of military preparedness appears to have been placed further down the list of important factors, at least outside of the Department of Defence. UN membership meant the Department of External Affairs assumed a more prominent role in decisions regarding Defence Forces deployment. External Affairs requested a 'brief paper' from the Department of Defence in March 1968, outlining 'the manner in which Ireland has been able to meet UN calls for Peace-Keeping Contingents at very short notice without having to maintain a "Stand-by" unit'.

Asked for his observations, Mac Eoin, whose experience encompassed fifteen months as ONUC Force Commander in Congo, was at pains to correct the perception that the Defence Forces were, in general, sufficiently well-trained and ready to deploy overseas. That, he informed Michael Hilliard,

Minister for Defence, had not been the case with Congo or Cyprus. As no individual unit within the Permanent Defence Forces had sufficient strength to provide a framework around which a unit for UN service could coalesce, battalions sent overseas had been ad hoc formations drawn from across the four regional commands. Personnel and equipment limitations meant that while future units could be raised and sent overseas at short notice, they would be suitable only for missions of a policing character.

Without sufficient time for training and integration over a period of months, Mac Eoin argued, units would be poorly prepared for deployment to one of the 'trouble spots of the world … In our case administrative and technical personnel often carry out the role of infantrymen for which they are NOT adequately trained.' Apart from the Niemba ambush, participation in Operation Morthor and the Battle of Jadotville, the missions undertaken in the Congo and Cyprus (to date) had largely been of a policing nature: 'Should such a mission escalate to combat, it must be clearly understood that our troops are NOT sufficiently well trained to give the kind of performance which the country would rightly expect of them … such an involvement must

Members of 38 Infantry Battalion on duty with ONUC in March 1963, securing road blocks and positions on the perimeter of Elisabethville. The troops are supported by two Irish Ford Mark VI armoured cars, built by Thomas Thompson & Son of Carlow in 1941. The turret was modelled on the Landsverk L180 armoured car. Eight Ford Mark VI were deployed to the Congo in January 1961, becoming the first Irish armoured vehicles deployed overseas.

During his trip to Ireland in the summer of 1963, President John F. Kennedy was particularly impressed by the drills performed by an honour guard of the 36th Defence Forces Cadet Class. Following his assassination in November 1963, his widow, Jackie Kennedy, requested that the cadets perform the same drills at his graveside during the burial. Members of the 37th Cadet Class were despatched to Washington. In this photo of the burial at Arlington Cemetery on 25 November, American service personnel convey President John F. Kennedy's coffin to his grave. Six members of the Irish Cadets are visible on the left, presenting arms. Among the mourners in the background are Jackie (head veiled and bowed), and President Kennedy's brother, Robert.

inevitably lead to unnecessary and grave losses in personnel because of a lack of combat efficiency':

> Without this <u>TIME</u> we are operating on a policy of make-believe. Indeed, it can be truly stated that we have already taken too many risks, that our unpreparedness could have placed us in more serious military situations from which we might not have been able to extricate ourselves with honour, even with grave casualties. [The Department of External Affairs] should be made aware of these critical facts, our present state of unpreparedness, the limiting factors on our capabilities for action and the steps we are duty bound to take to remedy such a known situation.[27]

Members of the advance party of 40 Irish Battalion, the first Irish force deployed for service with UNFICYP, explore the ruins of the ancient city of Salamis, 13 April 1964. The remainder of the battalion arrived in Cyprus between 19 and 21 April.

Commanded by Lt Col P.P. Barry and attached to UNFICYP, 40 Irish Battalion became operational on 22 April 1964, taking over responsibility for the Famagusta area in eastern Cyprus. This photograph shows members of the battalion escorting Turkish Cypriots from an area in Famagusta that had recently come under fire from Greek forces.

Off-duty personnel from 10 Infantry Group play volleyball at Lefka, Cyprus, during their tour with UNFICYP. 1 September 1968.

Mac Eoin's observations underline the extent to which the performance of Irish soldiers in Congo and Cyprus had risen above the limitations of their training and preparation; limitations imposed by repeated underinvestment in the Defence Forces.

'To patrol our territorial waters and to cover our principal harbours'[28]

At the time of its establishment in 1939, there was little sense that the Marine and Coast Watching Service would be anything more than a temporary innovation, to be disbanded once the Emergency conditions of the war had passed. Yet the policy put forward by the 1944 'Memorandum on the Defence Forces' envisaged a small naval service for patrol of territorial waters, a position amplified the following year when GHQ proposed that a naval service be established as a permanent component of the Defence Forces.

On 15 March 1946 the government approved the recommendation and authorized the reorganization of the Maritime Inscription as a Naval Reserve (An Sluagh Muirí). Two months later the role of fisheries protection was formally transferred to the Naval Service. On 26 November the government advised the President to appoint Henry Joseph Alexander Savile Jerome to temporary commissioned rank as Captain (Marine Rank) and OC of the Service, with effect from 1 December. The suggested command structure, whereby the Naval Service's commanding officer would have the same seniority as other Corps commanders and fall under Army control, raised some eyebrows:

> The only plausible case for the retention of the Naval Service under Army command would be one of expediency ... reason would dictate that the Army officers bearing the final responsibility for naval matters should possess some knowledge and experience of naval affairs. Such is not the case here at present ... The present Defence Forces Act is completely inadequate to deal with naval situations, and the spectacle was seen, during the Emergency, of the Minister being unable to commission officers in the Marine Service owing to the impossibility of giving them authority on board ship without their possessing a British Board of Trade certificate – a civilian license.[29]

HMS *Borage*, one of three Flower-Class corvettes purchased from the British Navy in 1946, was commissioned as the Naval Service's first new vessel on 15

LÉ *Clíona* (03) pictured with MTB M4.

Naval Service recruits relax together while one plays the accordion. The photo was taken at Haulbowline Naval Base, possibly in the 1950s.

November 1946 and renamed LÉ *Macha* (LÉ is the designation given to all ships in the Naval Service and stands for Long Éireannach – 'Irish Ship'). It was followed the next month by LÉ *Maev* and in January 1947 by LÉ *Clíona*, which together formed the backbone of the Naval Service for the next two decades. *Muirchú* and *Rannoch* were both sold in the summer of 1947, while each of the six Motor Torpedo Boats acquired during the Emergency had been disposed of by 1950.

Following the submission of a further memorandum from the Defence Forces on the future of the Naval Service, a government meeting on 24 June 1949 referred the matter for consideration, and report, to a committee comprising the Ministers for External Affairs, Agriculture, Finance and Defence. A year later, the committee had yet to meet. Rumours of the Service's impending demise were strong enough to prompt correspondence from concerned public bodies, including the Maritime Institute of Ireland.

Though supply lines from the British War Office overall remained strained, Irish officers continued to be welcomed to British military colleges for advanced training. Co-operation with the Admiralty enabled the completion of a major hydrographical survey of the Irish coastline between November 1948 and December 1952. As the Defence Forces lacked both the expertise and technical equipment for the survey, British military personnel were seconded to a project they labelled 'Operation Sandstone'.

In 1960 the Department of Defence assumed responsibility for marine rescue co-ordination from the Department of Transport and Power, establishing a co-ordination centre at Haulbowline. Peacetime functions of the Naval Service were further expanded in the 1960s, encompassing introductory courses for young, potential fishermen at Haulbowline (initiated in 1964), while from 1966 the service also began offering training in ship defence to merchant seamen.

Despite the evident need for and the good work of the Naval Service, some familiar problems threaded through the 1950s and 1960s. Several attempts were made to acquire vessels appropriate for seaward defence and minesweeping, tasks for which the corvettes acquired in 1946 became increasingly unsuitable as technology advanced and the vessels aged. Anxious to avoid the situation that had pertained during the Emergency, in 1954 the Chief of Staff counselled a steady build-up of the fleet: 'If we can build up a small efficient service, we could expand it on mobilization and be able to control and defend our ports, anchorages and coastal waters against minelaying and submarine attacks.'[30]

Advice was sought from the British Admiralty on several occasions, and two vessels were made available to the Naval Service in the mid-1950s: 'Alleged financial stringency and a need for economy measures brought the project to an end.'[31] Seán Mac Eoin was moved to inform the minister in 1965 that 'the Naval Service has not the capabilities either at present or potentially to meet its war and peace commitments'.[32]

Pay and conditions were a perennial problem. A survey of the Service in 1962 found that the 'deadly monotony' of fisheries patrols was one of the principal reasons for failure to retain recruits, with the merchant marine and British Navy offering greater pay and variety of service.[33] Haulbowline's nineteenth-century roots were increasingly an issue – it had no sports fields, recreation rooms, gym

A Naval Service officer oversees training with a 40mm 'pom-pom' gun, found on Flower-Class corvettes acquired in 1946.

or canteen. A recruitment drive in 1963 was dubbed a 'complete failure', with just twenty-three enlistments during the first nine months of 1964.[34]

The Service operated in a policy vacuum, with successive governments declining to seriously consider a series of proposals presented by the General Staff. Twenty years after the Service's establishment, the Chief of Staff appealed for clarity from the Minister for Defence: 'I am naturally anxious that a clear cut attainable mission for the Naval Service ... should be defined and so clarify a position which has caused me and my predecessors in office so much concern since 1946'.[35]

By 1968 the Naval Service's three corvettes had each been in service for more than two decades. Despite a major overhaul in the late 1950s, all three were long past their prime and were restricted solely to fishery protection. Replacement of the corvettes was an urgent priority, and in June 1967 the Minister for Defence, Michael Hilliard, presented a memorandum to government outlining the case for new ships. Following consideration, the government demurred on making a positive decision for the development of the Naval Service. On 8 August

1967 it established an interdepartmental committee, with representatives from Defence, Transport and Power, Agriculture and Fisheries, and Finance to consider and report to the Minister for Defence on how to provide for 'the minimum requirements in the matter of naval defence with the maximum requirements in the matter of fishery protection'.[36]

The urgency of the situation was heightened by the withdrawal from service of LÉ *Macha* in December 1968, followed by LÉ *Clíona* in July 1969. As the new decade dawned, the Naval Service had precisely one ship to its name.

'Some helicopters should be acquired ... for sea and air rescue work'[37]

In contrast to the Marine Service, the end of the Emergency brought relatively little change to the Air Corps. With the ongoing development of Rineanna Aerodrome as a transatlantic civilian airport, No. 1 Fighter Squadron had been transferred to Gormanston Camp in February 1945. Vickers Supermarine Seafires and Spitfires replaced the Hurricane as first line fighters in the late 1940s. Equipped with F24 aerial reconnaissance cameras, the Seafires provided support flights photographing the coast during the hydrographic survey of the late 1940s and early 1950s. No. 1 Fighter Squadron returned to Baldonnel in 1956. A short service commission scheme, which accelerated the training and qualification process for pilots and had first been introduced during the Emergency, was revived in 1953 and evolved to become the principal pathway for civilian pilots. Thirty-six pilots were released to fill vacancies in Aer Lingus between 1952 and 1960.

A major review of air defence planning was completed in 1952, though such was the deficit of anti-aircraft weaponry and radar equipment, the plans were described as 'theoretical' in value: 'The studies made have, however, given precise information as to the magnitude and extent of the anti-aircraft defence problem.'[38] The eight Seafires in service with No. 1 Fighter Squadron (down from eleven the previous year) were nearing end of life, and replacements were urgently needed. Nor could they be adequately replaced until hard-surfaced runways were installed at Baldonnel – a minimum necessity for the operation of jet fighters. Purchase of jet aircraft was essential not just to give the Air Corps some semblance of wartime operational capabilities, but also to fulfil an emerging implied task – the training of pilots for Aer Lingus.

Following several years of increasingly urgent warnings about the lack of aircraft available to the Air Corps, and the creeping obsolescence of those that were available, Lt Gen Liam Egan bluntly stated that as of the end of 1954, no operational fighter craft were available. Given the growing importance of air power and the state's near complete lack of anti-aircraft defences, Egan offered a masterclass in understatement when he noted 'our deficiency in operational aircraft is serious'.[39]

Though a request for funding for hard-surfaced runways was first referred to the Department of Finance in 1948, it was not until 1951 that plans for laying two hard-surfaced runways at Baldonnel were approved. Further obfuscation from Finance ensured that work did not actually begin until February 1954, however, and the first runway was completed in the summer of 1955. A second, shorter concrete runway was laid in 1956. To coincide with the completion of the runways and the construction of a control tower at Baldonnel, in July 1956 the Air Corps took delivery of three De Havilland Vampires, its first jet aircraft. Three more Vampires were delivered in early 1961.

Deployment of 32 Infantry Battalion to the Congo in July 1960 had relied on the United States Air Force for transportation, which exposed the limitations that still existed at Baldonnel Aerodrome. The lack of approach radar prompted the American pilots to refer to Baldonnel as a 'jungle airstrip'.[40] When requested to airlift 34 Infantry Battalion in January 1961, the United States Air Force agreed only on condition that it could operate from Dublin Airport. Approach and surveillance radar equipment were eventually installed at Baldonnel in 1963 and 1964.

Vickers Supermarine Spitfire Tr.9s in formation. The Air Corps purchased six of these two-seater training aircraft in 1950, which were delivered the following year. They remained in service until 1961, variously used as trainers and by No. 1 Fighter Squadron.

The Aérospatiale Alouette III is perhaps the most iconic aircraft of the Irish Air Corps. The first two Alouette IIIs entered service in November 1963, with the first search and rescue operation featuring the helicopter conducted the following month. The Air Corps acquired eight in total, which remained in service for a remarkable forty-four years before finally being retired in September 2007.

The emergence of the helicopter as an important tool both in military and civil operations was one which was closely monitored by the Air Corps and within GHQ. Liam Egan brought its importance to the attention of the Minister for Defence in 1955, referencing its prominence in the Korean War: 'It would appear that they will play an important part in any future war, both in direct support of the forces in the field, and in supply, reconnaissance and rescue work of all natures.'[41]

Established to examine Ireland's search and rescue network in the wake of a boating tragedy near Clare Island, Co. Mayo, an interdepartmental committee concluded in 1958 that the need for helicopters to assist in search and rescue operations would be too rare to warrant their purchase. Further maritime tragedies in the late 1950s and early 1960s forced a rethink of that conclusion, particularly after a Royal Air Force helicopter assisted with the rescue of the crew from the *Halronnel* after it was swept onto Tuskar Rock in October 1961. The Defence Forces' contribution to a second committee convened in 1962 strongly urged the addition of helicopters to its fleet. That recommendation was accepted, and the Air Corps received its first helicopters in November 1963.

203

A rare photo, taken by Paddy O'Meara, of an Air Corps De Havilland DH 115 Vampire in mid-air, with the distinctive roundel of the Irish Air Corps visible on the fuselage. Construction of concrete runways and a modern control tower at Baldonnel in 1955 and 1956 finally paved the way for the acquisition of jet aircraft, and in July 1956 the Air Corps received three Vampires at a cost of £146,000, with three more acquired in 1961. The Vampires saw service with No. 1 Fighter Squadron and also served as advanced training aircraft, and were withdrawn from service in 1976.

Helicopter Flight came into being on 26 November 1963 with the delivery of two Aérospatiale Alouette III helicopters – the first aircraft acquired by the Air Corps that were not manufactured in Britain. Inshore and offshore search and rescue operations were revolutionized as a result, and the Air Corps revitalized. Helicopter Flight's first search and rescue mission was conducted on 23 December 1963, and its first successful rescue completed in Dublin Bay on 8 August 1964. Following agreement between the Department of Defence and the Department of Health, the Air Corps initiated an air ambulance service in 1965, with Helicopter Flight carrying out most emergency transportations.

'Lessening the urgency of defence preparations'

Composed by the Chief of Staff's Branch in 1967, a review of all aspects of national defence noted that three separate detailed studies of the 'defence problem' had been completed by the Defence Forces since the beginning of the decade, as part fulfilment of the Chief of Staff's duty to advise the government on military matters. The review observed that while the recommendations contained within were typically accepted by government, the 'means to give them effect were not subsequently provided'.[42]

The parallels between the Defence Forces in the decade after the Civil War, and that after the Emergency, are striking. In both instances the national profile of an institution that, for a variety of reasons, had provided stability and focus in a time of crisis rapidly dwindled. In the late 1940s and 1950s, economic exigencies and the relatively abstract nature of the Cold War's threat to Irish security provided excuses for the denial of funding and equipment.

The 1967 review offered a realistic assessment of the Defence Forces' fortunes since 1946, and its prospects for investment in the absence of a major international war:

> It is inevitable that successive governments have been concerned more with economic, cultural and social development than with the problem of defence, which impose a drain on the national resources ... The success of international diplomacy to date in finding temporary solutions to critical international situations and the apparent absence of an immediate threat to our national security are factors which have resulted in lessening the urgency of defence preparations since the end of the Second World War.[43]

At the close of the 1960s the Defence Forces remained far below its establishment strength. Funding was typically sufficient to maintain ageing and obsolete equipment, with occasional investment in new technology such as automatic rifles, helicopters and communications equipment. Each component of the Defence Forces stood at a different stage in their development. While the Naval Service was in crisis, Helicopter Flight had provided the Air Corps with renewed purpose. Deployment with ONUC and UNFICYP had revitalized the entire service, and established the Defence Forces as a central pillar of Ireland's foreign policy objective of multilateral engagement.

Defence against external aggression, which had been foregrounded as the Defence Forces' primary role since 1939, had been joined by overseas peacekeeping. Its other operational duties were less well defined, a point made in the 1967 review: 'The allotting of clear cut, reasonably attainable missions to the Defence Forces, in order of priority, is of fundamental importance in deciding on the structure, training and equipping of the various components. Above all it is essential to morale.'[44] It was an observation that could have been made at any time since the end of the Civil War, and one that assumed even more importance at the end of the decade. The outbreak of the Troubles in Northern Ireland in August 1969 radically altered internal deployment and overall defence policy. Border security would, for the next three decades, place major new demands on the Defence Forces' role as an aid to the civil power, prompting a significant expansion in its strength from the early 1970s.

THE DEFENCE FORCES ON THE SILVER SCREEN

Beginning with the handover of Beggars Bush Barracks on 1 February 1922, the Defence Forces have been captured on film for over a century. Pathé News filmed the National Army assuming control of various barracks throughout 1922, and over the next two decades continued to document the activities of the National Army and the Defence Forces, from the Civil War to ceremonial events and on into the Emergency.

In 1939 the government released *Step Together*, a nine-minute-long recruiting film for the Volunteer Force. That was followed in 1942 by a series of eight Movietone newsreels filmed with the co-operation of the Army Publicity Section, covering topics such as the Air Corps, the Marine Service

PARAMOUNT PICTURES CORPORATION
WEST COAST STUDIOS

5451 MARATHON STREET · HOLLYWOOD, CALIF. 90038

AREA 213
469-2411

CABLE ADDRESS
"FAMFILM"

Production Office - 140
Intercontinental Hotel
Ballsbridge 4, Dublin

April 22, 1968

The Secretary
Department of Defence
Parkgate Street
Dublin 7

For the attention of: Mr. H. O'Carroll
Lands Section

Dear Sirs:

Re: Film Making - "DARLING LILI"

We wish to apply for permission to use the two bays of the magazine located at Casement Aerodrome for Special Effects equipment from May 1st until June 30th. We would appreciate a decision on this as soon as possible.

We also wish to apply for permission to use the gymnasium for lunch break from 12 noon to 2 p.m. each day from May 2nd to June 16th approximately.

Yours faithfully,

William O'Kelly.
William O'Kelly
Lt. Colonel Rtd.
Production Liaison Officer

Agreed

No

cc: Comdt. P. Monahan,
Dept. of Chief of General Staff

Production Liaison for Paramount Studios, Lt Col William O'Kelly, requests the use of facilities at Casement Aerodrome (Baldonnel) during the filming of *Darling Lili* in April 1968.

and the Local Defence Force. That year the Defence Forces also established its own film unit, whose activities were chronicled in the official history of the Emergency, *The Call to Arms*, published in 1945. Though the footage it produced lacks sound, it is in colour and provides a fascinating snapshot of the Emergency-era Defence Forces, including the Blackwater Manoeuvres of 1942.

Aside from newsreels and documentary footage, the personnel of the Defence Forces have long featured on the silver screen. Hollywood first came calling in the 1950s during the filming of *Knights of the Round Table*, a Metro-Goldwyn-Mayer production starring Ava Gardner and released in 1953. Some of the battle scenes were shot at Luttrellstown Castle, Co. Dublin, and featured more than 300 officers and men as extras. The deal struck with MGM included the promise of a substantial contribution to the Army Benevolent Fund.

The late 1960s and early 1970s saw multiple film productions that made use of the Defence Forces. In 1965 Ardmore Studios in Co. Wicklow provided a home for the filming of *The Blue Max*, a First World War film depicting

A ground scene during the filming of *Darling Lili.*

Filming for *The Blue Max*, a major Hollywood production starring George Peppard and Ursula Andress, took place in Ireland during 1965, at Ardmore Studios and Casement and Weston Aerodromes. In this photo four De Havilland Tiger Moths, painted in First World War-era German camouflage, are being filmed by an Aérospatiale Alouette II helicopter, just visible in the distance above the closest Tiger Moth.

the activities of a German fighter pilot. Weston Aerodrome in Leixlip and Baldonnel (renamed as Casement Aerodrome in March 1965) served as filming locations, as did the campus of Trinity College Dublin. More than 1,000 Defence Forces personnel were employed as extras, while the Air Corps provided facilities and technical support. Lynn Garrison, a Canadian stunt pilot who worked on the film, maintained the film's aircraft at Weston Aerodrome, where they proved attractive to filmmakers seeking to recreate the First World War. Garrison's fleet was utilized for the filming of *Darling Lili* in 1967 and 1968, starring Rock Hudson and Julie Andrews. Between 23 May and 6 June 1968, the Air Corps and Eastern Command supplied up to 90 men a day, including ten pilots, for filming at Baldonnel and Kings Inns, Dublin. Pilots were provided at a rate of £6 3s. per day.

This sudden flurry of filming disrupted training plans, with the 1967 annual training camp at Fort Dunree cancelled and transferred to the Leenane area to facilitate another filming request from MGM, who required 100 troops and a pipe band. Chief of Staff Seán Mac Eoin warned that this would have a detrimental effect on 9 Infantry Group's preparations for UN duty with UNFICYP later that year. Nonetheless, government policy was that all departments were to facilitate and co-operate with film producers and studios.

Requests for use of Defence Forces' personnel and facilities continued to come thick and fast. MGM were facilitated during production of *Alfred the Great* in Galway in August 1968, with 450 soldiers from Western and Southern Commands. Filming of *McKenzie's Break* in late 1969 required the use of Coolmoney Camp for five weeks over October and November, as well as Casement Aerodrome for two days. On some days of filming at least 260 personnel were required to represent German officers and British Guards in charge of a POW camp. Lynn Garrison's collection of aircraft was once again used during the filming of *Zeppelin* in August 1970, as were the Air Corps. On this occasion tragedy struck while filming aerial scenes off Wicklow Head, when a Royal Aircraft Factory S.E.5, flown by Air Corps pilot Jim Liddy, collided with a helicopter carrying the film crew. Five people, including Liddy, were killed in the accident.

Though few major Hollywood movies were filmed in Ireland during the 1970s and 1980s, Mel Gibson and Steven Spielberg famously drew on the personnel of the Permanent Defence Forces and the FCÁ while filming their epic movies *Braveheart* (1995) and *Saving Private Ryan* (1998). Gibson assembled up to 2,000 members of the FCÁ to create the film's battle scenes, later recommending Ireland to Spielberg as a filming location. With the help of the Defence Forces, Spielberg re-created the D-Day landings at Normandy on Curracloe beach in Wexford, depicted to devastating effect in the film's visceral opening sequence.

CHAPTER 6

1970–99
GUARDING BORDERS AND
BREAKING BOUNDARIES

The last three decades of the twentieth century saw the Defence Forces adapt and respond to fast-moving and dangerous domestic and international security environments. The outbreak of the Troubles in Northern Ireland in 1969 brought with it a need to strengthen Border security and to counter the subversive activities of terrorist groups within the Irish state, particularly the Irish Republican Army. On the international front, multilateral engagement with the United Nations remained one of the cornerstones of Irish foreign policy, as it had been since 1955. Civil war in Lebanon led to the deployment of Defence Forces units with the UN's peacekeeping force, UNIFIL, in 1978. Lebanon soon became as well known in Ireland in the 1970s and 1980s as Congo had been during the 1960s. Closer to home, Ireland's accession to the European Economic Community in 1973 raised the possibility of involvement in a new European security

Lt Noel Byrne of the Army Cavalry Corps and Insp C.S. Cavanagh of An Garda Síochána sit on the bonnet of a Garda car while consulting a map, prior to heading out on a Border patrol (1 April 1974).

and common defence architecture, a prospect that was raised throughout membership negotiations and one that the Irish government did not rule out. It was a development that would not materialize until the 1990s, however, and in a form different to that envisioned in the 1960s. The end of the Cold War in 1989 reshaped global geopolitics and the conduct of inter- and intra-state conflicts, increasing the complexity and number of UN peacekeeping efforts. Legislation enacted in 1993 enabled the Defence Forces to participate in UN-mandated peace enforcement missions, led by regional supranational organizations such as NATO and the European Union.

'Prepare the Army for incursions into Northern Ireland'[1]

Between 1969 and 1998 the scale of Defence Forces' operations within Ireland reached levels not seen since the Emergency. Ignited by violence on the streets of Derry in the late summer of 1969, the conflict in Northern Ireland (the Troubles) lasted for nearly three decades and was characterized by sectarian violence, terrorist attacks and the murder of civilians. In the early weeks and months of the violence hundreds of refugees from the Catholic and nationalist communities of Belfast and Derry fled across the Border, initially accommodated by the Defence Forces at Gormanston and Finner Camps, in Co. Meath and Co. Donegal respectively. Refugee numbers would continue to grow in the first half of the decade, reaching several thousand.

Political and public sentiment placed strong pressure on the Irish government to respond, creating a context in which the deployment of the Defence Forces into Northern Ireland to protect these communities was raised at cabinet. In a televised address on 13 August 1969, Taoiseach Jack Lynch declared that the government could not 'stand by' while the situation in Northern Ireland deteriorated. The Defence Forces were instructed to establish field hospitals along the Border and reservists were called up, though these moves were largely an attempt to placate hardliners within the government. In February 1970 the Minister for Defence, Jim Gibbons, instructed the Defence Forces to prepare plans for hypothetical incursions into Northern Ireland. In the course of preparing those plans, the General Staff concluded that the Defence Forces were incapable of mounting an effective cross-Border military operation:

> Critical deficiencies in personnel strength and in equipment, allied to the present very high incidence of duties, have created a situation in which training for combat is not possible. In these circumstances combat efficiency is very low ... The events since August 1969, have only served to confirm the lack of combat effectivity: when no one unit could from its own resources provide an effective force, and when it became necessary to form ad-hoc groups hastily drawn together and made up from personnel from administrative, technical and training staffs to provide sufficient numbers to protect and support the refugee centres and field hospitals ... Following a directive from the Minister for Defence, the General Staff had an 'Estimate of the Situation' prepared which assessed the situation in Northern Ireland and the capabilities of the Defence Forces to provide more positive assistance should the strife in Northern Ireland continue at the level of mid August 1969 or even deteriorate. The assessment indicated a very low standard of combat effectivity, and a critical situation in regard to personnel deficiencies and shortage of essential equipment, which precluded action.[2]

(*Above*) An Irish Air Corps Alouette III, Serial No. 202, drops members of the Army in Donegal during Border operations in November 1985. (*Opposite*) Armed with a Belgian-made FN FAL, first introduced to the Defence Forces in 1961, a member of the Defence Forces adopts a watchful position while on Border patrol between Castlefin, Co. Donegal, and Castlederg, Co. Tyrone, in November 1985.

There was little chance that the government would actually order an incursion across the Border, but the mere existence of discussions at cabinet illustrates the political and military problems presented by the Troubles and the changing nature of an emotionally charged and dangerous security environment. Deep divisions within the government over the means with which it could aid nationalist communities led to the Arms Crisis of 1970, one of the most damaging scandals in Irish political history and one in which the Defence Forces became entangled.

Rather than mounting cross-Border operations, which would inevitably have led to armed confrontations with British security forces in Northern Ireland, including the British Army, the role of the Defence Forces during the Troubles became one of ensuring the security of the Border. When the political climate was relatively favourable, some co-operation with British and Northern Irish security forces was also possible, particularly in a context where the IRA actively sought to provoke an engagement between the Irish and British forces.

Before 1970 the Defence Forces maintained no permanent military posts north of a line stretching from Gormanston, Co. Meath, to Galway city, except for Finner Camp, near Ballyshannon, Co. Donegal. By the end of the decade the demands of internal security saw that number rise to eleven as several new barracks and outposts were constructed, manned by three infantry battalions and a cavalry squadron.

Personnel numbers were increased in response to the Troubles and to elevated levels of subversive and terrorist activity within the state. Sustained recruiting campaigns brought the Permanent Defence Forces strength up from 8,242 in 1969 to 13,569 a decade later, reaching a high of 14,771 in 1977 – the largest number in uniform since the end of the Emergency. Statistics for 1975 indicate the scale of the commitment to internal security duties: 5,500 military parties were supplied for checkpoint duties, manning and setting up 10,000 joint checkpoints with Gardaí. In addition, more than 5,400 joint patrols were conducted along the Border, with instructions to detain anyone caught carrying arms illegally. Escort duties, typically for transportation of explosives, were provided on more than 1,000 occasions, while 300 requests for bomb disposal teams were met. Other roles assigned during the Troubles included escorts of large cash movements within the state, provision of

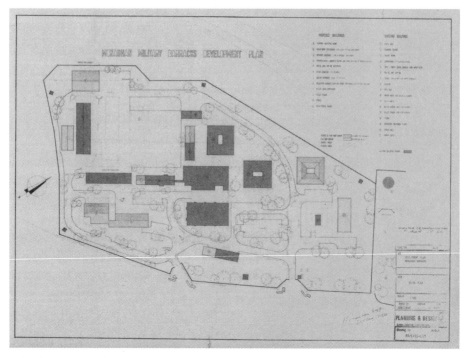

A development plan for Monaghan Military Barracks, drafted in March 1988. Built in the mid-1970s and formally opened by Taoiseach Liam Cosgrave on 13 December 1976, the barracks was one of several constructed close to the border with Northern Ireland during the Troubles. The barracks was permanently closed on 22 January 2009.

military guards for transportation and storage of industrial explosives, and guarding politically subversive prisoners at Portlaoise and other prisons.

Coastal patrols by the Naval Service assumed an even greater importance as the interdiction of ships suspected of gunrunning became one of the core duties of the Service. Aided by good intelligence, the capture of gunrunning vessels led to some significant strategic successes. As part of a joint operation with the Army, Air Corps and An Garda Síochána, and working with British intelligence, on 29 March 1973 the Naval Service seized arms destined for the Provisional IRA. As the MV *Claudia* arrived at Helvick Head, Co. Waterford, from Cyprus, it was trapped by LÉ *Deirdre*, LÉ *Fola* and LÉ *Gráinne* and diverted to Haulbowline, where almost five tons of guns, ammunition and explosives were unloaded. A similarly successful operation was mounted in September 1984, when the fishing vessel *Marita Ann* was intercepted off the coast of Kerry by LÉ *Emer* and LÉ *Aisling*, preventing the IRA from smuggling several tons of weapons, explosives and ammunition into Ireland. The acquisition of eight Cessna FR.172H (in 1972) and ten Siai-Marchetti SF.260WE (in 1977) allowed the Air Corps to provide improved aerial reconnaissance while assisting security operations along the Border.

During the early years of the Troubles the Defence Forces stationed four infantry groups along the Border. Personnel in these units were drawn from across the Commands, and a review of Border operations in late 1971 highlighted issues with these ad hoc arrangements. Drawn together at short notice, the infantry groups lacked identity and cohesion. Though equipment was generally satisfactory, some specialized items (such as smoke grenades and mine detectors) were wanting. The report's conclusion highlighted the impact of Border duty on the nature of the Defence Forces' Aid to the Civil Power (ATCP) responsibilities, as well as the growing wealth of knowledge and experience within its ranks when it came to Border operations:

> Aid to the Civil Power and internal security are operations in which all officers are interested and a high proportion have experience. Many new problems have come to the fore in the past few years and inevitably political factors arise in this type of operation. Because of the wide coverage given to this subject in the news media, other ranks are influenced by what they hear and see. Greater effort should be made to keep them fully briefed particularly as to the role of the Army and the policy of the State.[3]

In September 1973 the infantry groups were replaced by the newly raised 27 and 28 Infantry Battalions, headquartered at Dundalk and Finner Camp respectively. The Army's presence along the Border was augmented in October 1976 when 29 Infantry Battalion was activated, while the first new barracks built in the state since the 1930s were constructed at strategic locations along the Border, including Monaghan and Dún Uí Néill, Co. Cavan. Reorganization of the Defence Forces in 1979 saw a reduction in brigades to four, from the six created by the 1959 reorganization, along with the introduction of the Eastern Command Infantry Force (ECIF). Headquartered at Gormanston Camp, ECIF incorporated 27 and 29 Battalions. On 19 May 1986 large-scale manoeuvres were staged by ECIF along the Border as part of 'Operation Readiness'.

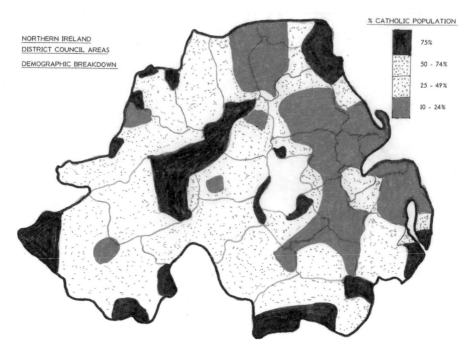

% CATHOLIC POPULATION

NORTHERN IRELAND
DISTRICT COUNCIL AREAS

DEMOGRAPHIC BREAKDOWN

75%

50 – 74%

25 – 49%

10 – 24%

This hand-drawn map, prepared in February 1986 to accompany a secret memo on Northern Ireland, offers a geographic breakdown of Northern Ireland's population by religion. The memorandum considered the possibility of a unilateral British withdrawal from Northern Ireland and the potential deployment of the Defence Forces to protect the nationalist population of Northern Ireland in the event of a widespread breakdown in law and order.

In addition to 27, 28 and 29 Infantry Battalions, other new units were formed in response to the Troubles. A select group of officers trained at Fort Benning with the United States Rangers in 1969 before returning to conduct the first Army Ranger course in Ireland. By the middle of the 1970s there were more than 300 fully trained Rangers in the Defence Forces, who formed Special Assault Groups (SAG) attached to each Command. In 1978 the SAGs were reconfigured into a special forces unit known as Sciathán Fianóglach an Airm/Army Ranger Wing and became operational in March 1980. While the Army Ranger Wing retains the counter-terrorism role from which it originated, it has since undertaken operations outside the state under UN-, NATO- and EU-led missions.

Numbers in the FCÁ averaged just under 18,000 during the 1970s. By 1979 it had become apparent that the experiment of integrating the FCÁ with the

Front page of the first issue of *Artillery Lines*, a newsletter produced by 7 Field Artillery Regiment of the FCÁ, then stationed at McKee Barracks. The FCÁ's 6 and 7 Field Artillery Regiments were amalgamated in 2005 to form 62 Reserve Artillery Regiment, which was later stood down in 2013 as part of a major reorganisation of the Defence Forces.

ARTILLERY LINES

7th FAR McKee Barracks, Dublin 7. Phone 774301   Vol. I No. 1 Oct. 1986

Comdt. Mick O'Beirne, Battery Commander

In the year of Our Lord 1950 Mick arrived at McKee Barracks to join the Cavalry, but due to the fact it was a Tuesday, for some reason they could not take him on. They asked him to come back next week, they did not know it then, be they lost a great man.

You see, it came to pass on Thursday of the same week Mick was passing Collins Bks., so he decided to join the Cavalry there. So he joined on the 23.3.50. He was a member for six weeks before he found out it was the arty. (The attesting officer was 2nd Lt. T. Lowen)

On 29.6.50 Mick was made a one star gunner and became an ACC. He stayed with the ACCs for about four years, in which time, he went to 2 star on 24.7.51, to 3 star 31.7.51. On 5.7.52 Mick became Cpl. one star and on 27.7.53 Cpl. two star. But then the big moment, Mick became Sgt. on 30.7.54.

Michael became Sig. Sgt. in '54 and I must say some of the great days of the Btys were in the fifties. Some of you will remember the old 22 sets and all the turning and netting calls, they seemed to take longer than the shoots. There are some great stories about laying line in those 'dark days', you see you had to have line, as the radios failed more often than they worked.

Mick did a transport course in '55. It lasted about eight months, he did very little more than ride around on a 500 B.S.A. solid frame motor bike for most of the course. Then they produced trucks and said sit in and drive, you are now doing your driving test. And of course, true to form, he passed with flying colours.

In the years that followed he drove six wheelers, quads, the 'New Austins' as they were known for about 20 years. He also drove Jeeps, Rovers and anything else they threw our way.

The 41st-42nd Btys, as we were in the old days prior to '59, it was said did not recruit men, they auditioned them. It is a well known fact that the Battery's were loaded with talent, and no better man than Mick, who was never slow when called upon to do his 'bit'. He made songs like 'Robinson Crusoe' and

'The straps of her bra' very famous indeed. I think it is true to say he knows more songs from the musicals than any other man living.

Mick gave his all to the unit and it was plain to all he would not remain a Sgt. for too long. And so it came to pass in 1958 he was commissioned, but he had to wait for nearly a year for the commissioning ceremony so you will find the date reads 19.5.59. On 16.9.63 Mick was promoted to 1st Lt. and of course reached the great exalted rank of Captain on 9.11.66. As Captain he covered every aspect of artillery and while doing all these things, it is very true to say, Mick's first thought was always for his NCOs and men. His

heart was always in the right place and indeed has remained so through all the years.

Mick took over as B.C. still as Captain on 20.2.78 and as annual camp in the Glen of Imaal came to a close, Mick was promoted Comdt. on 5.7.78.

Michael O'Beirne will retire from the FCA on 9th November 1986. It will be a sad day for the 7th F.A.R. and for the FCA in general. Mick has always been a great officer and gentleman and will always be remembered by those who have soldiered with him.

On behalf of the officers, NCOs, and gunners of the 7th Regiment I would like to take this opportunity to wish Comdt. Mick O'Beirne a very happy retirement and we are all looking forward to seeing him in the 'Visitors' room in Coolmoney. Adios AMicko.

Comdt. Bill McMahon

Members of the 41st/42nd Btys (now the 14th/19th Btys) firing 60 Pounders in the Glen of Imaal 1947.

Permanent Defence Forces, introduced in the 1959 reorganization, had failed. As part of the 1979 restructuring the FCÁ was given an establishment strength of 22,110 and regrouped on a Command basis, with a Directorate of Reserve Forces established at GHQ and dedicated FCÁ staffs in each of the regional Commands. Legacy issues remained unaddressed, however. Constant changes to command and training structures inhibited development, while equipment provision for the reserves was limited to cast offs from the Permanent Defence Forces, which were usually already obsolete. Despite the abandonment of the integrated brigade concept and the issues that remained, the FCÁ had already proven its value since 1969 and would continue to do so. With the resources of the Defence Forces stretched to their limits by operational duties before the raising of the three new battalions, deployment of FCÁ personnel on routine static duties at barracks and other posts allowed greater rotation of PDF personnel and provided opportunities for much-needed leave.

Terrorist activities in Ireland, typically by the Provisional IRA (PIRA) and occasionally Loyalist paramilitaries, provoked a number of tense stand-offs and firefights with the Gardaí and Defence Forces. During an operation on 16 December 1983 to locate and rescue businessman Don Tidey, kidnapped the previous month, Pte Patrick Kelly and Garda Gary Sheehan were shot and killed by the PIRA in Derrada Woods, Co. Leitrim. Pte Kelly was the first soldier to die under fire in Ireland since the Civil War, and was the only Defence Forces' casualty of the Troubles. Tragedy also returned to the Defence Forces' training grounds at the Glen of Imaal, in the Wicklow Mountains.

Members of 1 Tank Squadron conduct a bridgehead training exercise at Blessington Lake, 23 October 1984. Designed primarily for battlefield reconnaissance, the Defence Forces received its first Scorpion light tanks in 1980 and acquired fourteen in all. Its main armament, a 76mm L23 A1 gun, was powerful relative to the vehicle size and the Scorpion was considered ideal for Irish requirements.

Armed with a Belgian-made FN MAG 7.62mm general purpose machine gun, a soldier from 27 Infantry Battalion mans an Observation Point on the Louth–Armagh border in the early 1990s.

Five soldiers lost their lives at the Glen on 26 May 1977, while training in the use of mortars.[4] It was the worst loss of life in a single Defence Forces' training incident since the death of sixteen officers and men at the Glen on 16 September 1941. Further tragedy struck on 14 April 1979. This time the casualties were civilians, with three children killed when an unexploded shell detonated, injuring ten others. It followed several incidents in the Glen over the previous twelve months, when children were injured by other abandoned and unexploded ordnance and led to the introduction of improved safety and security arrangements.

Greater numbers in uniform and impending reorganization prompted changes to high-level command. At a cabinet meeting on 13 June 1978 the Minister for Defence, Robert Molloy, received government approval to upgrade the principal military offices of the Defence Forces. The Chief of Staff would in future hold the rank of Lieutenant General, while the Adjutant General and Quartermaster General would each hold the rank of Major General. The assistant Chief of Staff and officers commanding commands would henceforth hold the rank of Brigadier General. The Defence

Defence Forces personnel and members of An Garda Síochána man a Border checkpoint. The soldier nearest the camera is armed with an Austrian-made Steyr AUG A1, which entered service in 1988 as the Defence Forces' standard assault rifle, replacing the FN-FAL.

(Amendment) Act giving effect to these changes was signed into law on 20 February 1979.

The parameters of defence planning evolved to include the security risks posed by the Troubles. In a planning document drafted in 1973 several assumptions were made, including a requirement for the Defence Forces to meet an internal security problem involving interference with the democratic institutions of the state. The Planning and Operations Branch of the General Staff recommended that 'in this time of continuing crisis we must bring the Forces up to full Peace Establishments so that viable units will be available as soon as possible and in order to provide a platform from which to expand to meet eventualities.' Objectives established for the Defence Forces in the mid-1970s were:

1.   To demonstrate and assert the sovereignty of Ireland, the intention of the state to maintain its sovereignty and the duty and right of the state to maintain forces to assert its sovereignty.
2.   To assist the government in supporting and maintaining the Constitution and in upholding and advancing national policy.
3.   To be maintained at sufficient strength in men and equipment and be maintained at a level of organization and training to provide a significant deterrent against external aggression.

Members of 25 Infantry Group departing Cairo for Sinai as part of the second UN Emergency Force (UNEF II), deployed to Egypt at the conclusion of the Yom Kippur War of October 1973. 25 Infantry Group were on the ground in Cairo by 31 October.

4. To provide Aid to the Civil Power as required.
5. To assist civilian authorities in the event of emergency or natural disaster, to provide search and rescue services and contribute to national development.
6. To provide support to the Civil Defence.
7. To provide military support to any group, or community of nations with which the state is, or may be associated.
8. To provide professional counsel and advice [to the government].
9. To contribute to the material and moral well-being of the nation.
10. To provide certain community services (e.g. training Aer Lingus pilots), seamen and personnel trained in equitation, and to provide support services.[5]

While without any specific mention of the Troubles, the context was clear.

Planning also covered the potential withdrawal of British forces from Northern Ireland, or an aggressive action against the state by 'partisan or organized forces' from across the Border. The Anglo-Irish Agreement of 1985 had the opposite effect to that intended, and increased inter-communal tension in Northern Ireland. In response to a suggestion that the Defence Forces might be deployed into Northern Ireland to protect nationalist communities, Minister for Defence, Patrick Cooney, informed his cabinet colleagues that the Defence Forces were too poorly equipped and understrength for such an operation.

Though Cooney's assessment had been based on information provided by the General Staff, the assumption was challenged by the Director of Operations, Col S. Murphy, who argued that

> in the event of a unilateral withdrawal by Britain circumstances could arise which would create an irresistible pressure for intervention by the Defence Forces. It is clear that any intervention would be costly but it is equally clear that the Defence Forces have a capability for intervention to achieve certain objectives that would contribute to the restoration of peace and order in Northern Ireland.[6]

'We were always turning the other cheek, and then At Tiri happened'[7]

Though the Troubles had focused attention on internal security in a manner not seen since the early 1920s, the Defence Forces continued its primary overseas deployment with UNFICYP. In late 1973, as the UN sought to stabilize relations between Egypt, Israel and Syria in the aftermath of the Yom Kippur War, 25 Infantry Group's mission was radically altered just days after the arrival of the complete unit at Camp Innishfree in Cyprus. On 27 October Group Commander Lt Col Allen received a message from the Chief of Staff, Maj Gen Thomas O'Carroll: 'Consideration being given, subject to government and Dáil approval, which is likely to be affirmative, for movement of unit to new force in Egypt. Confirmation soonest but plan for it.'[8] Four days later 25 Infantry Group had landed in Cairo. They were now the Irish contingent of the new UN Emergency Force (UNEF II), tasked with keeping the peace at the conclusion of the Yom Kippur War.

By mid-November the battalion had established itself at Rabah Camp, Sinai, before moving to Benburb Camp in March 1974. Reverend Colm Matthews CF, chaplain with 25 Infantry Group, offered his impressions of Sinai:

When we saw Rabah the following morning in the sunlight, it was only fantastic. Beautiful big date palms towering over the tents, and a huge hill of sand rising out to the black. Rabah is on a long oasis, so there are lots of these date palms and salt swamps. There are about four hundred Bedouin living on the oasis; many of whom are here because they had to move back from the front and the mine fields.[9]

26 Infantry Group began arriving in the Sinai Desert at the end of April 1974, and had assumed responsibility for the Irish sector by 3 May. Just two weeks later, on 17 May, a major terrorist attack by loyalist paramilitaries saw four car bombs detonated in Dublin and Monaghan, killing thirty-four including an unborn child. Virtually all of 26 Infantry Group's personnel were withdrawn to Ireland in the immediate aftermath, and by September Ireland's commitment to UNEF II had ended.

Just four years later Irish troops returned in large numbers to the Middle East. Peacekeeping and the Defence Forces from the late 1970s is inextricably linked to Lebanon and the deployment of the UN Interim Force in Lebanon

25 Infantry Group were the first UN troops to cross the Suez Canal as part of UNEF II, pictured here doing so at 11.35 hrs on 9 November 1973.

(*Left to right*) Capt Eli, Assistant Senior Israeli Liaison Officer with UNEF, Maj Engelbert Torefalk (Finland), Capt Eero Vallaskangas (Finland), an unidentified member of 25 Infantry Group, Ops/Int Officer Capt Dan Rea and Lt Col Patrick Allen, Officer Commanding 25 Infantry Group. November 1973.

(UNIFIL) following Israel's invasion in March 1978. Ireland's initial commitment to UNIFIL consisted of 750 personnel. Tasked with confirming and monitoring the withdrawal of Israeli forces and bringing stability to south Lebanon, UNIFIL's work was complicated and frustrated by continuing hostilities and Israeli-backed operations over the next two decades.

To date forty-eight Irish soldiers have lost their lives in Lebanon, with Ptes Stephen Griffin, Thomas Barrett and Derek Smallhorne the first to be killed in action while serving with UNIFIL. Griffin died of wounds suffered on 9 April 1980 during the Battle of At Tiri (6–12 April), when Irish and Fijian peacekeepers clashed with South Lebanese Army (SLA) elements under the command of Gen Saad Haddad. The tactical use of the Panhard AML 90 armoured car by the Irish contingent had a decisive role in ending the battle after it engaged and destroyed an SLA 'half-track'. Barrett and Smallhorne were abducted and murdered while on a resupply patrol after the battle, in retaliation for the death of a South Lebanese Army soldier. At

Tiri remains among the most significant Irish engagements while on overseas duty, ranking alongside the Battle of Jadotville and the Battle of the Tunnel in Katanga in 1961.

Cpl Gregory Morris and Ptes Thomas Murphy and Peter Burke were murdered by their colleague, Michael McAleavey, while serving with UNIFIL in October 1982. The death of Cpl Dermot McLaughlin on 10 January 1987, while on duty at a UN observation post near the town of Brashit in Southern Lebanon, prompted a government review of Ireland's commitment to UNIFIL. Days after McLaughlin's death a detailed memorandum was presented to the government, presenting evidence that Israeli forces had deliberately targeted the position with tank fire in full knowledge that it was a UN post. As a result the withdrawal of the Irish contingent in Lebanon was briefly considered by cabinet, though ultimately rejected after consideration of the damage it would cause to Ireland's international standing.[10]

In addition to hostile fire, casualties also resulted from poor preparations both on the part of the Defence Forces and UNIFIL. On 21 March 1989 Cpl Fintan Heneghan, Pte Mannix Armstrong and Pte Thomas Walsh, members of C Coy, 64 Infantry Battalion, died when their vehicle drove over

Rabah Camp, Sinai, home to the Irish contingent of UNEF II, as photographed by Capt Chris Browne on St Patrick's Day, 1974.

a landmine. UNIFIL's contemporary investigation of the incident concluded that the battalion's standard operating procedures were appropriate, and that no blame could be attached to any UNIFIL personnel. When new evidence came to light in 2011 the Minister for Defence, Alan Shatter, appointed the Callanan commission to review the deaths of the three men. While making allowance for the difficulties of operating in a fast-moving, rapidly evolving security environment, the commission found several failures on the part of UNIFIL and the Defence Forces. Inadequate threat assessment procedures and poor force protection measures were identified, and the commission concluded that 'the training of the soldiers of the 64th Battalion in relation to the threat of IEDs [improvised explosive devices] was deficient'.[11]

In the intervening two decades, improved mission readiness training and equipment had already addressed most of the failings identified by the Callanan commission. Dedicated training in UN operations has also been provided at the Military College since 1993, following an internal analysis of the College's syllabi which found that cadets and officers received comparatively little training on UN-specific issues. As a result, the United Nations Training School in Ireland (UNTSI) was established to provide pre-deployment training for troops embarking on peacekeeping operations. UNTSI was one of the first such institutions established by any military, and its first international UN military observers and staff officers course, held in June 1995, was attended by officers from Brunei, Egypt, the Netherlands, Italy, Lebanon, Poland, Romania, Sweden, US, UK and Zambia.[12]

Members of 25 Infantry Group receive their first issue of desert boots at OP501, Sinai, in 1974.

The perilous state of public finances, especially during the difficult years of the late 1970s and 1980s, was an ever-present threat to overseas deployment. Proposals for cost saving measures within the Defence Forces, prepared by the Department of Finance in May 1978 as part of a wider programme exploring potential reductions in public expenditure, included the withdrawal of troops from Lebanon and the UN Truce Supervisory Organization (UNTSO), with anticipated savings of between £1m and £2m. Neither suggestion was implemented.

'Displaying the courage and professionalism which we know they possess'[13]

In the decade after the fall of the Berlin Wall the international order reshaped itself, and the 'traditional' style of peacekeeping missions gradually became less effective. The use of unarmed observers and lightly armed infantry groups to monitor ceasefires and maintain peace among warring factions became increasingly ineffective, given the rise in asymmetrical warfare. The United Nations began to cede initial leadership of peacekeeping missions to regional, supranational organizations such as the EU and the African Union.

Faced with such a major shift in geopolitics, successive Irish governments re-evaluated the state's commitments to peacekeeping operations. The Defence (Amendment) Acts of 1993 and 2006 widened the parameters under which the Defence Forces could deploy overseas, including 'peace enforcement' missions authorized under Chapter VII of the UN Charter, an evolution from the previous restriction to missions of a 'police character' authorized under Chapter VI of the Charter.

While membership of NATO has never been seriously entertained by the Irish government, the joining of NATO's Partnership for Peace (PfP) initiative in December 1999 ushered in a new era of overseas commitment for the Defence Forces. Established as a co-operative framework, PfP allowed security and defence co-operation between NATO member-states and non-NATO members of the Organization for Security and Co-operation in Europe. Membership proved controversial in domestic politics, though it has continued with relatively little comment since 1999. The first Defence Forces involvement in a NATO-led operation came with the deployment in May 1997 of a military police unit with Stabilization Force (SFOR), a UN-mandated mission in Bosnia. SFOR was tasked with overseeing implementation of the Dayton Peace Agreements, which had brought an end to the Bosnian War.

Four members of 47 Infantry Battalion on patrol near At Tiri, May 1980. The Battalion served in Lebanon with UNIFIL from May to October 1980. Two of the soldiers, wearing blue helmets, are in a Panhard AML 245 H90 armoured car (commonly referred to as the AML 90), one of twenty acquired by the Defence Forces between 1970 and 1975. The AML 90 is painted white as per UN regulations and carries the letters UN and a green shamrock on the glacis. Two more AML 90s are visible on the right-hand side of the photo.

Reflecting on forty years of Defence Forces' peacekeeping missions, Chief of Staff Lt Gen Gerry McMahon noted in 1996 that while the Irish experience, to that point, had been one of 'traditional classical peacekeeping', the Defence Forces were adapting to changing international conditions and to the evolving needs of the UN.[14] Irish soldiers had begun serving with missions under the remit of the EU and the Organization for Security and Co-operation in Europe, while also assisting NGO operations in Africa.

Between 1958 and 1996 the Defence Forces had served with twenty-nine different missions in forty countries, contributing more than 42,000 tours of duty. In a further sign of Ireland's commitment to the United Nations, on 16 October 1998 the Irish government signed a memorandum of understanding that committed up to 850 troops to the UN's standby arrangements for peacekeeping operations – thus implementing a plan first proposed in the mid-1960s. It was yet another indication of the signature place of peacekeeping in Irish foreign policy. In the 1990s alone, Defence Forces personnel participated in thirty-one separate missions overseas, under the auspices of the UN, the EU and NATO.

'Our soldiers need a far better infrastructure of training and accommodation'[15]

Recruitment campaigns of the early 1970s sought to increase strength in light of increased Border security commitments and to improve the image of the Defence Forces. High discharge rates during training and short terms of enlistment meant that turnover of troops was high. Following delivery in 1970 of a report by a working party on Defence Forces' pay, improvements in conditions of service saw pay for enlisted personnel increase by 10 per cent. New recruit pay was raised to £15 10s. per week, with food, accommodation and clothing allowances naturally also provided. Married men received a higher stipend.[16]

Analyses of personnel trends in 1971 and 1972 demonstrated that a career in the Defence Forces was more favourably viewed than in previous years, and that improvements in standards of clothing, equipment and barracks accommodation were encouraging enlisted soldiers to extend their service. For new recruits, the importance of having relatives or friends already in the service was a clear factor influencing a decision to enlist.

Lt Gen William Callaghan, UNIFIL Force Commander (seated, far right holding his glasses) listens to a briefing by Maj Conway of the United States Army on 9 June 1984. Seated with Callaghan are UN Secretary General Javier Perez de Cuellar, and senior UN officials Iqbal Akhund and Brian Urquhart. Callaghan (1922–2015) joined the Defence Forces as a cadet in 1939 and served as UNIFIL Force Commander from February 1981 to May 1986, when he was appointed head of the UN Truce Supervision Organisation (UNTSO).

The need to provide opportunities for education was also highlighted by a number of surveys conducted by both the Defence Forces and the Department of Education in the late 1960s and early 1970s. Literacy levels were found to be lower than expected, a consequence of the tendency for recruits to have left school earlier than was standard at that time. A report on recruitment trends compiled in 1971 noted that educational opportunities, such as that provided by the Army Apprentice School, were attractive for recruits:

> This is a very important factor also in motivating the recruit to enlist. He is aware that his educational level precludes him from employment other than labourer hence his desire to 'join the army to learn a trade and improve' himself.[17]

Noting that the British had recognized that nearly 90 per cent of their recruits had left school by the age of 15 or younger, and had introduced a remedial education course for new recruits, the report also suggested that 'the question of educational training could be examined with a view to preparing future NCOs for promotion'.

Reasons offered for joining the Defence Forces mostly related to self-improvement and self-esteem. In this regard the masculine stereotype was very evident: 'Combat uniforms and He-man image are very important … to attract this type of recruit the army should exploit the masculine stereotype – Rangers, combat uniforms, etc., and offer the opportunity of remedial education and "easy" trades.'[18] It was also an era of profound economic difficulty in Ireland. By 1990 an independent analysis found that pay was adequate and retention of personnel then at an 'acceptable level', with approximately 80 per cent of privates whose initial enlistments expired between 1985 and 1988 opting to extend their service.[19]

'There is an excessive degree of protectiveness of women's welfare'[20]

Recommendations to focus solely on masculine stereotypes in recruitment campaigns were soon outdated. By the mid-1970s the Defence Forces were out of step with their international counterparts when it came to the recruitment of women. Proposals to allow women join the Defence Forces surfaced by the middle of the decade, and a commitment to establish a women's service corps was included in Fianna Fáil's 1977 election manifesto. Two years earlier Dr Brigid Lyons Thornton had expressed surprise that she remained the only woman ever commissioned in the Defence Forces, a distinction she retained until 1980:

> It has always surprised me that some form of Woman's Army Corps has not been introduced. With the present security demands being made on the Army it surprises me even more that in the year 1975 there are still no plans for the use of women in the defence of the nation. As the only woman ever commissioned in the Army … I look back now and marvel at the liberal attitude of the Army authorities of that time. Although in their infancy, the new State and its Army were away ahead of their time.[21]

A member of Cumann na mBan and heavily involved in republican activities between 1916 and 1921, Thornton also studied medicine at University College Galway between 1915 and 1922. Following her graduation, Michael Collins (with whom she had worked closely during the War of Independence) offered her a commission in the National Army's medical service. In 1924 Thornton suffered a serious recurrence of tuberculosis, ending her military career.

In September 1977 a joint committee, consisting of representatives from the civil and military branches of the Department of Defence, examined the creation of a Women's Service Corps (WSC). It sought advice and information from military forces in other small European countries that had opened enlistment to women, including Denmark, Norway, Belgium and the Netherlands, while information was also received from the Western European Union. Information secured from the Department of Foreign Affairs noted that Norway was preparing to admit women on the same terms as men, though as non-combatant personnel, eligible for technical, administrative and certain operational jobs. The committee's first report, delivered on 10 February 1978, concluded that

> A Women's Service Corps, if properly established and developed, would have a useful role as part of the Defence Forces ... We regard the process of the selection and training of the first groups of potential officers and NCOs as a matter of the utmost importance to the future of the Corps and of the Defence Forces generally.[22]

The views of the committee members diverged, however, on the issue of equal pay and the duties considered suitable for women. Though the committee's formal report recommended non-combatant status for the WSC, generally restricted duties, and consequently lesser pay, a reservation urging equal pay for men and women was submitted: 'It appears to us ... that while women would not be liable to perform all the duties of male members of the Permanent Defence Forces they would, nevertheless, be performing work of equal value to that of men.'[23] The reservation was signed by two of the four civilian members of the committee and none of the three military members, but received the support of the Minister for Defence, Robert Molloy.

With the basic outline of the WSC's structure established by the committee, preparation of the necessary Defence Forces Regulation was ordered by the

The first eight women cadets received their commissions on 27 April 1981. Pictured here a week before the ceremony are (*back row standing, left to right*): Cadets Paula Cox, Oonagh Maher, Maureen McEnery, Maria O'Donoghue, Nicola Dunne, Carmel Hughes, Maree Flynn. Seated in the front row are (*left to right*): Comdt Jim Sreenan, Col Dermot Byrne (Commandant, Military College), Cadet Colette Harrison, Lt Col Noel Bergin, and Capt Paul Rossiter.

Chief of Staff, Lt Gen Carl O'Sullivan.[24] An establishment strength of 307 all ranks was proposed, with a minimum of three years expected before the WSC could be brought up to establishment. The cost, including pay and modifications to accommodation at the Curragh and other barracks, was estimated at £840,000.

Government approval in principle was granted on 12 June 1979, with a lower strength of 277 all ranks. The Defence (Amendment) (No. 2) Act of 1979, approved by the Oireachtas on 31 October, provided for the enlistment of women in both the permanent and reserve elements. Educational standards expected from applications for the first four cadetships offered within the WSC were higher than for male cadets, with a university degree required – a stipulation objected to within the Department of Finance as equivalent to gender discrimination.

By the beginning of December 1979, nonetheless, over 1,000 applications had been received. Four women were initially selected and began training on

A publicity photo showing one of four uniform outfits created by Ib Jorgensen in 1980 for the Women's Service Corps.

10 March 1980: Maria O'Donoghue, Colette Harrison, Maureen McEnery and Maree Flynn. On 27 April 1981 the first eight female cadets received their commissions, and on 29 October the first cohort of female recruits – 38 in total – passed out as members of the 4th platoon at the Curragh, under the command of Lt Maria O'Donoghue.

The WSC was, however, disbanded that same month, in recognition of the difficulty of maintaining a Corps that lacked appropriate command and administrative structures. Female recruits and officers would instead be posted to units on the same basis as that applied to male soldiers, subject to certain limitations. Recruitment of women thereafter was, however, slow. In 1991 there were just 89 female personnel in the Permanent Defence Forces (31 officers, 19 NCOs and 39 privates), constituting 0.7 per cent of total strength.

Along with An Garda Síochána and the prison service, the Defence Forces were initially exempt from the provisions of the Employment Equality Act (1977). The elevation of women soldiers to equal status with men was slow, mirroring broader societal trends. Initial policy dictated that women would

Ireland's first women soldiers to serve overseas with the UN, pictured at Dublin Airport on their return home (26 April 1983). *Left to right*: Pte Caroline Hayes, Lt Colette Harrison, Pte Mary O'Riordan. O'Riordan was awarded Joint Best Shot when her recruit platoon passed out.

only be employed in roles that excluded duties of an operational or security nature under arms. With just a few exceptions, women were not permitted to serve as officers in units of the Infantry, Artillery or Cavalry Corps, and were restricted to serving at Force Headquarters while on UN duty. In the Air Corps, women pilots were not permitted to fly in armed support roles, or to take part in Aid to the Civil Power operations. In 1989 a slight modification was introduced, with women allowed to serve as orderly officers in barracks, while competition for apprentice schemes was opened to all in 1991.

A statement prepared by the Adjutant General's office in 1990 reaffirmed this policy, thus restricting women to eligibility for just 55 per cent of possible appointments within the PDF and, by extension, hindering career progression or promotion. Though approved by the General Staff and Brian Lenihan, then Tánaiste and Minister for Defence, continuation of the policy was met with protest by female officers. It also attracted sustained criticism from the Judge Advocate General's office, which submitted a counter-report recommending the abandonment of such a discriminatory policy.

Pte Helen Lavin (*foreground*) of the FCÁ gets ready to fire, supervised by her instructor, Coy Sgt Andrew Scannell.

Recognizing the level of dissatisfaction with the status quo, and that international norms increasingly tended towards full integration of women soldiers, Chief of Staff Lt Gen James Parker convened a board in October 1991 to re-examine the issue. Its recommendations were for women to be allowed to fully participate in all aspects of Defence Forces' duties, including operational work, and to have equal access to the career educational system and promotion opportunities. Restrictions on deployment of women soldiers under arms were lifted in 1993, and the full integration of women achieved over the remainder of the decade.

'A smaller, lighter calibre weapon has now been adopted'[25]

In the late 1980s the Defence Forces and the Department of Defence began examining alternatives to the Belgian 7.62mm FN FAL assault rifle, which had been in service since 1961 as the Defence Forces main assault rifle. Seeking a smaller, lighter weapon, an extensive period of testing at the Curragh in March 1987 led to the selection of the Austrian-made Steyr AUG A1. It entered service

LÉ *Eithne* (P31) was commissioned on 7 December 1984. The ship was designed and built at Verolme Dockyard, Co. Cork, the last ship built in Ireland for the Naval Service. Verolme Dockyard ceased operations later that year. When commissioned LÉ *Eithne* was the only ship in the Naval Service with a flight deck, and remained in service until July 2022, when she was decommissioned alongside LÉ *Ciara* and LÉ *Orla* (both originally commissioned in January 1989).

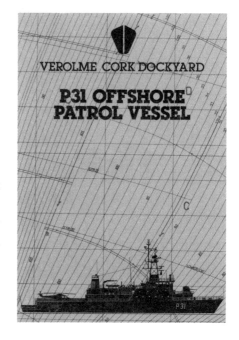

as the Defence Forces standard assault rifle in 1988. The Steyr fires NATO-standard 5.56mm ammunition, making procurement of supplies easier, and it has been augmented and updated through refits since introduction.

The late 1970s and 1980s saw the introduction of modern equipment in several other areas. Weapon data systems and computer equipment enhanced the capabilities of the Artillery Corps. So too did the introduction of the 105mm howitzer to replace the 25-pounder, which was deployed to the field artillery units of the reserve.

Fourteen Scorpion tracked reconnaissance vehicles were purchased between 1980 and 1985. This enabled the revival of 1 Tank Squadron, raised in 1959 but disbanded in 1973 owing to the obsolescence of its Churchill and Comet tanks. 1, 2 and 4 Cavalry Squadrons were established in the summer of 1983. Ten Timoney armoured personnel carriers, manufactured by Timoney Technology in Navan, Co. Meath, entered service between 1978 and 1983 and were typically used in patrolling the Border.

The obsolescence of the Defence Forces armoured cars was highlighted in Congo during service with ONUC. Sixteen Panhard AML 60s were purchased and saw service in Cyprus with UNFICYP from 1964. They were later joined by a further purchase of sixteen AML 60s and twenty AML 90s, which had larger calibre main armament.

As the LÉ *Maev*, LÉ *Macha* and LÉ *Clíona* were withdrawn from service, the very real possibility of the Naval Service being without a single operational vessel loomed in 1971. The Department of Finance had blocked the purchase

A CASA CN235, serial no. 252, pictured with Croagh Patrick in the background. The largest aircraft operated by the Air Corps, two CASAs were purchased in 1991 with assistance from EU funds and entered service in 1994. Primarily used for maritime surveillance and patrol, the CASA also fulfils a number of other functions, including air ambulance services.

of an interim vessel in 1969, and in April 1970 the Department of Defence noted:

> As far as fishery protection is concerned, public criticism has been severe and sustained and will become even more so if no vessel at all is available for an extended period. Naval defence is unlikely to become a public outcry in peace time but as far as the Department

240

of Defence is concerned … it is obvious that any naval capability, even of the most elementary kind, must be built up in peace time.[26]

Finance relented and an order was placed in August 1970, for delivery in April 1972, for a corvette-style coastal patrol vessel, known as the *Deirdre* class, and suitable for the rough seas of the Irish Atlantic coasts. Commissioned in June 1972, LÉ *Deirdre* (P20) was the first all-purpose naval vessel designed for Irish waters and built in Ireland.[27]

Changes to Ireland's maritime reach resulting from a United Nations Law of the Sea conference, and the obligation to patrol extended fisheries and maritime zones due to EEC membership, brought the need for an increased naval capability into focus. After intense evaluation of LÉ *Deirdre*, the Minister for Defence, Paddy Donegan, argued that a minimum of eight vessels – three similar to LÉ *Deirdre* and the remainder minesweepers – were needed to effectively patrol Ireland's fishery limits. Three *Deirdre*-class vessels were ultimately constructed: LÉ *Emer* (P21, commissioned in January 1978), LÉ *Aoife* (P22, November 1979) and LÉ *Aisling* (P23, May 1980), all of which saw service into the twenty-first century. Funding for each vessel was provided by the EEC. The P31 class LÉ *Eithne* – unique in having helicopter landing capacity – entered service in 1984, followed by LÉ *Orla* (P41) and LÉ *Ciara* (P42) in 1988.

The balance of where re-equipment fell between Army, Air Corps and Naval Service could change over time. In 1975 the Air Corps replaced its ageing de Havilland Vampires with six Fouga CM Magisters, which operated in a light strike and advanced training role. Painted in silver and with its signature iconic swallow tail, the Fouga was the embodiment of the Irish Air Corps internationally for a quarter of a century. The 'Silver Swallows' air display team won a number of notable international awards flying the Fouga; when the last Fouga was withdrawn from service in 1999, the Air Corps lost its jet aircraft capability.

Perhaps the most significant change in Air Corps capabilities in the 1990s came with the arrival of two CASA CN-235 100M aircraft at Baldonnel. They represented a major increase in the state's ability to patrol its Exclusive Economic Zone, enabling fisheries protection patrols of increased endurance in conjunction with the Naval Service as well as more traditional coastal patrols, military transport and air ambulance missions.

'The Defence Forces have traditionally enjoyed high esteem and trust'[28]

In the early 1970s the influential public servant T.K. Whitaker addressed students and staff at the Military College. Then governor of the Central Bank, Whitaker was a former secretary of the Department of Finance and one of the architects of the state's economic expansionism of the 1950s and 1960s. Pressed as to why Ireland's spending on defence was less than half that of the EEC average, Whitaker explained that government policy was to prioritize the modernization of Irish industry and the economy, especially in light of Ireland's accession to the EEC. Ireland was effectively gambling on peace, trusting that international affairs would not require government to deploy a well-equipped and modern military in defence of the state.[29]

Beginning in the early 1970s and extending through the next three decades, the scale of Defence Forces operations at home and the number of duties it was required to fulfil steadily increased. Overseas deployment expanded beyond the Middle East, to Africa, Asia, Central America and Europe. Despite the limited procurement described above it remained under-resourced, while from the early 1980s personnel numbers were allowed to fall once more.

By the end of the 1980s morale in the Defence Forces was at a low ebb, prompting a sustained campaign to allow the establishment of representative associations for officers and enlisted personnel, as well as a formal commission to investigate pay and conditions. On 16 May 1991 Brendan Daly, Minister for Defence, signed Defence Forces Regulation S6, which permitted Irish soldiers to join representative associations. Among the issues championed by organizations such as the Permanent Defence Forces Representative Association (PDFORRA) were sub-standard accommodation and poor pay and conditions.[30]

Under pressure to address these issues, the government appointed a commission to 'carry out a major review of the remuneration and conditions of service of the Defence Forces' in July 1989. By the time it had finished its work, the Gleeson Commission (named for its chairman, Dermot Gleeson) had carried out the most detailed review of the Defence Forces since its foundation. In addition to its recommendations for improving pay, the commission noted flaws both in the relationship between the civil and military branches of the Department of Defence, and the excessively bureaucratic nature of decision making within the Defence Forces:

The centralized bureaucracy and the slow processing of decisions through extended chains of command, create a sense of powerlessness and disillusion among military personnel, resulting in lower morale and widespread feelings of frustration. Discontent and frustration in the face of what is perceived as an insurmountable bureaucracy were frequently cited as causes of complaints by both officers and enlisted personnel. Relatively minor expenditure proposals which have been approved by the military management are subject to further close scrutiny by the Department of Defence.[31]

The Gleeson Commission prompted a period of sustained scrutiny, at a time when public perception of the Defence Forces was damaged by the 'army deafness' issue, when more than 15,000 personal injury claims made by retired and serving personnel were settled at a cost of more than €270m. Multiple reviews conducted during the 1990s by the Efficiency Audit Group (EAG), led by accountants Price Waterhouse, identified awkward and challenging administrative structures. One review observed that there was a

In 1974 the Air Corps purchased six Aérospatiale Fouga Super Magisters as replacements for its De Havilland Vampires. The Fougas were delivered between August 1975 and November 1976, and fulfilled a variety of roles for the Air Corps until the last Fouga was withdrawn from service in 1999. The Air Corps has had no jet aircraft in service since that date. Four inverted Fougas fly in Diamond formation.

fundamental problem at the heart of the statutory regime in the Department of Defence. The Secretary, as Accounting Officer, is accountable for the spend of the Defence Votes. He is not, however, responsible for the actions of the military whose activities account for 97 per cent of the Vote ... Conversely, the Chief of Staff, Adjutant General and Quartermaster General are directly answerable to the Minister for Defence for the control of staff and for the objectives and outputs of the Defence Forces, but cannot control the budgets allocated to those outputs which are largely under the control of the Secretariat.[32]

Less welcome was the recommendation, contained in a 1994 EAG report, that the Defence Forces should be reduced by 3,000 personnel and close up to half of its barracks. Four years later the EAG had rowed back on this drastic step, and recommended an investment package of £235m in the Air Corps and Naval Service over ten years. Such radically divergent recommendations, delivered just a few years apart, were emblematic of the overall lack of clarity in broader defence policy (which in turn dictated procurement priorities), particularly in light of the emerging Peace Process in Northern Ireland and beginnings of a reduction of the Defence Forces' presence on the Border. Greater clarity was promised by the government's commitment to publish a White Paper on Defence.

Initiated by the government in response to the Gleeson Report and subsequent findings of the Efficiency Audit Group, the 1996 Defence Review Implementation Plan was intended to provide widespread reform of the Defence Forces. On 1 December 1998 the Permanent Defence Forces implemented a major reorganization that included radical downsizing. Establishment was dropped from 13,500 to 11,500, though two years later there were just 10,772 personnel in uniform.[33] The closure of six barracks was announced, while the regional commands that had been put in place in the 1920s were scrapped, replaced by a three brigade structure. Among the units disestablished in 1998 were several with a rich history stretching back to the early years of the Defence Forces, including the Survey Company Corp of Engineers, established in 1931 to foster co-operation with the Ordnance Survey.

Closures and reorganizations saved money and a large proportion of those savings were reinvested in the Defence Forces, but there was a reluctance to truly ask 'whither Ireland' when it came to its defence policy and military

Painted in silver and with its signature iconic swallow tail, the Fouga was the embodiment of the Irish Air Corps internationally for a quarter of a century. During an 'Air Spectacular' at Fairyhouse Racecourse in August 1983, the Fougas of Light Strike Squadron carried out the first formation loop ever completed by the Air Corps, and in 1987 the Silver Swallows Air Display team was formed, which performed both at home and abroad over the next decade. The 1997 (and final) Silver Swallows team, pictured with four Fougas and the tail of a CASA 235 in the background (*left to right*): Capt Graeme Martin (team leader), Capt Peter McDonnell, Lt Paul Whelan, Lt Christian Keegan.

forces and still no sign of a coherent plan for the future of the Defence Forces. The plethora of reports delivered between 1989 and 1997 generally focused on the minutiae of administrative practise, rather than tackling the broader question of defence policy in the post-Troubles era, and a changing geopolitical environment no longer defined by the Cold War. The purpose and nature of neutrality in the twenty-first century was given scant consideration, even after Ireland's engagement with the NATO/OSCE PfP initiative. Nevertheless, the potential implications of an increased commitment to any common European security infrastructure were becoming notable, and would be seen in European referenda in the first two decades of the twenty-first century. Inured to such uncertainty by decades of long experience, the Defence Forces prepared to enter the new millennium with a greatly reduced responsibility for internal security, and with peacekeepers deployed on missions in the Mediterranean, the Middle East, Asia and Africa.

BEGINNINGS: AN COSANTÓIR

'Keep your copies of *An Cosantóir* in a safe place. You will want them for reference later'. That was the advice carried in the first issue of *An Cosantóir* ('The Defender'), a new Defence Forces journal launched on 27 December 1940. The journal was originally conceived and published by Southern Command, with its initial circulation confined to that command's personnel. Heavily modelled on *An tÓglách*, it is no coincidence that the OC of Southern Command at this time was Col Michael J. Costello, former editor of and frequent contributor to *An tÓglách* – the first issue featured no less than three contributions from Costello. From its very first issue *An Cosantóir* invited contributions from members of the Defence Forces and the Local Security Force (and later the Local Defence Force), on current defence problems and exercises, military history, and instructional articles for training purposes.

Issued on a weekly basis and printed by *The Tipperary Star* newspaper, forty-eight issues appeared between 27 December 1940 and 6 December 1941. Early issues continued to mine *An tÓglách* for content, while the humorous cartoons of B.S.C. Thomson even made a brief reappearance in March and April 1941. Such was the journal's popularity and rapid spread beyond Southern Command, by July 1941 its strapline had been altered to declare that it was now published 'under the auspices of the Army

Foreword by Maj Gen Dan McKenna, Chief of Staff, published in the first issue of *An Cosantóir* on 27 December 1940.

An COSANTÓIR

Vol. 1.   DECEMBER 27th, 1940.   No. 1.

LOYALTY
By MAJOR GENERAL D. McKENNA, Chief of Staff.

THE present expansion of the Army has brought into its ranks men of every political party and men of every creed and class. This unification of the different elements of the community is in itself one of the greatest factors in our defensive strength to-day.

The magnificent response to the appeal for recruits for the Army, and the even more splendid rallying of our manhood to the ranks of the Local Security Force, bear witness to the loyalty of her sons to Ireland's cause.

By this common loyalty to our country we are united in a great bond of comradeship. No personal feelings or prejudices must be permitted to mar this unity. Our loyalty must be given without condition and without reserve.

We must seize every opportunity to show that we are good comrades, that we are worthy members of the organisation to which we belong, and that Ireland's cause is greater than any personal motive or private jealousy.

We must learn to know and appreciate the good which is in each of our comrades. Each must contribute his share to the fostering of good comradeship as the cement of common loyalty. Thus, whether we are in the Army or in the Local Security Force, we shall create a spirit of soldierly unity that will in later times be a proud and pleasant memory.

It is in this manner only that patriotism effectively functions and loyalty is practically expressed.

The matter contained in "An Cosantóir" is supplied from Headquarters of the Southern Command. The views expressed are those of the individual contributors unless the contrary is clearly stated.

Contributions are invited from members of the Army and the L.S.F.

Manuscripts must be legibly written on one side only of the paper and must bear the name and address of the sender. Typewritten articles are preferred.

The most suitable subjects are—
(a) Current local defence problems and exercises.
(b) Instructional Articles on Training.
(c) Military History.

The Editor cannot be responsible for rejected manuscripts, but every effort will be made to return them when stamps are enclosed for the purpose.

Manuscripts intended for publication must be submitted for censorship.

Communications for the Editor should be addressed to The Editor, Headquarters, Southern Command.

Communications respecting advertisements and supplies of "An Cosantóir" should be sent to the Advertising Manager, "An Cosantóir," Paramount Printing House, Clarke's Bridge, Cork.

Printed and Published by the Paramount Printing House, at their offices Clarke's Bridge, Cork—December 27th, 1940.

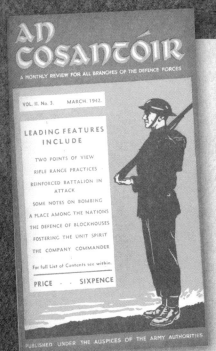

The cover of the March 1942 issue of *An Cosantóir*. Colour covers were possible following its move to Alexander Thom's in Dublin for printing at the end of 1941.

Authorities'. Responsibility for publication passed to the Army Intelligence Service in December 1941, and paper shortages then forced a move to monthly issues from January 1942. Repurposed as a review for all branches of the Defence Forces, printing was transferred to Alexander Thom and Co. in Dublin, which allowed for the addition of a colour cover. The price rose from two to six pence – 'remarkable value when you consider that you will be getting approximately three times the amount of reading matter contained in the present size' (*An Cosantóir*, 6 December 1941). Circulation began to drop immediately after the Emergency ended, an unsurprising result of demobilization. As the journal began to lose money for the first time, its future seemed in doubt. In 1948 a new production structure was put in place, with a body of officers acting as proprietors and responsible for printing and publication. Circulation almost doubled to 1,400 in the year ending 31 March 1949, securing its future. *An Cosantóir* has evolved to become the official magazine of the Defence Forces, in continuous publication since its first issue appeared in December 1940.

The cover of the August 1979 issue of *An Cosantóir*, featuring Cpl W. Barry of A Company, 29 Infantry Battalion, while on Border patrol. Cpl Barry carries a Gustaf M45 9mm submachine gun, which was in service with the Defence Forces from the early 1960s until the late 1980s.

CHAPTER 7

2000–22
INFLECTION POINTS

The history of the Defence Forces can be characterized as an ongoing search for a defined shape and mission. Prior to the turn of the millennium, government policy on defence and for the evolution of the state's military capabilities had largely been reactive. Development of the signature traits of the Defence Forces, including peacekeeping duties, search and rescue capacity, maritime patrol, and counter-terrorism capabilities, were largely driven by urgent need in response to external factors. The proliferation of reports on the Defence Forces during the early and mid-1990s heralded a turning point, ultimately resulting in the publication of a developmental framework in the government's White Paper on Defence (2000). Intended to facilitate the development of a 'balanced and flexible military organization', the White Paper provided, for the first time, a clear policy and cohesive set of operational objectives.[1]

Conversely, it allowed the General Staff and representative associations to highlight longstanding problems with pay and

During a visit to McKee Barracks on 15 October 2004, UN Secretary-General Kofi Annan is greeted by a member of the Army Bomb Disposal Team. Laid out on the ground between them are examples of explosive ordnance.

conditions and retention of personnel. Despite some initial progress on implementation, the economic downturn of 2008–10 and ensuing climate of economic austerity curtailed much of the momentum that had been established. In the meantime, the emergence of serious allegations of bullying and sexual harassment forced a reckoning with disciplinary issues among a minority of personnel. The individual experiences of the men and women of the Defence Forces have mirrored the ups and downs of the organization. The formation of representative associations, for all ranks, had proved to be an important milestone. Yet both establishment and actual strength have continued a steady decline from the highs of the late 1970s and early 1980s. While this can be partially attributed to the easing of tensions in Northern Ireland and the reduced need for a Border presence after the signing of the Good Friday Agreement in 1998, it is also reflective of government efforts to rationalize expenditure on defence.

'To provide value for money military services'[2]

The development of defence policy has rarely been the sole preserve of the Department of Defence. Since the end of the Civil War the Department of Finance has exercised considerable influence on the evolution of the Defence Forces, as it has across the wider public sector. Since the late 1950s the Department of External Affairs (renamed Foreign Affairs in 1971) has gained an increasing level of influence. Participation in UN-led or UN-mandated peacekeeping missions has become a central plank of Irish foreign policy, with the Defence Forces serving as the sharp end of diplomatic soft power.

Defence thus featured heavily in the government's 1996 White Paper on Foreign Policy, which emphasized the potential for Irish participation in European common defence arrangements, or with NATO-led missions for conflict prevention and crisis management. With the formation of a Fianna Fáil/Progressive Democrats coalition following the 1997 general election, the programme for government pledged to 'stop the reactive ad hoc planning that has characterized the management of our Defence Forces'.[3]

Two Pilatus PC-9Ms fly in formation alongside LÉ *Eithne* in August 2006. Acquired as an advanced turboprop trainer, in 2004 the Air Corps received eight PC-9Ms capable of carrying LAU-7 rocket pods and .5-inch FN heavy machine guns under each wing, as seen here.

Publication of a White Paper on Defence Policy – the first in the history of the state – was promised within one year of the government taking office. Finally unveiled in February 2000, the White Paper clearly defined the operational objectives of the Defence Forces:

- to defend the state against external aggression – resource allocation for this role to be dependent on the government's assessment of external threats;
- to aid the civil power;
- to participate in UN missions in the cause of international peace;
- to provide a fishery protection service in accordance with the state's obligations as a member of the EEC;
- to carry out such other duties as may be assigned from time to time, including search and rescue, the ministerial air transport service, aid to the civil authority.

It also defined the mission of the Department of Defence: 'to provide value for money military services which meet the needs of government and the public and encompass an effective civil defence capability'.[4]

Veterans of UN peacekeeping operations participate in a wreath laying ceremony at McKee Barracks in July 2009, in honour of Irish soldiers killed while on UN duty.

The Defence Forces provide a guard of honour at the Garden of Remembrance, Dublin, on 17 May 2011 during the State visit of Queen Elizabeth II and the Duke of Edinburgh. Since the foundation of the state in 1922, the Defence Forces have fulfilled an important ceremonial function at major state events, and were especially prominent during activities to mark the centenary of the 1916 Rising.

The White Paper imposed a further reduction in strength to 10,500, with a commitment to reinvest savings in equipment and infrastructure. Reaction from opposition benches, and from former senior members of the Defence Forces, was not complimentary. Frustration within GHQ was also evident, and had been flagged well in advance. The Defence Forces' submission to the Department offered a blunt assessment of proposed reductions in strength and organizational change, particularly the contemplation of a two- or even single-brigade structure. Lt Col Betson, Director of the Strategic Planning Office, argued that the proposals would result in an 'unbalanced' Army, seriously out of step with international norms. With regard to the 'value for money' that would be achieved by reducing personnel, Betson pithily observed that 'a flexible and affordable Defence Forces will not necessarily result in an effective and efficient organization'.[5]

Chief of Staff Lt Gen David Stapleton requested an urgent meeting with the Minister for Defence, Michael Smith, at which he pressed for several formal clarifications to the White Paper. Citing implications for morale, Stapleton sought a guarantee that the proposed reduction of 1,000 personnel would be managed internally, and an assurance that establishment strength would not be reviewed again for at least a decade. He also emphasized that to maintain a strength of 10,500, it was necessary to always have 250 soldiers in training to cover 'wastage', which then stood at *c*.1,000 per annum. A force of 10,500 represented 'the strength requirement to meet current roles and tasking and the current threat assessment ... The three brigade structure remains the basic organization necessary to meet Defence Forces (PDF and FCÁ) tasks and responsibilities for the duration of the White Paper.' Stapleton also used the meeting to underline the Chief of Staff's role as the principal military adviser to the minister and person responsible for day-to-day operational control of the Defence Forces. In a memo to the minister outlining the agreements reached at the meeting (which was subsequently reported in the national press), Stapleton concluded with a statement freighted with meaning: 'I understand that the White Paper as published will be amended on the major issues above as necessary.'[6]

Six of the Naval Service's fleet on exercise off the south-west coast of Ireland, during joint manoeuvres with the Air Corps in June 2011. Pictured (*from foreground to background*) are LÉ *Emer* (P21), LÉ *Aoife* (P22), LÉ *Aisling* (P23), LÉ *Ciara* (P42), LÉ *Orla* (P41) and LÉ *Roisín* (P51). As of July 2022, all except LÉ *Roisín* have been decommissioned. Commissioned in 1999, LÉ *Roisín* gave its name to a class of offshore patrol vessel and is one of two such vessels in service, alongside LÉ *Niamh*.

Members of 104 Infantry Battalion pay their respects, on 6 July 2011, at the memorial erected in Tibnin to the Defence Forces' personnel who lost their lives while on duty with UNIFIL between 1978 and 2001. The deployment of this battalion of c.440 personnel to Lebanon in 2011 marked a significant recommitment to UNIFIL, the Defence Forces having scaled back operations in 2001.

As well as providing a clear set of policy objectives and developmental goals, the process of drafting the White Paper also marked a turning point in the relationship between the civil and military elements of the Department of Defence. The combination of both within the Department has long posed specific challenges that require careful management and compromise. Though competing priorities have occasionally been evident since the 1920s, reaction to the White Paper suggested that the disconnect between both elements was wider than had perhaps been realized. This may in part have been due to the removal, in the 1954 Defence Act, of the statutory obligation for the Council of Defence to meet at least once every six months. The Council was summoned by the Minister for Defence on just eight occasions between 1954 and 1990, and both the Gleeson Commission and EAG had commented on the need for more effective integration of military and civil managements within the Department. Greater harmonization within the Department was promised by the appointment of a Defence Forces strategic management

Zeina Islambouli (*left*) accompanies UNIFIL's IRISHBATT on 4 May 2012. Islambouli was one of eight journalism students, based at Beirut's Lebanese University, who participated in a UN programme to bring students together with the sixteen UNIFIL contingents, as part of a project to explore the different duties and cultures of UNIFIL.

committee in 1996. Though it met on only fourteen occasions between 1996 and the end of 2000, following the White Paper the committee streamlined its processes and has evolved to become a key forum for policy development and implementation.

'The culture of the PDF has to change'[7]

Few organizations in the modern Irish public sector have fostered as strong an emphasis on continuous training and providing life-long learning opportunities as the Defence Forces. Recognition of the importance of continuing education had come as early as the summer of 1922, when Michael Collins initiated efforts to establish an officer training corps and attempted to establish links with the Swiss military. Since the late 1920s officers have studied overseas at various military colleges, broadening the knowledge base within the Defence Forces. Alongside the work of the Army School of

Instruction/Military College, the opening of the Army Apprentice School in October 1956 provided vocational training for more than four decades. Strategic partnerships with the university sector have allowed personnel to further their educational and professional development, particularly in the field of professional military education. The opening of the University Service Administrative Complement (USAC) at NUI Galway in 1969 has allowed commissioned officers to gain an undergraduate degree at an early point in their career. Further collaborations with Maynooth University (since 2002) and IT Carlow (since 2012, now known as South East Technological University) have helped to foster a culture of further or continuing education and professional military development opportunities for officers and enlisted personnel.

Evidence of a culture of disciplinary problems, including sexual harassment of female recruits, emerged in 2000. The following year saw the establishment of an external advisory committee by the Minister for Defence, to investigate the prevalence of bullying and harassment within the Defence Forces. The committee's findings were stark, including 'unacceptable levels of harassment, bullying, discrimination and sexual harassment'.[8]

LÉ *Samuel Beckett* (P61) at anchor as night falls. *Samuel Beckett* was the first of four new offshore patrol vessels acquired between 2014 and 2018, with a design updated from the *Róisín*-class patrol vessels acquired in the late 1990s/early 2000s. It was joined by LÉ *James Joyce* (P62), LÉ *William Butler Yeats* (P63) and LÉ *George Bernard Shaw* (P64).

LÉ *William Butler Yeats* (P63).

An Independent Monitoring Group (IMG) was appointed in 2002 to oversee the implementation of reform. Among the challenges highlighted by the IMG's first report, delivered in 2004, was a widespread lack of confidence in the existing internal procedures for investigating and addressing grievances. It was an issue that had been flagged as early as 1989, when the Gleeson Commission urged the appointment of an independent appeals body, or a military ombudsman. The prevailing sentiment was that the grievance procedures then in place were unfit for purpose and, indeed, potentially career-damaging.

In September 2005, following a sustained campaign from PDFORRA and other representative organizations, the government appointed Paulyn Marrinan Quinn as Ombudsman for the Defence Forces. Ireland was the first country in Europe to create an ombudsman for its military forces. The impact of the revelations of bullying and sexual harassment was deep and long-lasting. Under the guidance of the IMG, however, which issued further reports in 2008 and 2014, the Department of Defence and the Defence Forces created what were then regarded internationally as models of best practice. Indeed, in its 2008 report the IMG expressed concern that 'the pendulum may have swung too far in one direction in the last four years. The result may be that the essential robust nature of military training is in danger of being lost.'[9] Challenges remain, however, including the necessity to tackle the legacy of previous institutional failures, as highlighted by the RTÉ Radio documentary 'Women of Honour', broadcast on 11 September 2021.

An Bord Snip Nua

Responding to the global economic crisis of 2009/10 and the ensuing recession, a government-appointed public-expenditure advisory group, chaired by Prof Colm McCarthy and commonly known as An Bord Snip Nua, sought further reductions in defence spending. Proposals included the cessation of Irish participation in the UN mission to Chad (MINURCAT) and the rationalization of the Defence Forces' overseas commitments to

Chol Mayomdit (*left*), an officer with the South Sudan National Police Service (SSNPS), and a member of the Defence Forces conduct a controlled detonation of unexploded ordnance in Rajaf, South Sudan, on 25 October 2013. Having gained independence in 2011 following a lengthy civil war, South Sudan inherited large swathes of land dotted with landmines and other unexploded devices. With support from various organisations, including the Defence Forces, the United Nations Mine Action Service (UNMAS) began a three-year project in 2013 to train members of the SSNPS in conventional munitions disposal.

An Agusta Westland AW139 during joint Naval Service and Air Corps manoeuvres in June 2014. The Air Corps acquired its first two AW139s in November 2006, and later purchased four more. The AW139 can be used in a variety of roles, including air ambulance, search and rescue, and troop and heavy equipment transportation, and can be armed with two 7.62mm general purpose machine guns.

a 'smaller number of key missions'. A further staffing reduction of 500 in the Defence Forces was to be achieved by 'natural wastage and non-filling of non-essential vacancies'. The group also proposed that 'a smaller, more focused Reserve Defence Force could deliver a more usable capability to the Defence Forces for less expenditure': its recommendation was for a two-thirds reduction in the RDF.[10]

Focusing on the Defence Forces' property portfolio, the group noted that though ten barracks had been closed since the late 1990s, twenty-four remained occupied across the country, with alleged administrative inefficiencies – an uncanny echo of the advice delivered by successive Chiefs of Staff to the Minister for Defence during the 1920s and 1930s. An Bord Snip Nua made several other cost-cutting recommendations, including the closure and sale of Cathal Brugha Barracks in Rathmines and the abolition of the Army Equitation School. Savings from the latter were estimated at €1m per annum.

Strength in the Permanent Defence Forces had hovered around establishment for the first decade of the new millennium, before falling below 10,000 in 2009 for the first time since 1972. The overall strength of the Reserve continued to fall after the turn of the millennium. Among the factors contributing to the ongoing decline was the reduction in value of the annual gratuity paid to members of the FCÁ, as the economy continued to grow and wage levels increased.

Seeking ways to revitalize the Reserve, a government-appointed group was tasked in 1997 with developing 'a blueprint for a more effective, efficient and value for money Reserve Defence Force'.[11] The group delivered a lengthy report in August 1999, with a series of suggested reforms and a six year implementation plan. Its programme of reform, while never fully implemented, resulted in the creation of a new Reserve Defence Force (RDF) in October 2005 and the disbanding of the FCÁ, then just one year short of its 60th anniversary. An Slua Muirí was renamed the Naval Service Reserve on 1 October 2005.

UN Secretary-General, Ban Ki-moon, during a visit to the United Nations Training School, Ireland (25 May 2015). The school was established in 1993 as part of the Military College at the Defence Forces Training Centre in the Curragh. Accompanying the Secretary-General are his wife, Yoo Soon-taek, and Minister for Defence, Simon Coveney TD.

Members of 48 Infantry Group, deployed with the United Nations Disengagement Observer Force (UNDOF), conducting a search for unexploded ordnance in the foothills of the Mount Hermon mountain range, 11 August 2015.

The strength of the RDF has steadily declined since 2005. With an establishment strength of 4,069, as of March 2022 personnel numbers in the RDF stood at 1,380 in the Army Reserve and 114 in the Naval Service Reserve, with a further 271 personnel in the First Line Reserve – collectively just 43 per cent of establishment. Implementation of the Single Force Concept, introduced to fully integrate the Permanent and Reserve Defence Forces, has been inconsistent and slow.

Reorganization of the Defence Forces in 2012 saw a further reduction in establishment strength to 9,500, the lowest figure since the 1960s. To achieve this reduction, 4 Brigade was abolished and the country reduced to two brigade operational areas. 1 Brigade remained headquartered in Collins Barracks, Cork, while 2 Brigade remained at Cathal Brugha Barracks, Dublin.

Personnel numbers have stood below establishment since 2013. As of March 2022 the strength of the Permanent Defence Forces stood at 8,398. Of these, 576 were then serving overseas, while there are 595 female soldiers in the Defence Forces, constituting 7 per cent of total strength. The imperative to cut public expenditure saw a reduction in the budget for defence from €888m in 2008 to €686m in 2013 – a cut of 22.7 per cent.[12] Though the defence budget has increased in recent years, relative spending has since fallen from 0.56 per cent of GDP in 2013 to 0.27 per cent in 2020, well below the EU average of 1.2 per cent.[13]

Peacekeeping in the twenty-first century

In the seven years that preceded the economic crash of 2008, expenditure on equipment for modernization of the Defence Forces exceeded €390m. Reinvestment of savings that accrued from the closure and sale of barracks and reductions in personnel from the late 1990s had been a key promise of the White Paper, and one on which the Department of Defence handsomely delivered. Among the major items procured for the Army were Mowag armoured personnel carriers, the Javelin anti-tank weapon system, and various support weapons, along with updated force protection, including small arms and body armour/helmets. For the Air Corps, eight Pilatus PC-9 turboprop training craft were delivered in 2004 at a cost of €60m. With its fleet of Alouette III helicopters nearing the end of their serviceable life, replacement began with the acquisition of four Agusta Westland AW139 helicopters in 2006 and 2007, capable of fulfilling multiple roles.

In the wake of the failure of several peacekeeping missions during the 1990s, particularly in Rwanda, Somalia and Bosnia, the UN initiated a review of its peace and security activities. The resulting Brahimi Report recommended several major reforms in UN operating procedures, including a commitment to deploy UN troops in sufficient force to ensure their own protection and that of local populations. Together with the advent of the Good Friday Agreement in 1998, which reduced the Defence Forces commitment to internal security, the sustained investment in equipment allowed for a pivot towards deployment on more robust peace enforcement missions under Chapter VII of the UN Charter. In October 1999 the Army Ranger Wing (ARW) was despatched to East Timor as part of UNAMET, and since the turn of the millennium the ARW have frequently been used as an initial entry force on peacekeeping operations, drawing upon their elite skills to prepare the ground for further troop deployments.

In November 2003 the Defence Forces deployed more than 400 troops to Liberia with UNMIL, a Chapter VII peace enforcement mission. Providing a Quick Reaction Force alongside a Swedish contingent, Irish personnel completed more than 2,700 tours of duty with UNMIL over the next five years. The ARW supplied a special operations task group under the direct command of UNMIL's Force Commander. Members of the ARW also deployed to Chad on 20 February 2008 as part of a UN-mandated, EU-led peacekeeping mission (EUFOR Chad/CAR). Conditions in Darfur and Chad

Elements of 111 Infantry Battalion in the Glen of Imaal, conducting a combined arms night shoot on 11 October 2017, as part of their training prior to deployment to Lebanon with UNIFIL.

had led to the displacement of nearly 400,000 refugees, with peacekeepers deployed to protect these refugees and the NGO personnel attempting to provide aid and assistance. Two Irish officers were appointed to the mission's command: Lt Gen Pat Nash was appointed Operational Commander, based in Paris, while Col Derry Fitzgerald served as Deputy Force Commander.

Since the late 1970s the main Defence Forces commitment overseas has been to UNIFIL. Ireland's contribution initially ended in 2001 after a period of twenty-three years' continuous service, until a significant escalation in

Maj Gen Michael Beary, Force Commander and UNIFIL Head of Mission (centre), accompanied by Imran Riza, Deputy Head of Mission, Lebanese Army representatives and local students, pictured on 19 March 2018 at the opening of a photo exhibition in Mamlouk House in Tyre, South Lebanon. The exhibition marked UNIFIL's 40th anniversary. Having joined the Defence Forces in 1975, Beary served as UNIFIL Head of Mission and Force Commander from 2016 and 2018.

hostilities between Israel and Lebanon in 2006 saw the government authorize deployment of 34 and 36 Infantry Groups to Lebanon until November 2007. When that commitment ended, a small number of Irish personnel continued to serve with UNIFIL headquarters in Naquora.

At the request of the UN a Mechanized Infantry Battalion of more than 440 personnel (104 Battalion) deployed to Lebanon in June 2011, and Ireland's commitment to peacekeeping in the Middle East has since been maintained through UNIFIL and the United Nations Disengagement Observer Force (UNDOF) in the Golan Heights. The number of troops serving overseas on UN-mandated missions between 2016 and 2018 typically averaged 534, with a rise to 671 in December 2018. In September 2019 Brig Gen Maureen O'Brien was appointed Deputy Force Commander for UNDOF, and assumed the role of Acting Force Commander between October 2019 and March 2020. In May 2021 O'Brien was promoted to Major General, the second highest rank in the

Defence Forces, and appointed as military advisor on peacekeeping to the Secretary-General of the United Nations.

Legal authority for the deployment of the Defence Forces on overseas missions was originally provided for in the Defence (Amendment) (No. 2) Act of 1960, subject to what is now known as the 'triple lock' mechanism – deployment is only possible on missions with a UN mandate, a formal government decision and with the approval of the Oireachtas. Additional legislation in 1993 and 2006 was required for deployment on Chapter VII missions and peace support missions under the auspices of supranational regional organizations. The 'triple lock' mechanism was formally written into Ireland's national declaration on the European Union's Lisbon Treaty. Irish troops are now potentially committed to working with UN-, NATO- and EU-led missions. In 2021 Defence Forces' personnel were deployed on 7 UN missions, 3 EU military missions, 6 EU civilian missions, and 1 NATO mission.

There can be little doubt that the addition of peacekeeping operations to the remit of the Defence Forces mission revitalized the organization. Enthusiasm for service overseas has been palpable among all ranks since the 1960s. In its annual report to the Chief of Staff for 1962, Planning and Operations Branch observed that the support of UN operations 'continued to be the outstanding military feature' of the year, with personnel operating in Congo, the Middle East and West New Guinea. Peacekeeping duties were,

An Air Corps Agusta Westland AW139 fills a bambi bucket with water at Lower Lough Bray while assisting firefighting operations in the Dublin and Wicklow Mountains in June 2018. Aid to the Civil Power (ATCP) functions such as this are an important element of the Defence Forces' duties.

Three Mowag Piranha III mobile reconnaissance vehicles, armed with an Mk44 Bushmaster II 30mm cannon, and 7.62mm machine guns. The Defence Forces acquired several variants of Mowag from 2001, primarily armoured personnel carriers. These Mowags were photographed in October 2018 during an Operational Capabilities Concept exercise, conducted under the auspices of NATO's Partnership for Peace (PfP) initiative, allowing the Defence Forces to benchmark itself to international standards through both internal and external evaluation.

however, stretching resources to their limits. With Congo tours lasting six months and replacement units in training at home in advance of deployment, the effective number of troops committed to Congo was between 1,600 and 1,800 per annum: 'It is true to say that this has thrown a great strain on the units at home and great difficulties are experienced in organizing, training and other military activities.' The report went on to lament the equipment available for training, and consequent implications for the Defence Forces' primary role of protecting the state: 'With the combat effectiveness of our units gravely suspect, we lack essential weapons and equipment to engage even in a CD [civilian defence] role.'[14]

Sixty years later the Commission on the Defence Forces arrived at similar conclusions, and the parallels between the disposition of the Defence Forces in the 1960s and the present day run deep. If participation in overseas missions has provided the Forces with an impetus and mission that would otherwise be lacking, it may also have had the unintended consequence of distorting development and distracting from its primary role: 'Our Defence Forces are largely staffed and equipped for constabulary and overseas taskings, rather than for defence of the State from external aggression.'[15] The Defence Forces' own assessment of its capabilities concluded that the combined elements of the Army, Air Corps and Naval Service were 'not equipped, postured or realistically prepared to conduct a meaningful defence of the State against a full spectrum force for any sustained period of time'.[16]

Though future development of the Defence Forces is likely to focus on addressing any existing operational imbalances, overseas deployment on peacekeeping and crisis management missions is certain to remain at the heart of service in the Defence Forces. As of 2022, Irish soldiers have completed a cumulative total of more than 74,000 overseas tours of duty, spanning sixty-four years of continuous service since the deployment of five officers to Lebanon with UNOGIL in June 1958.

An Air Corps recruit grimaces during a training exercise in the Glen of Imaal on 2 December 2019.

An Air Corps Pilatus PC-12 in flight. The Air Corps acquired four PC-12s at the end of 2020, which are capable of fulfilling a variety of roles and have a range of up to 1,500 nautical miles. During the Covid-19 pandemic, the PC-12 delivered PCR samples to testing centres in Germany. The PC-12 in this photo displays 104 Squadron's new flash on the fuselage beneath the cockpit canopy. 104 Squadron is part of No. 1 Operations Wing and is tasked with Army Co-operation.

The view from inside an Air Corps helicopter en route, with a delivery of COVID-19 vaccine, to a remote island location on 26 April 2021. The Defence Forces played a vital role in the state's response to the Covid-19 pandemic, providing personnel and logistical support for testing and contact tracing, and later in the successful national roll-out of the vaccine.

'There is a disconnect between stated policy, resources and capabilities'[17]

Publication of a second White Paper on Defence in 2015 came in response to the increasing impact of globalization on the international security environment, and in recognition of the fact that development of the Defence Forces since the economic crash of 2008 had been driven by financial constraints, rather than the ambitious modernization agenda laid out in 2000.

Five years later the Defence Forces were once more placed under the microscope. Appointed in December 2020, the Commission on the Defence Forces was tasked with conducting a detailed assessment of the current needs of the Forces, to ensure that it remains 'agile, flexible and adaptive in responding to dynamic changes in the security environment' and to develop a strategic vision for development beyond 2030.[18] Challenged to be 'potentially radical' in its analysis by the Minister for Defence, Simon Coveney, it delivered its report in February 2022, three months later than originally intended.

Combined with the Defence Forces' visibility during the Covid-19 pandemic, the Commission's work has brought a level of attention to the work of the

LÉ *Samuel Beckett* (P61) sailing from Dún Laoghaire Harbour on 1 September 2021 during the celebrations marking the 75th anniversary of the Naval Service. Commissioned in 2014, LÉ *Samuel Beckett* is named for the playwright and author, and was deployed to the Mediterranean as part of Operation Pontus/EUNAVFOR-Med Operation Sophia in 2015 and 2016. During the Covid-19 pandemic the vessel was docked at Sir John Rogerson's Quay in Dublin for use as a testing centre.

Escorted by Capt Shane Flood and Aide de Camp Col Stephen Howard, with 2/Lt Zara Bolger carrying the flag of 1 Brigade, President Michael D. Higgins inspects the Captain's Guard of Honour, comprised of members of 3 Infantry Battalion. The inspection took place during a ceremony, held on 16 January 2022, to mark the centenary of the handover of Dublin Castle by the British Government to the Provisional Government of the Irish Free State.

Defence Forces not seen since the end of the Troubles. Its report included the assessment that:

> ... the relatively high levels of ambition for Ireland's military capabilities, as set out in the [2015] White Paper, are not supported by the resources provided for the Defence Forces. This has led the Commission to conclude that there is a disconnect between stated policy, resources and capabilities.[19]

In the commission's assessment, merely attempting to maintain current military capabilities would leave Ireland 'unable to meet its desired level of military deployment overseas, weak on Aid to the Civil Power and Aid to the Civil Authority capabilities and, most importantly, without a credible military capability to protect Ireland, its people and its resources for any sustained period'.[20]

Alterations in command structure were also proposed to remedy structural challenges that dated back to the 1920s. The Commission's report highlighted elements of the Defence Forces' command and control system that ran contrary to international best practise. Its recommendations included the elevation of the Naval Service and Air Corps to services on a par with, rather than adjuncts, to the Army, thus 'contributing to a joint strategic command'. The Commission also noted 'with concern' that the formal chain of command excludes the Chief of Staff.[21]

The final stages of the Committee's deliberations occurred at a time when tensions in Europe were rising at a rate not seen since the end of the Cold War. In late 2021 and early 2022 more than 100,000 Russian troops massed on the Russian border with Ukraine before staging an invasion. Ireland's geopolitical importance to the technological infrastructure of Europe was

An aerial shot of a ceremony held at Casement Aerodrome (Baldonnel) on 23 March 2022, marking the centenary of the Air Corps, at which nine officers received their wings. Five of the historic aircraft formerly in service with the Air Corps are on display between the two First World War-era hangars. At bottom left is a De Havilland Vampire, while at bottom right is a Fouga Super Magister. From left at the top of the picture are a Cessna FR.172H, an Aérospatiale Alouette III helicopter, and a Siai-Marchetti Warrior. The nine newly commissioned officers are standing between the Vampire and the Fouga.

273

Two Pilatus PC-9M fly over Casement Aerodrome (Baldonnel) on 3 May 2022, during a ceremony to mark the centenary of the handover of Baldonnel from British forces to the National Army. On the left stands a statue, in silhouette form, of Michael Collins. The nose of a De Havilland Vampire is also visible on the far left, bearing the distinctive Black Panther badge of No. 1 Fighter/Light Strike Squadron.

highlighted when the Russian navy declared its intention to conduct exercises within Ireland's extended economic zone. The announcement was seen as deliberately provocative, emblematic of Russian efforts to find the soft spot in the EU's defences. The manoeuvres, held in the vicinity of deep sea cables that provide crucial trans-Atlantic communications, exposed the challenges Ireland faces in effectively patrolling and actively monitoring its territorial waters and skies.

'The Defence Forces will play a significant role'[22]

The Defence Forces remain something of an enigma in Irish public consciousness, one of the most frequently discussed yet least understood elements of the public sector. Unlike foreign policy – with which the Defence Forces have become inextricably linked over the past six decades – there has never been a concerted effort to outline the Defence Forces' mission to the wider public. Overseas activities ensure a high profile, yet there remains a broader confusion about the role and purpose of the Defence Forces. This confusion ties in with misconceptions about the reality of Irish neutrality, and indeed the necessity of having an effective military for the preservation of national sovereignty and the maintenance of that neutrality.

Assessing the future of the Defence Forces a decade ago, one observer predicted that it would continue to scrape by on meagre resources, to 'make and mend, much as they have done since their foundation.'[23] One of the underlying themes that threads through the past century has been the effect of underinvestment in the Defence Forces, other than in times of national crisis. Since the turn of the millennium, however, that paradigm has shifted. Though financed in part by savings accrued from personnel reductions, significant investment in equipment between 2000 and 2008 was followed by several important acquisitions and upgrades for the Army, Naval Service and Air Corps between 2010 and 2020.

Pictured at the launch of the report of the Commission on the Defence Forces at McKee Barracks on 9 February 2022: (*left to right*) Jacqui McCrum (Secretary General, Department of Defence), Simon Coveney TD (Minister for Defence), Lt Gen Seán Clancy (Chief of Staff), and Aidan O'Driscoll (Chairperson, Commission on the Defence Forces).

Between 2015 and 2019, artist Amelia Stein shot a series of portraits of members of 3 Infantry Battalion, the oldest unit of the Defence Forces and known as 'The Bloods'. The photos were taken at James Stephens Barracks, Kilkenny, and exhibited in the city's Butler Gallery in 2020. Pictured are Pte Ciara Nevin, Pte Evans Wallace, and Pte James Dooley with Fionn, an Irish Wolfhound and battalion mascot.

With the territorial integrity and sovereignty of the state largely unthreatened since 1923 (leaving aside the genuine fears of invasion during the Emergency), the Defence Forces have found purpose in overseas service and the provision of aid to the civil power and authority. The effective yet unobtrusive manner in which it fulfils these obligations brings little notice or acclaim, perhaps because they are accomplished in an efficient and effective manner. When called upon at short notice, whether for peacekeeping duties overseas, or during the Civil War, the Emergency, or the Troubles, the Defence Forces have invariably provided exemplary service. The national crisis engendered by the Covid-19 pandemic provided a new perspective on the capabilities of the Defence Forces, and the extent to which the state relies upon its military in times of emergency. The adaptability and flexibility demonstrated by the personnel of the Army, Air Corps and Naval Service, as they met the logistical challenges of the pandemic, stand as a testament to their professionalism.

In its report, the Commission on the Defence Forces highlighted a number of organizational challenges that required attention, from both within and without the Defence Forces. It also observed that demands on defence capabilities were becoming increasingly 'sophisticated and dynamic', and recommended internal reforms matched by adequate investment. In welcoming the report, Chief of Staff Lt Gen Seán Clancy anticipated a new era for the Defence Forces:

> We are undoubtedly at the start of something new, which will have lots of steps, twists and turns to it; but today in a Defence Forces ... that has a continuous appetite to do better, that strives every day to lead excellence, we sit looking over the horizon awaiting a positive decision on a level of ambition from Government on the future of the Defence Forces, which must of course be backed by proper resources.[24]

The recommendations of the Commission on the Defence Forces mark an inflection point, one which indicates an evolutionary moment perhaps equalled only by the transition, between 1922 and 1924, from the Irish Republican Army to the Irish Defence Forces.

BEGINNINGS: MILITARY ARCHIVES

Operating under the National Archives Act of 1986, Military Archives has been the official repository for records of the Defence Forces, the Department of Defence, and the Army Pensions Board since 1990. Military Archives traces its roots to December 1924, however, when Col Michael J. Costello and Comdt William Brennan-Whitmore presented a persuasive plea for the establishment of a Military Archives Section within Army Intelligence. Prompted by the identification of valuable historical documents in Dublin Castle, including papers from the British War Office, Brennan-Whitmore made an eloquent case for their preservation:

> [What] will future generations of our race say of us if, through our negligence, we allow invaluable State documents to be lost? ... all State documents, whether of the old regime or the new, which have reached the historical stage – that is to say, are no longer current – and relate to matters of military interest, should be in the care, and under the control of the Intelligence Branch; that the Intelligence Branch should be charged with setting up an Historical, or Military Archives Section, and the head of the Intelligence Branch charged with the care, preservation and historical utility of every page.[1]

There was a practical side to the preservation of documents, which were invaluable aids to the deliberations of bodies such as the Army Pensions Board. It also allowed the Defence Forces, then still in its infancy, to begin

Launch of new Military Archives building construction. (*Left to right*): A representative of GEM construction, with Heather Humphries TD (Minister for Arts, Heritage and the Gaeltacht), Simon Coveney TD (Minister for Defence), Comdt Padraic Kennedy, OIC of Military Archives, and Maj Gen Michael Beary, GOC 2 Brigade, inspecting plans for the refurbishment of the old Military Hospital in Cathal Brugha Barracks, to house Military Archives.

collecting documentary evidence in support of its origins and legitimacy. Contemporaneous intelligence files record that the opponents of the Treaty, including Éamon de Valera, were also 'working hard on an archives from their point of view'.[2]

Military Archives was given a secure footing under the stewardship of Col Jeremiah 'Ginger' O'Connell, who served as its first director from 1935 to 1944. During the Emergency, O'Connell drew up plans to relocate the Archives' collections, then stored at Griffith Barracks, in the event of a threat to Dublin: 'A couple of lorries would serve for this purpose and we could load in a couple of hours. If, say, a day's warning were given they could be so made up as to be loaded in about half an hour.'[3]

The philosophy underpinning Military Archives was perhaps summed up in a report on its work in 1948 and 1949. As well as liaising with the Bureau of Military History and cataloguing collections (including the papers of Michael Collins), Archives had dealt with various requests for information: 'The number of inquiries average from two to three a week and sometimes deal with matters which can hardly be regarded as strictly official, but information, if available, is always supplied as a matter of good "public relations" policy'.[4]

The efforts of successive directors from the early 1980s ensured that Military Archives survived, despite fluctuating fortunes in financial support and staffing provision. Those efforts were rewarded on 24 April 2016, when long standing ambitions for a permanent home for the archive were finally realized. On that day, President Michael D. Higgins attended Cathal Brugha Barracks to officially open the new complex housing Military Archives. As well as providing state-of-the-art facilities for the safe preservation of archival collections, the former barracks hospital was converted to accommodate a library, conservation facilities, office space and a reading room, open to the general public.

CHAPTER 8

1922–2022
MEMORIES OF THE MEN AND WOMEN
OF THE DEFENCE FORCES

Among the unique collections held in Military Archives are two that have directly recorded the personal recollections and experiences of the men and women who have served in the Defence Forces over the past century – the Bureau of Military History (BMH) and the Military Archives Oral History Project (MAOHP). Between 1947 and 1957 the BMH assembled material documenting the history of the Irish revolutionary movement, 1913–21.[1] It collected 1,773 witness statements, twelve voice recordings and a valuable collection of contemporary documents.

Though much of the BMH material stuck to the specified date range of 1913 to 1921, many of the witness statements gathered by the BMH offered recollections that touched upon the split in the IRA after the Treaty was signed in December 1921, the formation of the National Army in early 1922, and the subsequent Civil War.

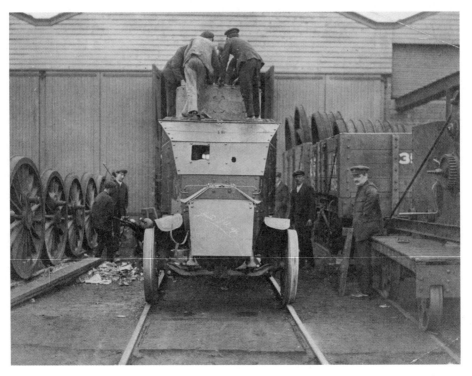

A Lancia armoured car at Great Southern & Western Railway's Inchicore Works, being converted for use on railway tracks for the Railway Protection, Repair and Maintenance Corps. This photo was originally published in the *Sunday Independent* on 3 December 1922.

An extract from one of those statements, by Joseph Lawless, is included below. Together with the statement by Seán Mac Mahon and the extract from Art Magennis's unpublished memoir, they differ from the remainder of the testimonies presented here in that they are carefully composed, written accounts. Mac Mahon's statement – drawn from Military Archives' Army Inquiry Committee papers – is also notable for being composed in April/May 1924, almost contemporaneously with the events it describes. It was, in effect, an affidavit presented to the Army Inquiry Committee to refute charges that the mutiny of March 1924 was a result of 'muddling, mismanagement and incompetence' by the Army's most senior officers.

The nine remaining extracts are drawn from interviews collected by the MAOHP.[2] Established in 2015 with the aim of recording and preserving the history and traditions of the Defence Forces, the project was conceived as a natural extension of the Bureau of Military History. At time of writing the MAOHP has collected more than 350 interviews with retired and serving personnel of all ranks, and several interviews with others who have worked closely with Irish UNIFIL personnel in Lebanon. The memories and witness accounts that have been captured span from the Emergency up to the Covid-19 pandemic, providing an exceptional insight into the varied careers and experiences of Defence Forces personnel over the past eighty years.

The excerpts below have been transcribed by the author for this book, and any editorial interventions – to clarify dates or to provide full names – are identified by [square brackets]. An ellipsis indicates that matter has been omitted. Brief biographical details are given for each contributor where they first appear, along with the rank they held either when the interview was conducted, or at which they retired.

General Seán Mac Mahon (1893–1955) joined the Volunteers in November 1913, participated in the 1916 Rising and was appointed as the IRA's Quartermaster General (QMG) in 1919. He retained the post of QMG in the National Army and succeeded Richard Mulcahy as Chief of Staff in August 1922. He held this position until March 1924, when his commission was withdrawn by the government in the wake of the Army Mutiny. Exonerated by the Army Inquiry Committee of 1924, Mac Mahon's commission was restored and he was appointed OC of Southern Command. He resigned from the army in 1927. Here he recalls the task of establishing the National Army, and preparations for the handover of Beggars Bush Barracks by the British on 1 February 1922:[3]

From the date that the Treaty was signed it was discussed freely throughout the Volunteer organization, and opinion was sharply divided in the great majority of areas, and even General Headquarters Staff divided on the matter. This made the position very difficult and, when the Treaty was ratified by An Dáil, General Headquarters had a huge task before it. There was the task of keeping order in the country, the task of taking over from the British, the task of setting up a force of even a few thousand men to take over the different barracks, and the task of setting up machinery to handle even such a small regular force ... under normal conditions such tasks would have required every effort to see through but with the Volunteer ranks rent from top to bottom throughout the country the task seemed a hopeless one ...

During the month of January, I, as Quartermaster General, received instructions to arrange for the taking over of Beggars Bush Barracks from the Auxiliaries on 1 February 1922. Every step towards putting the Treaty into force was hindered by the anti-Treaty military leaders. I could get no assistance from the Officer Commanding, Dublin City Brigade,[4] in the matter ... During pre-Truce days we had a unit in Dublin (Active Service Unit) between 50 and 60 strong, and which was on whole time service. This unit was under the officer commanding, Dublin City Brigade, but was also controlled directly by General Headquarters for special service when required ...

Having discussed the situation with General Mulcahy, who was then Chief of Staff, and about this time became Minister for Defence, it was decided that these men who we understood to be all pro-Treaty should be recalled from leave and formed into the first unit of the regular Army for the purpose of taking over Beggars Bush Barracks ... This matter having been decided the next thing to be considered was a place of assembly. We had no premises capable of holding 50 men where they could be shaped rapidly into a regular military unit.

After some delay we discovered a vacant workhouse at Celbridge which we took over and set up as the first barracks of the regular Army. Much work had to be done to get the workhouse into shape ... the next matter that required attention was the provision of uniforms, equipment, arms, etc., for the unit and all this had to be dealt with within the few days at our disposal before 1 February 1922. On that day, however, in spite of all the difficulties which had to be overcome the first unit of the regular Army was armed, fully equipped and ready to march through the city to take over Beggars Bush. I may add that the final touches were not completed until 4am on the morning of 1 February.

Colonel Joseph Vincent Lawless (1896–1969) *was a member of the Fingal Brigade of the IRA, participated in the Howth gun running of 1914 and the Battle of Ashbourne during the 1916 Rising. He was interned at Frongoch and, after his release, continued as an active member of the IRA during the War of Independence.*

A large group of National Army troops in a personnel carrier, accompanied by an Army chaplain. Several of the soldiers appear to be nervously looking at the road. The photo was possibly taken on Charlesville Road, outside Limerick city.

He was arrested again in December 1920 and interned at Collinstown Aerodrome, Arbour Hill and finally Rath Camp (the Curragh), from which he escaped in October 1921. Lawless was later part of the team that designed the Ford and Dodge armoured cars that were built in Ireland during the Emergency. Here he recalls the split in the IRA in 1922 and his decision to join (and later re-join) the National Army:[5]

I had joined the National Army as a Captain of the Mechanical Transport Corps, but in my frequent visits to Fleming's of Drumcondra, I continued to meet the officers of the South Tipperary Brigade, all of whom were avowedly anti-Treaty. Naturally this led to discussion on the question and, while neither side could convince the other, I think we all agreed to admit each other's sincerity and personal right to act according to our convictions …

The IRA, the guerrilla force which had done the fighting and still had arms in its hands, was, of its nature, identified with the political partisans of the dispute. In this lay the danger that was recognized by thinking men of either side and so an effort was made to stabilize the military end of the situation by the calling of a convention at the Dublin Mansion House in March 1922, where representatives of all the IRA brigades of Ireland would decide the attitude of the army on the political controversy and place its control on a firm basis.

The convention, however, proved itself to be a fiasco. There was evidence of efforts to pack the convention with delegates who were not freely elected … and it was clear that the lines of cleavage were already drawn … Civil war began to be spoken of vaguely, as a sort of stiffening of the arguments for and against the Treaty, but I doubt if any of those who used this phrase had any conception of the horrors of civil war …

I discussed the situation with Seán Lemass … one evening as we left Beggars Bush Barracks after duty. Seán was also a captain in the newly formed National Army at the time … I do not remember much of what was said between us except the final sum up … Finally, I said that if we, the old IRA officers, should decide to take our stand on the abstract argument against the Treaty and walk out of the Army, then the government would have to replace

A civilian offers cigarettes to National Army soldiers sitting in the back of a lorry. The soldiers are not wearing official uniforms, suggesting that this photograph was taken in the early stages of the Civil War.

us with whatever material came to hand, and there was plenty of alternative material in the ex-British officers and opportunists of all kinds, who would then become the directing influence in an Irish army to which we would become mere spectators.

Joseph Lawless in Rath Camp, 1921. From a collection of photos taken in the camp using Lawless' camera.

Seán said: 'I think that is the proper way to look at it; we'll stay in the Army and do our best to exert our influence from inside', and we shook hands on that fact. Yet, within a couple of weeks we had both left the army, he to join the anti-Treaty forces who had taken possession of the Four Courts, and I to essay a return to civilian life ...

I did not, in fact, hand in my uniform, nor did I hand in any formal written resignation, but I walked out of Marlborough Hall [in March 1922] and did not return ... It was with quite a shock that I awoke on the morning of 28th June to the sound of heavy gunfire in the city, and soon learned that civil war had indeed begun ... I sat in my office at the garage in a state of mental upheaval. I felt that in such a cataclysmic state of affairs I could not take active part on either side, and yet there must be something I ought to do if I could only get my mind clear as to what that was ...

I made my way towards Portobello Barracks the following day to offer my services in any capacity, and meeting Peadar MacMahon, who had just then been promoted to the rank of Commandant General, he arranged that I would be allowed to resume my rank of captain and requested that I should accompany him to the Curragh as his transport officer. I arrived at the Curragh on or about 10 July 1922, in command of a convoy of some 30 vehicles laden with arms and equipment, which material was for the equipment of the new units then being formed under the title of the Volunteer Reserve. The realities of civil war had now to be faced. Although I had no heart in the fratricidal struggle, I realized that I must make my contribution towards the supremacy of the Government of Dáil Éireann as representing the democratic majority of the people of Ireland.

Seán Mac Mahon on the policy of state executions and the progress of the Civil War:[6]

During the period of fighting [in Dublin in the summer of 1922] and while this huge task was still before us, the work of organizing an Army had to be undertaken ... Appeals were made for recruits. They came pouring in and had to be rushed to positions in most cases even before they were uniformed to say nothing about being trained. Men were taught the mechanism of a rifle very often on the way to a fight. I may also mention that the material that came to us in the first rush of recruits was very often not of the best ...

During the month of September, an Dáil met and approved of proposals for setting up of Military Courts to deal with the Irregulars. In connection with this I may mention that the carrying out of executions was perhaps the most severe test on our troops. In an Army such as ours, which had been built in a hurry without the necessary training, and which had no time or means for fostering discipline it made us think carefully as to how the first executions should be carried out. It was proposed that the first execution should be carried out by a squad of officers as so much depended on it at the time and we could not afford to run any risk of our men refusing to carry out the work. It was, however, decided that a firing squad would be picked from the men of the best unit we had in Dublin and that proved successful.

From September on we had to adopt new methods of warfare to get after the Irregular columns which were moving around attacking our troops, looting, and destroying property. During the winter months the conditions under which our troops worked proved to be demoralizing and the form of operations which had to be carried out was very severe on both officers and men. We had occupied numerous towns and villages and established small posts in them in order to try and prevent Irregular columns from swooping down and looting such places.

A group of National Army soldiers alighting, outside the Belfast Banking Company on College Green, Dublin. A group of interested onlookers have gathered alongside the car.

These small posts had a very demoralizing effect on our men.

Towards the end of 1922 and in the beginning of 1923 the Irregulars concentrated on the use of explosives and also on holding up and looting trains, the burning of houses and other forms of destructive warfare. This form of warfare was very difficult to counteract but steps were taken to deal with it.

Mac Mahon on the difficulty of establishing discipline in the army under wartime conditions:[7]

When the Treaty was signed and ratified by Dáil Éireann the Army stood as the Dáil's right arm to enforce the Treaty, even against its own mutineers.

The Army fought again and won. It brought the country into line behind the Government elected by the people. It disposed of its surplus manpower necessitated by the fight and then came the 'Mutiny'. Was it the first mutiny that occurred? No! It was one of many mutinies but it was the first which occurred under normal conditions, and the first on which persons in positions of responsibility focused public attention, and into which an Inquiry was ordered by the Government …

We had mutinies in the Army before the Regular force was established. We had a minor mutiny during the first week of the regular Army's existence. We had a major mutiny again before the Army was two months old and I may say we had mutinies and numerous happenings bordering on mutiny from the time the fight started in 1922 …

We dealt with all such incidents and succeeded in bringing the Army up to the fine point of discipline where it was able to stand the shock of the removal [in March 1924] of its most senior officers and the Minister for Defence, General Mulcahy, its latest Commander in Chief.

Three National Army soldiers tend to a wounded man during the Civil War, who is dressed in civilian clothing but wearing a gun belt.

Lieutenant General Gerry McMahon DSM (1935–2017) enrolled in the Cadet School in 1953. During his career McMahon toured with UN missions in Congo, Cyprus, and Lebanon, while also serving as Commandant of the Military College, Director of Planning and Research, and Quartermaster General. McMahon was appointed Chief of Staff in 1994 and retired from the Defence Forces in 1998. Here he recalls a story told to him, by Col Seán Clancy, about the reaction in the Defence Forces to the election of Fianna Fáil to government in 1932:[8]

We do recognize a central plank ... is civil control of the military. Now, I often wondered about this. Where did it have its beginnings? It's generally accepted in all democracies, but not in all nations. You see it every day. But we have always accepted it. Seán Clancy was a Lieutenant Colonel, ex-CO of the 5th Battalion, which I commanded in Collins Barracks in the 80s.[9] It was the only unit I've ever commanded, and I was delighted to be able to command it. A fine unit. At a gathering of old COs of the 5th Battalion I met Seán Clancy, and he wanted to make a presentation of some documents he had, which were germane to Sarsfield Barracks in Limerick, the naming of Sarsfield Barracks. So I set up a meeting with him, I brought him down to Limerick and he made the presentation. But going down that day in the car, I brought him down to Limerick, we talked about all this. And he said that when Fianna Fáil first went into government, not when they first went into the Dáil but when they took over, remember it was only ten years after the Civil War, he went down to Parkgate Street which was Defence Forces headquarters, or Army headquarters as it would have been called at the time. He went down that morning and he met General [Michael] Brennan, who was Chief of Staff.[10] And he said, 'I suppose we'll be moving on the Dáil'. Now, he never told me whether he was saying it as a joke, as a wind-up, or whether he was serious. But he said, 'I said this to him', and he said Brennan turned around to him and said, 'We're a democracy. We, the Defence Forces of this democracy, are obliged to defend that democracy and defend the citizens. And the citizens have spoken. From that democratic vote, they have voted Fianna Fáil in. So we will do what the government tells.' This coming from a man who ... was very much on the other side in the Civil War.

Commandant Arthur 'Art' Magennis DSM (1919–2019) was a native of Co. Down. He enlisted in the Defence Forces in June 1940, serving for two tours both in Congo and Cyprus. He was awarded the Distinguished Service Medal, with honour, for his actions during his first tour of Congo with 35 Infantry Battalion.[11] Magennis retired from the Defence Forces in 1979. In this extract from his unpublished memoir, he recalls his decision to enlist and being posted to patrol the border with Northern Ireland in 1941:

World War Two commenced and the world outlook changed completely. For my friend Desmond Waters and me the really big event was the big gathering in College Green in Dublin which was addressed by the leading Free State politicians: de Valera, Cosgrave and Norton. We listened to the speeches on radio. They outlined the policy of neutrality we would pursue, the effect that would have on our lifestyle and above all the necessity for a defence force sufficiently strong to defend the country. By the time the radio broadcast was finished we had both decided we would be on the train to Dublin as soon as we had raised the necessary cash ...

[My] unit stayed in the Clondalkin post until the Spring [of 1941] when we moved up to the Border area. The morning we moved was one to remember. The fact that we were moving into an operational role for the very first time had sent a tremor of excitement through the Squadron. Well, it did so through me, and I felt the excitement of the occasion through my body, from my belly to my head ... [Gibbstown House] became Squadron Headquarters and

Official accreditation for the Military Tattoo, held in the RDS, Ballsbridge, in September 1945. More than 200,000 tickets were sold for the military exhibition, which had the overt goal of raising funds for the Army Benevolent Fund but also served as an attempt to raise public awareness of the work of the Defence Forces during the Emergency, and to emphasise its role in warding off invasion during the Second World War.

MILITARY
TATTOO
1945

OFFICIAL

No. ....

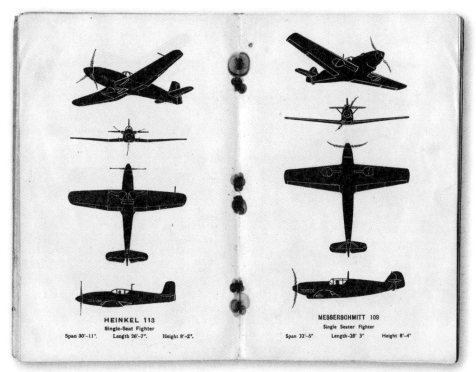

HEINKEL 113
Single-Seat Fighter
Span 30'–11".   Length 26'–7".   Height 8'–2".

MESSERSCHMITT 109
Single Seater Fighter
Span 32'–5"   Length–28' 3"   Height 8'–4"

Extract from a booklet, depicting the outline silhouettes of German aircraft, produced by the Department of Defence to assist the Coast Watching Service and others in the identification of aircraft during the Emergency.

officers' quarters, and the outbuildings other ranks' accommodation. The farmyard became the parade ground and a large galvanized shed the vehicle park ... Capt Charlie Hewston, squadron second in command, gave us a short talk on how our task, patrolling the Border area, would be carried out. I have no recollection of the content of that talk because his voice did not carry very well, but it went something like: 'One motor troop per day would be on Border patrol, half the troop by daylight and half from dusk until dawn. Great care must be observed to remain on our side of the Border.' I remember thinking, but to myself, 'How do we know where the State border is? Is it marked with whitewash or paint? Better not say anything in case everybody laughs at me for not knowing that there are clear signs marking it.' I had seen the maps of the Border area when I was marking the grid lines on the sheet sixteens [Ordnance Survey maps], and the Border was not plotted.

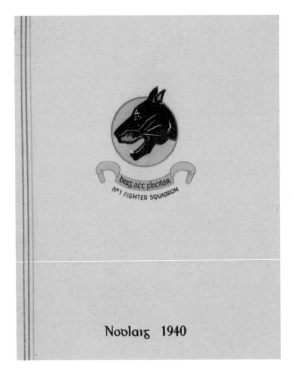

Noolaig 1940

Christmas card of the Air Corps No. 1 Fighter Squadron, 1940, featuring the Squadron's Black Panther badge along with its motto, 'Beag ach Fíochmhar' ('Small but Fierce').

Anyway, better keep quiet and learn from experience, Lt Harrington, the troop commander, would be sure to know …

I was very proud to be a Trooper in 2 Motor Squadron patrolling my side of the Border. It wasn't all patrolling. A lot of daylight hours were devoted to tactical training at a minor 'war games' level. A few men would be placed in a secret location with a few rounds of blank ammunition with orders to fire as a patrol approached, and the patrol would be taught how to handle the situation. These small Troop exercises developed into Troop against Troop and then into Squadron level manoeuvres.

Having received his commission, **Gerry McMahon** *recalls his first impressions on arrival at Custume Barracks, Athlone, in January 1956:*[12]

I would say that my immediate feeling was one of disappointment. I said to you earlier that we were protected from the realities of life. As a 2 Lt, platoon commander, B Company, 6 Infantry Battalion, you'd a vision that you were going down, that you'd a platoon, which was 34 men, which is a lieutenant's command, and that there'd be a platoon for you, and that you would train them and go on exercises. Go on operations if you were to be called on operation, although there were virtually no operations going on until the first Border thing at the end of the 50s. You arrived in the 6th Battalion, which should have had about 500 soldiers. It had little over 100. So what did they do? They went away on courses, they administered themselves. But it was, to my mind, it was soul destroying. And what had happened was, that after the Emergency the Defence Forces was cut, I've forgotten the exact numbers now, to about 16,000 we'll say, from three times that, from two divisions down to that. Then it was allowed, because we were in the terrible 40s and 50s, the Defence Forces were allowed to kind of just wither on the vine through lack of money.

Sergeant Joe Mallon *joined the Defence Forces in 1958, following in the footsteps of his father, who had served during the Emergency. Mallon served with 32 Infantry Battalion, the first Irish battalion to serve in Congo, and later returned with 38 Infantry Battalion. He also served with 11 Infantry Group in Cyprus, and 51 Infantry Battalion in Lebanon. Here he recalls volunteering to go to Congo in July 1960:*[13]

Dan Buckley was the adjutant at the time, and he came out in front of us and read out, that the United Nations had requested the government to send a battalion to the Congo, with the United Nations. Anyone that wanted to volunteer, take a pace forward. Of course me being a young lad looking for excitement, took the pace forward. Now that was on a Monday, back to the Curragh, and I think on the Friday we were on the planes from Baldonnel to the Congo. Vaccinations, inoculations, extractions, the whole lot … I remember there was a line of troops from Ward 8 in the Curragh, anyone that knows Ward 8, right back down to the ball alley, guys waiting to go in and get their needles and extractions … It was all a big rush. We had no kit and equipment. We went on the planes with the packs on our backs, and our bulls wool and our peaked cap, and I remember the first time we ever seen a plastic bag … as we went on the plane we got a plastic bag with an apple, an orange and a sandwich. And that kept us going to wherever we were going next.

Members of 3 Armoured Car Squadron, bound for Congo, prepare to board a US Air Force C-124 Globe-master at Dublin Airport, April 1963.

Mallon *on his first impressions of the Congo:*[14]

The first impressions when we got off the plane, we thought we were going to smother because of the hot air. We panicked actually, and you could see it, you know, see the air. And then it took us about a week before you got acclimatized to it, and then your ears, I think it was a couple of days and my ears were still cracking from the noise of the engines ... And then what happened was, with the heat, we were only after getting these inoculations and vaccinations, they start taking effect with the heat, and there was lads going down ... I remember one chap done guard, I'll never forget it, and he went out while he was resting off, in a swimming togs, fell asleep, turned around while he was asleep, and the roars of that chap. They had to put him on these rubber mattresses, he was all blisters.

Mallon *recalls when he first heard news of the Niemba ambush, which occurred on 8 November 1960 and resulted in the death of nine Irish soldiers:*[15]

I think we were in Kamina when we got that word. It was devastating, because we weren't sure how many were killed ... At that time, we were in trenches, actually, in Kamina, because they were going to attack to take the base ... As far as I can remember, when we were with 38 Battalion I think Trooper [Anthony] Browne's[16] body was found ... Things happened in the Congo and you wouldn't think about them then. It was when you came home the hair would stand on the back of your neck thinking about them.

Captain Thomas Croke DSM *enrolled in the 40th Cadet Class and joined the Air Corps after he was commissioned in September 1967. He received his wings on 1 April 1969. On 5 August 1972 Croke and his crewmen, Terry Kelly and John Ring, embarked on a search and rescue mission to try and reach two brothers who had become trapped on a ledge at Powerscourt Waterfall, Co. Wicklow. One of the brothers died while attempting to climb down before the helicopter arrived, but the crew were successful in reaching the surviving brother. They received the Distinguished Service Medal, with distinction, for their actions. Croke recalls the difficulty of the mission:[17]*

We got a call to say that there were two boys trapped on the Powerscourt Waterfall. Looking at the weather I thought this is going to be a problem with downdrafts, so we better make the aircraft as light as possible for the rescue ... As we approached Powerscourt Waterfall the downdrafts were horrendous. The wind was blowing over the waterfall at 44 knots. 35 knots is a gale force wind ... I couldn't see the survivors at all, so I decided, okay, I'm going to land at the foot of the waterfall where I could see the Garda car. Fortunately the Guards had a pair of binoculars, and they were able to say to me, 'You see the tree halfway up the waterfall there? He's at the base of that' ... As we went into the tree, the normal collective pitch limit is .75 for a hover, .80 for transition. But you could go up to 1, but the danger was you were going to cause damage to the engine. We were pulling up towards .95

and we weren't even in at the hovering point ... I have to be honest and say I've never been so scared in all my life ... At that stage as we were trying to get in and thinking, we can't get this wrong, this poor chap at the tree needs us. It wouldn't look good for the Air Corps to fail him, no matter what the explanation we could give ...

We went back into the tree, which was well into the valley, as I said it was halfway up the waterfall. The power was there to do the rescue, but it was very, very close to limits again. That was just with three of us on board. Terry was pattering me ... Because of where the pilot is sitting, he can't see directly under him. He's looking forward and a verbal description, which is described as patter, is given by the winch operator ... I started descending vertically, and it was very rough with the down drafts, coming over the top of the waterfall and down along the mountain, and around the trees and all the rest of it. But I became aware of branches growing up out of the corner of my eye. Because as you remember the Alouette III was all glass down to the floor, all Perspex. Out of the corner of my eye I could see the trees growing, and I said to Terry, 'Terry I can see branches growing up the side of the airplane'. And Terry just said, 'No no, it's okay, you can keep coming down'. We kept coming down, we had fabulous trust in each other ... Terry said, 'Steady steady, he's in contact with the survivor.' Very quickly John got the strap around the survivor and gave the thumbs up, and Terry just said, 'Up gently', which was the sign for the aircraft to take the weight of the two off the ground ... The job wasn't done at that stage because we had to lift vertically, and then back off from the cliff while winching in the survivor and the winch man. I was relieved when Terry said, 'They're at the door, they're on board, up and around' ...

We flew to St Vincent's Hospital, and sadly on the way in we discovered that it was this chap's brother who had fallen and was killed ... On Wednesday morning a letter arrived to Heli-flight, from the mother of the chap that I'd saved, the mother also of the chap who'd died, thanking me for saving her son, and telling me that the chap who had died was a gifted mathematician who was due to start in Oxford or Cambridge that September, a month later. I thought, imagine a woman sitting down to write that letter, three days after her son has been killed. That letter meant so much to me, that she would actually go to that trouble.

Croke *on flying missions in co-operation with An Garda Síochána during the Troubles:*[18] During the Troubles I was in Finner Camp, you might remember there was an attempt to bomb the RUC station in Strabane[19] ... The Guards needed photographs of the RUC station. We were asked to take the Garda photographer into the Border. Now, we have photographs with the exact Border delineated on the photographs, so we were able to go right into the Border, hover at reasonably high level and get the photographs that the Guards wanted. We were there for obviously a couple of minutes and then returned to Finner, but the word came back that the RUC were saying if you ever do that again they would shoot us down and say that they didn't realize that we were Irish helicopters. This was at a very early stage in the Troubles. And that's when the decision was made, if you remember, all the Alouettes had a tricolour on the bottom of the machine to identify them as Óglaigh na hÉireann helicopters. It was another event that I can remember of being involved with the Guards, and they were just so helpful and so appreciative of what we could do for them. I was involved doing the Herrema[20] searches. Constant searches with the Guards to try and spot where they were until they were actually found in Monasterevin.

An Air Corps Aérospatiale Alouette III during a search and rescue mission.

Commandant Michael Walsh *served with An Fórsa Cosanta Áitiúil before enrolling in Cadet School in 1976. During his career he served with the Artillery Corps and Military Police Corps and on numerous overseas mission, including with 57 Infantry Battalion in Lebanon. Here he recalls his training in the Cadet School:*[21]

My CS was a man named Sam Shannon. Sam was a Congo veteran ... we never were told about that. The other CS was Packie Burke. Packie was a Jadotville veteran ... Packie was a strange man. But now I can understand some of the training he gave us, the viciousness, the defence of positions and all that ... It's only recently I realized what the hell Packie was on about ... We were discussing it recently at a class reunion, and people were asking about the Cadet School and what we thought of it. My complaint, we didn't utilize the knowledge of the NCOs. Veterans of the Congo, which remember was only sixteen years before that, and in some cases fourteen, twelve years, guys who had seen serious action in the Congo and they were our instructors. Not once in the thirteen months that I was there did a senior NCO ever come up and give us a lecture on battle tactics, or on psychology, or their own opinions on it. Not once ... Now I would hope that they utilize experience an awful lot more.

Captain Maria O'Donoghue *joined the Defence Forces in March 1980 as one of just four members of the first women's cadet class, recruited for the newly formed Women's Service Corps. O'Donoghue was one of eight women to make further history when, on 27 April 1981, she received her commission. She retired with the rank of captain in 1999. Here O'Donoghue recalls her arrival at the Curragh in March 1980 and initial training:*[22]

The first day, it was 10 March 1980, a lovely bright Spring morning, and my parents drove me from Athlone to the

Curragh ... We were brought over to our lines. The CQMS showed us to our rooms and remarked on the bed pack that was on the bed, and said something to the effect that you're going to have to make that every day. I thought he was joking, I started laughing. Little did I know ... Then we were brought down to one of the training rooms in the Cadet School and sworn in ... The next day we collected our kit, and because we needed some items of clothing that weren't included in the old Q2, I think it was called, where you got the schedules of dress and all the rest of it ... We got combats that were tailored for us. The boots had to be specially made in our sizes because we had obviously smaller feet. The funny thing is, we even got issued with the old wobble brush and razor blades, all of that sort of stuff that the guys got ... We also did some classes with the 56th Cadet Class, who were in place at the time. They had started their cadet training back in the previous October, I think, so they were six months ahead of us or so. We did some training with them, classroom training mostly. And then we had our own square bashing, arms familiarization, all of that we did on our own ... Four of us joined up initially. There was myself and Colette Harrison, Maureen McEnery and Maree Flynn ... After a few months in the Curragh, we were sent to the British army to be trained ... When we went to Camberley[23] then in September [1980] to do our officer cadet training, the British army was changing itself a little bit, and it was beginning to think about women occupying more positions in the military than they had heretofore. The Women's Royal Army Corps had been non-combatant, and it was now beginning to explore the possibility of women becoming arms bearing and holding more operational roles. We did quite a bit of our training in Sandhurst[24] with the male officer cadet classes in there.

Sergeant Michael Jones MMG joined the Defence Forces in 1974. His father and two brothers also served in the Defence Forces. Michael and his brother Thomas were serving with 46 Infantry Battalion in Lebanon when, in April 1980, the De Facto Forces (South Lebanon Army) attacked UNIFIL troops protecting the village of At Tiri. He recalls his experiences of the battle and the aftermath:[25]

Once you're in the [armoured] car it limits your boundaries to information, the only information you're going to get is over the radio. The first night there, to my recollection, nothing happened ... It was the next morning, this DFF [De Facto Forces] head, he came up and he was kind of rabble rousing his own people to go in and take the village. They wanted this village and that was it. And the mukhtar was there and he was saying no, no, you're not coming in. They would have come in and the mukhtar would have disappeared, and anyone that would have voiced opposition to them coming in, they would have disappeared as well. We were there, the second day was fairly peaceful as well. It was only on the third day that it really kicked off, big time. We had dug in now at this stage.

(0:53:00)
We had all the entrances to the village blocked ... [The DFF] herded women and children up the left hand road, and there was four or five DFF behind them and they were firing into the bank on the roadside, herding them up ... We could see them coming up, and they were bang-banging into the road, the people weren't impressed at all. This was before the [DFF] Super Sherman arrived ... you see the sweat bursting out on the back of your hand. This thing could have done a lot of damage, for the simple reason, and it's only when I pointed it out to the lads afterwards, you see, it fires a solid shot. [Our AML-90] fires a fused round, so it has to travel a certain distance before it [explodes]. So he closed the distance between himself and the 90. He probably knew well because the Lebanese Army used AMLs in the 1990s ...

(1:03:45)
There'd be five minutes of gun fire, and then it'd stop ... They fired in a few rounds of phosphorous mortar then, which we didn't like at all ... [Sgt Spud Murphy] closed the hatch, and he hadn't it closed a minute, a round hopped off it. The Army had a terrible habit of painting the inside of the vehicles with cheap gloss paint. Armoured vehicles come with a dusty matt paint, but when you put your hand on it you leave a dirty mark on it, so the Army decided to paint it with gloss. Sure it was like shrapnel, we were peppered in gloss paint.

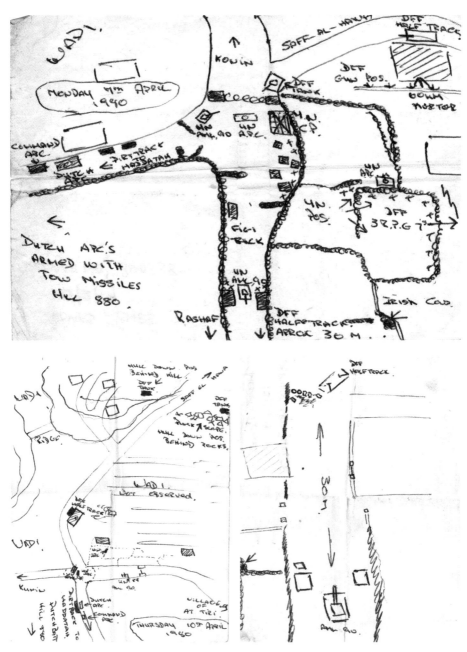

Hand-drawn maps by Sgt Thomas Jones, brother of Michael, illustrating troop and armoured car dispositions over several days during the Battle of At Tiri, April 1980.

Jones recalls the change in atmosphere following the evacuation of Pte Stephen Griffin, a member of 46 Infantry Battalion, who was badly wounded on 9 April and died shortly after. Griffin was one of two members of UNIFIL who lost their lives during the battle (1:14:46):

It was gloves off ... Everyone, including the DFF, realized something had changed. Something definitely had changed in the whole set up. And then of course when the 90 went up and engaged the half-track, that was it. There was no more firing over their heads or firing into the air, it was centre of the observed mass and that was it ... The house that we were parked behind started to take fire, and I knew that there was two of our lads [Ray Power and Joe Hines] inside... I shouted at the two of them evacuate the building, get out of the building, get out of the building. Because you could see the .5 rounds coming through the back wall. And the two boys just came out the top window, just jumped straight out the top window, landed on the road ... We were huddled in behind the APC ... It was all over by then, it all kind of stopped, there was quiet for a while. And then it all kicked off again.

On 8 April Trooper Gerry Mitten was attempting to transport the injured Pte McCarthy from the far side of the village of At Tiri when they came under fire. Jones and his colleague, Lt Tony Bracken, both received the Military Medal for Gallantry, with distinction, for rescuing their two fellow Irish peacekeepers while under heavy fire (1:23:10):

As soon as he turned on to the main road the half-track here opened up on him ... The Land Rover got a burst of about three or four HMG [heavy machine gun]. One of the rounds, which was an armour piercing round, it came in the front of the Land Rover, it travelled along the top of the engine block. But when it came through the bulkhead, where your gears, levers and the whole lot are all there, it shed the jacket. The tungsten core shed its jacket, and the core went in between his legs and into the seat cushion. But the copper jacket caught him on the side of the leg, and it was like you got a butcher's knife, and just below the knee just went into the bone and all the way down and the meat just peeled away. So he bailed out. I could see that happening so I was up and out and [Tony Bracken] came along. There was no words spoken, the two of us just walked out the road ... We tried to make ourselves as small as possible, they were still banging away. When we got out close to the jeep, I think Tony shouted, 'Is there anyone there?' And Gerry Mitten lifts up his leg and he says,

'Look', he says, 'Look at me leg, look at me leg'. We went over and we got out our field dressings. Tony was binding up Gerry's leg and the whole lot, and he says, 'There's another fella in the back.' There wasn't a word from the back of the Land Rover ... He was looking after Gerry Mitten's leg so I had to go round and have a look, and there was no noise whatsoever coming from this Land Rover. I was dreading looking around to see. I looked in anyway and young McCarthy was there. 'Have they stopped?', he says, 'They hit us, you know, the bullets were coming in the front. I think Gerry is wounded.' ... And that was it. It was a small little incident in a week of incidents that didn't seem very significant, except for what they were at the time.

Jones on the necessity of UNIFIL's actions at the village of At Tiri (1:32:50):

Had it to be done, or should it have been left alone? Yeah, it had to be done. Had to be done. Because on later trips going out to At Tiri, armoured Sisu ambulance, bringing the doctor out there. All old people, all the young people gone. All the houses boarded up. We did right that day to keep them out ... We were always turning the other cheek, and then At Tiri happened. It was different then, and I think we saved lives. I won't be as dramatic as saying we took lives to save lives, it just happened that way. It was just a certain set of circumstances that caused people on both sides ... Don't forget one of the DFF was killed, and you say oh well we saved lives by killing this fella. No we didn't, we lost two more. Smallhorne and Barret.[26] We lost them over killing him ... I wasn't the same person when I came home ... I never really considered the medal mine, I always considered it for the lads that didn't come home ... You never told the people at home what was going on ... Even to this day, you just don't tell the family what goes on ... The people in the country have no idea what we did, or what we went through. I think that's part of it, of the soldier not bringing home his war stories.

Maria O'Donoghue on the initial attempts to integrate women into the Defence Forces:[27]

There was some uncertainty, even amongst ourselves, some uncertainty about what we'd be doing, what a career was going to look like in the Defence

Forces for women. What the opportunities were going to be for us. There wasn't huge clarity on that at the time. Even down to how we were going to be employed, what our status would be in terms of combat. At the time we were precluded from doing regimental duties, for example, even though we were trained in the weapons and that sort of thing. We were the same, allegedly, but definitely there was a difference in how we were treated and deployed. And I'm not saying that in an accusatory manner, I think it was just symptomatic of the uncertainty with which all of us were operating at the time. And in the absence of clarity, I think the hierarchy erred on the side of caution where we were concerned ... I think there was quite a bit that wasn't thought through. I'm conscious that it was a political decision for women to join the army. I don't know what the prevailing school of thought amongst the military hierarchy was at the time, but it was a political decision and, like always, the military swings up its arms and complies. But I think there was a new complexity about integrating women into the army, that maybe not everything was completely thought through ... I don't think I ever had a sense of it being something special or anything. When I look back on it now, I can really appreciate how at twenty-one, twenty-two years of age, it was a big deal to rock up into an all-male organization and expect that the circumstances would all be in place for things just to work seamlessly. We had to do a bit of figuring out as we went along ... The doors have been opening over the last forty-odd years. It felt slow at times, particularly in the early days when we were young and enthusiastic. But they have opened. As [Major General Maureen O'Brien] herself said in one of the interviews yesterday, the opportunities were there, and she took them.[28]

*In 1994 **Comdt Michael Walsh** was seconded to GOAL, an Irish NGO, with whom he worked as a logistics officer in Goma during the Rwandan genocide. Situated in the Democratic Republic of Congo, Goma is just a few miles from the border with Rwanda:*[29]

We arrived in ... and met Paul Keyes and Tom Boyce, two Irish officers, had just spent the day burying the dead ... and we said, how many? And they gave a conservative figure of two thousand ... Out to the camps the following

Members of the Army Ranger Wing on patrol in Chad while serving with EUFOR Chad/CAR, mounted in a Ford F350 special reconnaissance vehicle.

day, the camps were about four or five miles outside of Goma town, and it was horrific. Working, trying to put order on the place, and seeing the madness of it. I wasn't there five minutes and a nurse came to me and says to me 'Do you know how to put a butterfly drip in?' I said no. She said, 'I'll teach you once.' I remember saying to her 'Jesus I'll hurt the child.' She says to me 'He's going to fucking die anyway'... And I learned how to do it. I was the only one with small kids, and you learned very quickly how to do it ... That was one of our primary jobs that day, and then worked out we would go out collecting the dead. We all took our turn at that. And then found different jobs. And then sat down, and kind of realized, this is not working ... We know the army way, so we need to organize. We need someone to do transport, someone to do the operations side ... We needed to do what we

307

knew we were good at. So that's what we did, broke up the tasks that way ... At worst we were burying, our group, three and a half thousand in one day. Physically, three and a half thousand people. And the smell of that is something that would stick to you for the rest of your life. You got up in the morning and you stuck Tiger Balm up your nose. I was off the fags when I went out there. When I came home I was on eighty a day.

Flight Quarter Master Sergeant Tracey Walsh enlisted on 11 April 1994 at Gormanston Camp and trained with the first mixed female/male platoon in the Defence Forces, subsequently joining the Military Police. Walsh served overseas in Lebanon and Bosnia, later transferring to 2 Brigade HQ and subsequently to 3 Ops Wing in the Air Corps. Here she recalls her time in Lebanon in 1996:[30]

The first [peacekeeping] mission that I was on was in the Lebanon, that was from April to November 1996. I was stationed in Naqoura ... It was a multi-national company, it's amazing, you learn so much from dealing with other nationalities ... We arrived about a week after the Grapes of Wrath had occurred, the Israeli operations.[31] There was one or two of the Fijian soldiers that had been involved in it that we were working with, and to hear them talking about it, they'd gone through such a horrific experience. I remember we went up to Qana, there was a ceremony on and there were a few of us that were sent up to the ceremony, as I said it was only a week or so after, and where the ceremony was on was the graveyard ... While we were sitting there

a child came up, a little girl, and she was playing with me. She was maybe three or four. I had no Arabic or anything, I just got down on my knees and was playing with her. We were probably there for half an hour, joking and playing. Afterwards one of the local people came up to me and said, 'Thank you.' And I remember saying,

FQMS Tracey Walsh (*right*), with her sister Sgt Leona Walsh and Capt Eugene Mohan.

An Air Corps Agusta Westland AW139 flies over Emergency-era coastal identification sign No. 7 at Hawk Cliff, Dalkey, Co. Dublin. Restored by a local community group in 2019, this sign was one of eighty-three created as navigational aids for British and American pilots during the Emergency, and is one of the few that still survives.

'For what?' And he told me the little girl had lost all her family, that was the first time she had smiled since it happened. Bringing it home, that someone so small, three or four years old, and everything they knew in the world was gone. Their house was gone, their family was gone … That is something that will always stay with me. I can always see that smile, I can always see her face smiling.

Between February 2008 and December 2010, the Defence Forces deployed the Army Ranger Wing and 97, 98, 99, 100, 101 and 102 Infantry Battalions with EU and UN-led peacekeeping missions to Chad and the Central African Republic (EUFOR Chad/ CAR & MINURCAT). **Fr Jeremiah 'Jerry' Carroll,** *chaplain to the Air Corps, recalls an incident when Irish troops protecting a refugee camp were confronted by the Janjaweed militia:*[32]

309

Members of 91 Infantry Battalion in a Panhard AML 90 armoured car while on duty with the United Nations Mission in Liberia (UNMIL) in July 2004. The Irish contingent provided UNMIL's Quick Reaction Force (QRF).

When they discovered that they couldn't get into the refugee camp, I don't think they were expecting to find us there, their intelligence wasn't much better than ours. They were as surprised to find us there as we were to find them outside our camp that afternoon. We were told they were two days away to the north of us. They had pointed their weapons in our direction. I can remember lying beside a machine gunner, who was there with a GPMG [general purpose machine gun], from Finner Camp. And sweat rolling down his eye, his left cheek, and just lying beside him just handed him a bottle of water, and chatting away to him. And he chatted with me with one eye open, and the other eye looking through the range finder of his GPMG, he would not take it off his target. And he spoke to me with his right cheek hugging the butt of the GPMG. And just waiting for the word, he had his earpiece on, just waiting for the word. Sitting in the mortar nest too afterwards with the guys, we had 81mm rounds there ... I remember the sergeant asking me to sit outside the sandbags, his left hand on his left earpiece, waiting for the word, getting orders and details and co-ordinates. There was a few technicals out there, one with an anti-aircraft gun pointing in our direction, and he'd been given the co-ordinates for that. His right-hand finger was up, he just told the guys they had to prepare the round and the guys had it over the muzzle of the mortar, ready to fire. All they'd to do was drop it. That went on, we stood there for at least a good minute, felt like an hour. All he had to do was drop the finger. That's all he needed to do, and that mortar would have landed in the front seat of the technical outside. It didn't come to pass. They decided to reverse, do a U-turn, and went back off into the bush.

Carroll reflects on his personal experience of working as a chaplain with the Defence Forces:[33]

People often ask me as a priest, how do you justify your calling as a priest, and spend your time as a military chaplain in war zones and that's associated with destruction? I explain to the guys I belong now, I'm an ordained missioner, it's my life to be a missionary. I belong now to what is probably the biggest missionary organization to leave the shores of this land, and it is the Irish Defence Forces, and they do terrific work. They do wonderful work, quietly but very professionally, by way of peacekeeping. And if there's no peace to be kept, they will make it, as in the case of Chad. And they do it very, very well, quite often in very dangerous, very testing, very demanding circumstances, without the use of weapons but with the tongue. They're great at talking things down, they do it very, very well, and it's good to be part of that.

Chief Petty Officer Ruairí de Barra joined the Naval Service in 1998, following in the footsteps of his father and of three brothers who had joined the Defence Forces before him. Here he talks about the demands of the job when posted to a ship:[34]

When you're attached to a ship, your job doesn't really change whether you're at sea or not. When you're on the ship and you're posted to a ship, it's constant. The ship is the biggest thing in your life, it's constant ... your phone is never off, you're always on call ... When you're on the base, when you're not attached to a ship, it's a great relief, because you have more of a chance of finishing at five or six o'clock in the evening than you would on a ship. On a ship your day doesn't end, you know. You certainly don't leave it at work, you must take it home. And I don't just mean physically work, but you take the ship home with you in your head ... There's no budget for maintenance, it's as if it doesn't come up on the radar. The maintenance that we do in the Naval Service, it's breakdown maintenance. We run the items into the ground. We have never funded it properly, we will never fund it properly, all we care about is sea days. We certainly don't care about the individuals or the machinery.

De Barra *recalls serving aboard LÉ* Eithne *when it was deployed to the Mediterranean, in May 2015, as part of Operation Pontus, a bilateral mission with Italy to rescue refugees attempting to cross the Mediterranean Sea. The mission served a precursor to the Naval Service's participation in EUNAVFOR-Med Operation Sophia, which continued until 2019.*[35]

Eithne was at sea, and I was on leave ... There'd been a horrible tragedy just a couple of weeks before where 800 people had drowned in one incident, from a ship ... On Monday morning they called a meeting on *Eithne*. They assembled the heads of department, which is the senior NCOs and the officers, and they said, 'We're leaving for Libya on the Friday, who's coming?' Everyone put up their hand ... We had to wait for a memorandum of understanding from the Italians, that allowed me to get some extra work done. I designed a freshwater system for the migrants on the decks. We arranged to take some stores for how to deal with bodily waste ... We were preparing as best we could, but you can't prepare for the unknown. And then the unknown happened, which is coming across your first migrant vessels, realizing that the numbers they're calling out over the radios are absolute nonsense ... seeing what 350 people look like on the flight deck of LÉ *Eithne*, from one vessel. Seeing the injuries that they have. Crush injuries, burns, chemical burns ...

You come up on the boat and you can see the people in the darkness. You see their heat signatures on the infrared. You instantly realize that the number is hokey that you've just been given. And it proceeded and it went on. And the numbers started growing. You had 50, 75, 100 ... the numbers are climbing and climbing, the operation is going on and I was going, sweet mother of God, what are we up on top of here ... By the time we were finished we were approaching 3,500 people, 63 days later. The numbers were staggering. The nationalities were staggering. The range of people, where they came from, the range of backgrounds. From an eighty-seven-year-old to a two-week-old baby. Asked the man what in God's name are you moving with the two-week-old baby? And he was a Syrian man and he said, 'They'll butcher us, they're lunatics. They're cutting people's heads off. I have to go, my brother has a shop in Germany and I've sent my money to him and we'll get there and be alright.'

De Barra on the effect of the mission on the crew of LÉ Eithne:[36]
You discuss it in the military way … And then as an NCO you move round over the course of the day when people are quiet and try to take them aside, and try to see how they're feeling. And what I've always found is that when the chips are down, you'll have known who your good operators are. When push comes to shove, they push back. And you'll see those people come to the fore again, and again, and again. And the drill grounds, the empty vessels, you'll see them crumble. And that's when you have to go in and you have to make sure that they're ok. Because they're part of ship's company too.

On 28 June 2015 the LÉ *Eithne* rescued 593 refugees from six separate craft. Originally present in the Mediterranean under Operation Pontus, a bilateral agreement with Italy, the Naval Service later joined the EUNAVFOR-Med Operation Sophia. Between 2015 and 2019, the Naval Service rescued more than 18,000 refugees in the Mediterranean. Operation Sophia was drastically scaled back in 2019, depriving the Naval Service of a major operational focus.

De Barra *on the humanitarian imperative of the mission in the Mediterranean:*[37]
These [people] are traumatized, they're in tatters. You'd be a stone not to feel for them. How callous the people that say let them drown. The fucking assholes. You can't. The only thing required for evil to prosper is for good men to do nothing ... You would have to wonder what is wrong with the world that we would allow this situation to occur.

Maria O'Donoghue *on the future of women in the Defence Forces:*[38]
I think the number is 6 per cent of the Defence Forces now is made up of women, I think that's great progress. I think there's still opportunity for more, and I think as military organizations become more technical, less about brute force and physical size, et cetera, and more technology enabled, that there's an opportunity for women to be much more integrated and to occupy a much higher percentage of the establishment of the military ... I think it's fantastic when I see how well women are represented on overseas tours. I think it's absolutely great that now it's just standard, whereas back at the time we had to agitate a bit and make a bit of a pain out of ourselves in order to do that. Actually, even making a pain out of ourselves didn't really make much difference a lot of the time. So it's great to see that.

Major General Maureen O'Brien, on the day of her promotion to the rank of Major General and appointment as Deputy Military Adviser to the UN Under Secretary General for Peace Operations, 25 May 2021. O'Brien joined the Defence Forces as a cadet in 1981 and was the first woman to attain the rank of Major General, the second highest in the Defence Forces. O'Brien had previously been the first woman promoted to the rank of Lt Col (2011) and to be appointed Officer Commanding an infantry battalion (27 Inf Battalion, 2012).

National Army soldiers, possibly on board the *Lady Wicklow* or the *Arvonia*, en route either to Fenit or to Passage West in August 1922. One soldier appears to be writing a letter or a report. The soldier looking directly at the camera stands out not just for his smile, but also because he is not wearing an army hat.

A group of National Army soldiers enjoy a break from duty and a hot drink from a mobile canteen, *c*. August 1922. The soldier from the previous photograph taken on board a ship, who had been smiling broadly, here is far more subdued.

National Army soldiers and officers on board the *Arvonia*, en route to Passage West in August 1922. Stencilling on the side of the Lancia armoured car in the background indicates that it is from the National Army's General Headquarters, then located in Portobello Barracks. Two soldiers, one holding a cup of tea and with what appear to be driving goggles on his hat, sit on a Rolls Royce armoured car (1920 pattern), named 'The Manager'. Its Vickers .303 inch machine gun, with shield plating, can be seen beneath the name. Fourteen armoured Rolls Royce were received from British forces in 1922 and 1923, one of which was captured and destroyed by the anti-Treaty IRA. The final Rolls Royce 'Whippet' (as they were known) was withdrawn from service in 1954.

General Richard Mulcahy, far left, leans down to speak to his eldest son, Risteárd. The photo was taken as the Signals Corps was exercising in the fields behind Lissenfield House, Rathmines, the Mulcahy family home. Printed in the 19 May 1923 issue of *An tÓglách*.

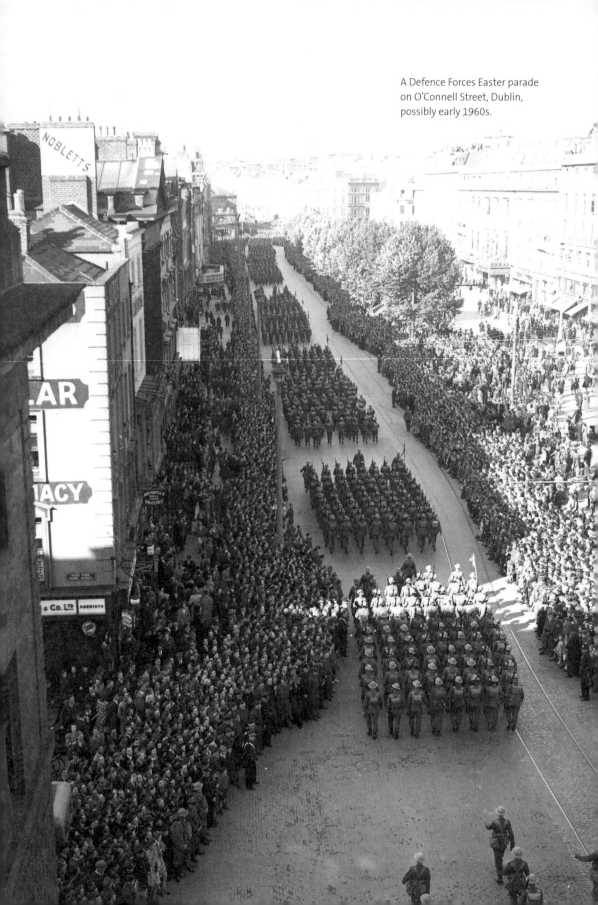

A Defence Forces Easter parade
on O'Connell Street, Dublin,
possibly early 1960s.

APPENDICES

Commanders in Chief and Chiefs of Staff, 1919–2022

The President of Ireland, an office established by the 1937 Constitution, is the Supreme Commander of the Defence Forces. Though all officers are commissioned by the President, the role is largely ceremonial and military command of the Defence Forces is exercised by the government through the Minister for Defence. At time of writing the Chief of Staff serves as the principal military adviser to the Minister for Defence, and is responsible for supporting the Minister in the discharge of his command, but does not exercise command responsibility. Changes to the command and control structure of the Defence Forces are widely anticipated in the wake of the report of the Commission on the Defence Forces (published in 2022).

In the list below, DSM denotes a recipient of An Bonn Seirbhíse Dearscna (the Distinguished Service Medal). The medal was introduced on 18 February 1964 and may be awarded to officers, non-commissioned officers and privates of the Defence Forces, and to members of the Army Nursing Service and Chaplaincy Service, in recognition of individual or associated acts of bravery, courage, leadership, resourcefulness or devotion to duty (other than any such acts or duty performed on war service) arising out of, or associated with, service in the Defence Forces and not meriting An Bonn Míleata Calmachta (Military Medal for Gallantry). For a list of recipients of An Bonn Míleata Calmachta, currently the highest honour in the Defence Forces, see below. A comprehensive guide to all medals issued since 1922 is found in *Medals of the Irish Defence Forces* (Defence Forces Printing Press, 1st ed., 2010).

Commander in Chief
General Michael Collins: 13 July 1922 – 22 August 1922
General Richard Mulcahy: 23 August 1922 – 3 August 1923

Inspector General and General Officer Commanding the Forces
General Eoin O'Duffy: 10 March 1924 – 30 September 1924

Chief of Staff

General Richard Mulcahy (Volunteers/Irish Republican Army): December 1917/ January 1918 – January 1922

General Eoin O'Duffy: February 1922 – July 1922

General Richard Mulcahy: July 1922 – August 1922

General Seán Mac Mahon: August 1922 – March 1924

Lieutenant General Peadar MacMahon: March 1924 – March 1927

Lieutenant General Daniel Hogan: March 1927 – February 1929

Lieutenant General Seán Mac Eoin: February 1929 – June 1929

Major General Joseph Sweeney: June 1929 – October 1931

Lieutenant General Michael Brennan: October 1931 – January 1940

Lieutenant General Daniel McKenna: January 1940 – January 1949

Lieutenant General Liam A. Archer: January 1949 – January 1952

Major General Liam S. Egan: January 1952 – December 1954

Lieutenant General Patrick A. Mulcahy: January 1955 – December 1959

Lieutenant General Seán Mac Eoin: January 1960 – December 1960 (appointed ONUC Force Commander, January 1961 – March 1962)

Lieutenant General Seán Collins-Powell: January 1961 – March 1962

Lieutenant General Seán Mac Eoin DSM: April 1962 – March 1971

Major General Patrick J. Delaney: April 1971 – July 1971

Major General Thomas L. O'Carroll: July 1971 – July 1976

Lieutenant General Carl O'Sullivan DSM: July 1976 – June 1981

Lieutenant General Louis Hogan DSM: June 1981 – April 1984

Lieutenant General Gerald O'Sullivan DSM: April 1984 – February 1986

Lieutenant General Tadhg O'Neill DSM: February 1986 – October 1989

Lieutenant General James Parker DSM: October 1989 – April 1992

Lieutenant General Noel Bergin DSM: April 1992 – December 1994

Lieutenant General Gerald McMahon DSM: February 1995 – August 1998

Lieutenant General David Stapleton DSM: August 1998 – September 2000

Lieutenant General Colm Mangan DSM: September 2000 – February 2004

Lieutenant General James Sreenan DSM: February 2004 – June 2007

Lieutenant General Dermot Earley DSM: June 2007 – June 2010

Lieutenant General Seán McCann DSM: June 2010 – August 2013

Lieutenant General Conor O'Boyle DSM: August 2013 – September 2015

Vice Admiral Mark Mellett DSM: September 2015 – September 2021

Lieutenant General Seán Clancy: September 2021 – present

Overseas Missions, 1958–2022

The Defence Forces have participated in UN-mandated peacekeeping and peace enforcement missions in every year since 1958, a commitment unmatched by any other member of the UN. The level of Ireland's commitment to the missions listed below at any one time has ranged from a single officer to a battalion with supporting services. Personnel have also been deployed on secondment in support of humanitarian operations run by non-governmental organizations (NGOs).

Current Missions	Deployment Commenced	Completed Tours to Date (as of April 2021)*
United Nations Truce Supervision Organization(UNTSO)	December 1958	596
United Nations Interim Force In Lebanon (UNIFIL)	May 1978	38,218
United Nations Headquarters, New York (UNNY)	November 1978	28
Organization for Security and Co-operation in Europe (OSCE, Vienna)	January 1984	48
United Nations Disengagement Observer Force (UNDOF)	September 1991	2,352
Kosovo Force (KFOR)	June 1999	2,866
Common Security & Defence Policy/ Partnership for Peace (CSDP/PfP, Brussels)	January 2000	72
European Union Military Staff (EUMS Brussels)	March 2001	95
United Nations Observer Mission in Congo (MONUSCO)	June 2001	106
European Union Force in Bosnia & Herzegovina (EUFOR BiH)	December 2004	534
European Union Training Mission, Mali (EUTM (Mali))	March 2013	253

* Figures for completed tours, both for current and past missions, date from April 2021 and are extracted from the report of the Commission on the Defence Forces (Dublin, 2022), p. 181. Every effort has been made to verify these figures, but due to the nature of overseas deployments, changes in the names and bodies exercising operational control of different missions, and gaps in the records, these figures should not be taken as definitive. The Defence Forces' records indicate that its personnel have completed more than 74,000 overseas tours of duty since 1958.

Current Missions	Deployment Commenced	Completed Tours to Date (as of April 2021)
United Nations Multidimensional Integrated Stabilization Mission in Mali (MINUSMA)	September 2019	56
EU NAVFOR Med Irini	April 2020	6
Total		**45,230**

Past Missions	Deployment Commenced	Deployment Ceased	Tours Completed
United Nations Observer Group in Lebanon (UNOGIL)	June 1958	December 1958	50
Opération des Nations Unies au Congo (ONUC)	July 1960	June 1964	6,191
United Nations Temporary Executive Authority (UNTEA)	August 1962	October 1962	2
United Nations Force in Cyprus (UNFICYP)	March 1964	May 2005	9,655
United Nations India Pakistan Observation Mission (UNIPOM)	September 1965	March 1966	14
Second United Nations Emergency Force (UNEF II)	October 1973	September 1974	573
United Nations Inspection Teams (UNTSO Secondments, Tehran)	June 1984	July 1988	9
United Nations Military Observer Group in India and Pakistan (UNMOGIP)	September 1987	June 1992	2
United Nations Relief and Work Agency (UNRWA)	February 1988	June 1992	2
United Nations Good Offices Mission in Afghanistan and Pakistan (UNGOMAP)	April 1988	March 1990	8
United Nations Iran-Iraq Military Observer Group (UNIIMOG)	August 1988	March 1991	177

Past Missions	Deployment Commenced	Deployment Ceased	Tours Completed
United Nations Transition Assistance Group (UNTAG)	March 1989	April 1990	20
United Nations Observer Group in Central America (ONUCA)	December 1989	January 1992	57
Office of the Secretary General in Afghanistan and Pakistan (OSGAP)	March 1990	December 1994	5
Second United Nations Angola Verification Mission (UNAVEM II)	July 1991	September 1993	18
European Union Monitoring Mission (EUMM Yugoslavia)	July 1991	December 2007	223
United Nations Mission for the Referendum in Western Sahara (MINURSO)	September 1991	July 2021	208
United Nations Advance Mission in Cambodia (UNAMIC)	November 1991	March 1992	2
United Nations Military Liaison Office, Yugoslavia (UNMLO Y)	January 1992	April 1992	7
United Nations Observer Mission in El Salvador (ONUSAL)	January 1992	May 1994	6
United Nations Transitional Authority in Cambodia (UNTAC)	March 1992	November 1993	36
United Nations Protection Force (UNPROFOR)	March 1992	February 1996	29
United Nations Iraq-Kuwait Observer Mission (UNIKOM)	April 1992	March 2003	69
United Nations High Commission for Refugees, Yugoslavia (UNHCR Y)	December 1992	March 1993	4
Second United Nations Operations in Somalia (UNOSOM II)	August 1993	January 1995	177
European Union Election Unit in South Africa (EUNELSA)	January 1994	May 1994	2

Past Missions	Deployment Commenced	Deployment Ceased	Tours Completed
Organization for Security and Co-operation in Europe (OSCE Georgia)	April 1994	September 2008	23
Irish Rwandan Support Group (IRSG RWA)	August 1994	December 1994	39
United Nations Mission in Haiti (UNMIH)	September 1994	March 1996	6
International Conference on the Former Yugoslavia (ICFY)	October 1994	March 1996	5
United Nations Office of the Secretary-General to Afghanistan (OSGA)	December 1994	July 1996	2
Organization for Security and Co-operation in Europe (OSCE Bosnia)	January 1996	September 2017	56
United Nations Transitional Authority in Eastern Slavonia (UNTAES)	February 1996	January 1998	10
United Nations Preventive Deployment Force (UNPREDEP)	February 1996	February 1999	8
United Nations Military Observer Mission in Prevlaka (UNMOP)	February 1996	December 1999	10
United Nations Special Mission to Afghanistan (UNSMA)	July 1996	October 1999	3
United Nations Special Commission (UNSCOM)	September 1996	March 2003	5
Stabilization Force (SFOR BiH)	January 1997	December 2004	636
Organization for Security and Co-operation in Europe (OSCE Albania)	January 1997	January 2008	14
Organization for Security and Co-operation in Europe (OSCE Croatia)	January 1998	April 2016	24

Past Missions	Deployment Commenced	Deployment Ceased	Tours Completed
Organization for Security and Co-operation in Europe (OSCE Kosovo)	December 1998	April 2016	12
1st Irish Honduras Support Group (IHSG)	January 1999	May 1999	27
United Nations Missions in East Timor (UNAMET/INTERFET/ UNTAET/UNMISET)	June 1999	May 2004	318
United Nations Interim Mission in Kosovo (UNMIK)	July 1999	April 2009	20
2nd Irish Honduras Support Group (IHSG)	January 2000	February 2000	15
Organization for Security and Co-operation in Europe (OSCE Yugoslavia)	January 2001	January 2008	8
3rd Irish Honduras Support Group (IHSG)	January 2001	February 2001	16
Organization for Security and Co-operation in Europe (OSCE Former Yugoslav Republic of Macedonia)	July 2001	December 2005	5
United Nations Mission in Ethiopia and Eritrea (UNMEE)	November 2001	June 2003	630
International Security Assistance Force, Afghanistan (ISAF)	January 2002	December 2014	196
United Nations Mission in Côte d'Ivoire (MINUCI)	June 2003	June 2004	8
Operation Artemis, Democratic Republic of Congo	July 2003	September 2003	19
United Nations Military in Liberia (UNMIL)	November 2003	January 2008	2,746
United Nations Operation in Côte d'Ivoire (UNOCI)	June 2004	March 2017	38

Past Missions	Deployment Commenced	Deployment Ceased	Tours Completed
African Union Mission in Sudan (AMIS, Darfur)	July 2004	December 2007	20
United Nations Joint Logistics Centre (UNJLC)	January 2005	May 2005	5
Tsunami disaster relief, Indonesia	January 2005	December 2006	3
European Union Force, DR Congo (EUFOR Congo)	June 2006	January 2007	7
KFOR, Framework Nation Head-quarters	August 2007	July 2008	58
EU Force Chad/Central African Republic (EUFOR Chad/CAR)	October 2007	March 2009	1,677
United Nations Mission in the Central African Republic and Chad (MINURCAT)	March 2009	December 2010	1,684
EU NAVFOR Atalanta	June 2009	December 2009	2
European Union Training Mission, Somalia (EUTM, Somalia)	April 2010	April 2014	42
United Nations Supervision Mission in Syria (UNSMIS)	May 2012	August 2012	6
United Nations Mine Action Service (UNMAS)	August 2013	September 2014	15
Resolute Support Mission (RSM), Afghanistan	January 2015	March 2016	14
EU NVAFOR MED SOPHIA	October 2017	April 2020	277
Total			**26,255**

An Bonn Míleata Calmachta
(Military Medal for Gallantry)

An Bonn Míleata Calmachta (Military Medal for Gallantry) was introduced in 1944 and is the highest honour that can be bestowed on the personnel of the Defence Forces. It may be awarded to officers, non-commissioned officers, and privates of the Defence Forces, and to members of the Army Nursing Service and the Chaplaincy Service, in recognition of the performance of any act of exceptional bravery or gallantry (other than one performed on war service) arising out of, or associated with, military service and involving risk to life and limb.

There are three classes associated with the medal:

a)   with Honour
b)   with Distinction
c)   with Merit

Recipients

Trooper Anthony Browne: ONUC (Congo), with Distinction

Captain Adrian Ainsworth: UNIFIL (Lebanon), with Distinction

Lieutenant Anthony Bracken: UNIFIL (Lebanon), with Distinction

Corporal Michael Jones: UNIFIL (Lebanon), with Distinction

Private Michael John Daly: UNIFIL (Lebanon), with Distinction

Commandant Michael Lynch: UNIFIL (Lebanon), with Distinction

Private Paul Coventry: UNIFIL (Lebanon), with Merit

Private Thomas Metcalfe: Ireland, with Merit

Ministers for Defence, 1919–2022

Richard Mulcahy: 22 January 1919 – 1 April 1919

Cathal Brugha: 2 April 1919 – 9 January 1922

Richard Mulcahy: 10 January 1922 – 19 March 1924

William T. Cosgrave: 20 March 1924 – 20 November 1924 (President of the Executive Council and Minister for Defence)

Peter Hughes: 21 November 1924 – 23 June 1927

Desmond FitzGerald: 23 June 1927 – 9 March 1932 (W.T. Cosgrave, President of the Executive Council, served as acting Minister from 26 April to 8 September 1927 due to Fitzgerald's illness)

Frank Aiken: 9 March 1932 – 8 September 1939

Oscar Traynor: 8 September 1939 – 18 February 1948

Thomas O'Higgins: 18 February 1948 – 7 March 1951

General Seán Mac Eoin: 7 March 1951 – 14 June 1951

Oscar Traynor, 14 June 1951 – 2 June 1954

General Seán Mac Eoin: 2 June 1954 – 20 March 1957

Kevin Boland: 20 March 1957 – 12 October 1961

Gerald Bartley: 12 October 1961 – 21 April 1965

Michael Hilliard: 21 April 1965 – 2 July 1969

James Gibbons: 2 July 1969 – 8 May 1970

Jerry Cronin: 9 May 1970 – 14 March 1973

Patrick Donegan: 15 March 1973 – 1 December 1976

Liam Cosgrave: 2 December 1976 – 16 December 1976 (Taoiseach and Minister for Defence)

Oliver J. Flanagan: 16 December 1976 – 5 July 1977

Robert Molloy: 5 July 1977 – 12 December 1979

Pádraig Faulkner: 12 December 1979 – 15 October 1980

Sylvester Barrett: 16 October 1980 – 30 June 1981

James Tully: 30 June 1981 – 9 March 1982

Patrick Power: 9 March 1982 – 14 December 1982

Patrick Cooney: 14 December 1982 – 14 February 1986

Patrick O'Toole: 14 February 1986 – 10 March 1987

Michael Noonan: 10 March 1987 – 12 July 1989

Brian Lenihan: 12 July 1989 – 31 October 1990 (Tánaiste and Minister for Defence)

Charles Haughey: 1 November 1990 – 5 February 1991 (Taoiseach and Minister for Defence)

Brendan Daly: 5 February 1991 – 14 November 1991

Vincent Brady: 14 November 1991 – 11 February 1992

John Wilson: 11 February 1992 – 12 January 1993 (Tánaiste and Minister for Defence)

David Andrews: 12 January 1993 – 15 December 1994 (Minister for Defence and the Marine)

Hugh Coveney: 15 December 1994 – 23 May 1995 (Minister for Defence and the Marine)

Seán Barrett: 23 May 1995 – 26 June 1997 (Minister for Defence and the Marine)

David Andrews: 26 June 1997 – 8 October 1997

Michael Smith: 8 October 1997 – 29 September 2004

Willie O'Dea: 29 September 2004 – 18 February 2010

Brian Cowen: 18 February 2010 – 23 March 2010 (Taoiseach and Minister for Defence)

Tony Killeen: 23 March 2010 – 20 January 2011

Éamon Ó Cuív: 20 January 2011 – 9 March 2011 (Minister for Defence, for Social Protection, and for the Environment, Heritage and Local Government)

Alan Shatter: 9 March 2011 – 7 May 2014 (Minister for Defence, and for Justice and Equality)

Enda Kenny: 7 May 2014 – 11 July 2014 (Taoiseach and Minister for Defence)

Simon Coveney: 11 July 2014 – 6 May 2016 (Minister for Defence, and for Agriculture, Food and the Marine)

Paul Kehoe: May 2016 – 27 June 2020 (Minister of State with responsibility for Defence)

Enda Kenny: 6 May 2016 – 14 June 2017 (Taoiseach and Minister for Defence)

Leo Varadkar: 14 June 2017 – 27 June 2020 (Taoiseach and Minister for Defence)

Simon Coveney: 27 June 2020 – present (Minister for Defence, and for Foreign Affairs)

Secretaries and Secretaries General, Department of Defence, 1922–2022

Cornelius B. O'Connor (Acting Secretary): 4 August 1922 – 30 June 1923

Cornelius B. O'Connor: 1 July 1923 – 30 March 1927

Lt Gen Peadar MacMahon: 31 March 1927 – 30 March 1958

Hugh C. Brady: 31 March 1958 – 5 June 1965

Stiofán Ó Cearnaigh: 6 June 1965 – 30 June 1975

Padraig Ó Murchú: 1 July 1975 – 30 April 1977

Michael P. Healy: 1 May 1977 – 1 June 1981

Richard O'Sullivan: 2 June 1981 – 18 March 1985

Michael J. Somers: 28 March 1985 – 21 May 1987

Gerard Scully: 22 May 1987 – 19 January 1991

Seán Ó Brosnacháin: 20 January 1991 – 5 June 1995

David J. O'Callaghan: 6 June 1995 – 30 September 2004

Michael Howard: 1 October 2004 – 1 October 2013

Maurice Quinn: 2 October 2013 – 23 August 2020

Jacqui McCrum: 24 August 2020 – present

Two Eastern Command personnel enjoy a light-hearted moment with an accordion while sitting on a BSA M20 motorcycle. The BSA M20 was first introduced to the Defence Forces in 1939; this photo probably dates from the early 1960s.

NOTES

References are provided for direct quotations, and for statistics provided in later chapters. For an overview of other sources consulted, see the Bibliographical Note below.

Introduction

1   *An tÓglách*, 16 Dec. 1921.
2   *An tÓglách*, 25 Apr. 1922.

Chapter 1 – 1922–3: Raising the National Army

1   *An tÓglách*, 7 Apr. 1923. Beggars Bush was indeed the first barracks to be handed over to the National Army, though the British Army had begun handing over barracks to IRA units from the middle of January.
2   *An tÓglách*, 28 Oct. 1922.
3   *Dáil Debates*, vol. T, cols. 423–4 (10 Jan. 1922).
4   Undated account by J.J. O'Connell on his role in setting up the National Army, and events leading up to the Civil War (National Library of Ireland, MS 22,126/2).
5   *An tÓglách*, 13 Jan. 1922.
6   *Dáil Debates*, vol. S2, col. 253 (26 Apr. 1922).
7   *An tÓglách*, 31 Mar. 1922.
8   *Freeman's Journal*, 7 July 1922.
9   *Dáil Debates*, vol. 1, col. 2433 (29 Nov. 1922). See also IE/MA/DOD/A/01278; IE/MA DOD/A /07460; IE/MA/DOD/A/07535; Lisa Godson, 'Wearing the Green: uniforms, collectivity and authority (25 May 1922)' in Darragh Gannon and Fearghal McGarry (eds), *Ireland 1922: independence, partition, civil war* (Dublin, 2022), pp 141–50.
10 General Order No. 5, July 1922 (IE/MA/CW/ OPS/1/1/2).
11 Richard Mulcahy's statement to the Army Inquiry Committee, 29 Apr. 1924 (IE/MA/ AMTY/3/21).
12 For Army appointments, including official notices of the appointment of the War Council and Army Council, see NAI, TAOIS/3/1318. See also IE/MA/AMTY/3/21; UCDA, P7/ B/177/161–177. For a comprehensive overview of the development of the National Army's administrative structures during the Civil War, see Patrick Long, 'Organization and development of the pro-Treaty forces, 1922– 1924', *Irish Sword*, 20 (Winter 1997), pp 308–30.
13 Ministry of Finance memo, 27 May 1922 (IE/ MA/DOD/A/6852).

14 Thomas Gorman to Richard Mulcahy, 2 Sept. 1922 (IEMA/DOD/A/6852).
15 Richard Mulcahy to W.T. Cosgrave, 28 Mar. 1923, second letter (IE/MA/AMTY/3/21).
16 Donald Barrett of the anti-Treaty Cork No. 1 Brigade, referring to the landing of National Army troops at Passage West on 7 August 1922. Quoted in Michael Hopkinson, *Green against green: the Irish Civil War* (Dublin, 1988), p. 164.
17 Richard Mulcahy to Seán Mac Mahon, 26 Sept. 1922 (IE/MA/DOD/A/7365). The four motor launches were purchased for £4,400. ML–1 and ML–3 were valued at £850 for insurance purposes.
18 Statement by Seán Mac Mahon to the Army Inquiry Committee, 6 May 1924 (IE/MA/AMTY /3/27).
19 James Moore to Hubert Cook, 9 Aug. 1922 (Commissioners of Irish Lights Archive, WR/ 2/5).
20 Minutes of a meeting held at Beggars Bush Barracks, 23 Mar. 1922 (IE/MA/DOD/A/12004).
21 Statement by Cahir Davitt to the Army Inquiry Committee, 24 Apr. 1924 (IE/MA/AMTY/3/ 60).
22 *Dáil Debates*, vol. 2, col. 49 (8 Dec. 1922). These four executions were carried out as reprisals for the murder, on 7 December, of Seán Hales. A TD for West Cork, Hales was a veteran of the IRA who had briefly been commissioned as a General in the National Army before concentrating on his political career. None of the four men executed by the state were afforded trials.
23 Richard Mulcahy to W.T. Cosgrave, 28 Mar. 1923, second letter (IE/MA/AMTY/3/21).
24 Seán Mac Eoin to Richard Mulcahy, 4 Sept. 1922 (UCDA, P7/B/73).
25 Emmet Dalton to Richard Mulcahy, 19 Sept. 1922 (UCDA, P7/B/73).
26 Secret and confidential report re Kenmare case, Cahir Davitt to Gearóid O'Sullivan, 3 July 1923 (IE/MA/AMTY/3/60). Davitt was appointed Judge Advocate General in August 1922.
27 Statement by Cahir Davitt to the Army Inquiry Committee, 24 Apr. 1924 (IE/MA/AMTY/ 3/60).
28 Richard Mulcahy's message to the Army (*An tÓglách*, 24 Feb. 1923).

29 James Langton, *The forgotten fallen: National Army soldiers who died during the Irish Civil War* (Dublin, 2019).
30 *An tÓglách*, 23 Feb. 1923.

Specialist Corps of the Civil War
1 Patrick Hogan to Richard Mulcahy, 22 Dec. 1922 (NAI, TSCH/3/S1943).
2 IE/MA/CW/OPS/07/16.
3 Kevin O'Higgins to the Army Inquiry Committee, 12 Apr. 1924 (IE/MA/AMTY/3/55).
4 *An tÓglách*, 21 Apr. 1923.

Chapter 2 – 1923–32: Reorganization, Professionalization and Retrenchment
1 *Dáil Debates*, vol. 4, col. 1296 (24 July 1923).
2 See, for example, Paul Hegarty, 'Joint Force Command: the need for change', *Defence Forces Review* (2019), pp 103–4. As of time of writing, legislation is in preparation to bring command and control structures in line with international best practise, as recommended by the Commission on the Defence Forces, which reported its findings to the government in 2022.
3 Quotation from the preamble to the Indemnity Act, 1923 (No. 31 of 1923).
4 Previous estimates for the number of men enlisted in the National Army at the end of the Civil War have been as high as 60,000. Richard Mulcahy gave a figure of 'approximately 52,000' for the Army's strength in April 1923 (IE/MA/AMTY/3/21).
5 Draft manuscript letter by Seán Mac Eoin, *c.*Dec. 1923 (UCDA, P151/240).
6 'History of events', 13 Sept. 1923 (IE/MA/AMTY/2/2).
7 'Document', June 1923 (IE/MA/AMTY/2/2). Emphasis in original.
8 Undated note by Mulcahy, *c.*Dec 1923–Mar. 1924 (UCDA, P7/B/261).
9 *Dáil Debates*, vol. 6, col. 1897 (11 Mar. 1924).
10 *Irish Times*, 20 Mar. 1924.
11 Seán Mac Mahon's statement to the Army Inquiry Committee, 6 May 1924 (IE/MA/AMTY/3/27). Mac Mahon was the only one of the three officers to resume his commission after the committee's work was concluded, but was not reappointed as Chief of Staff. He resigned from the Army in 1927 due to ill health.
12 *Report of the Army Enquiry Committee* (Stationery Office, June 1924).
13 *Dáil Debates*, vol. 7, cols. 3110, 3150 (26 June 1924).

14 'Memorandum on the development of the forces in the period 1923–1927', *c.*1927 (IE/MA/HS/A/876).
15 Eoin O'Duffy to the Executive Council, Report no. 11, 30 Sept. 1924 (IE/MA/CREC/6).
16 Joseph Vize to Richard Mulcahy, 22 May 1923 (IE/MA/DOD/A/7635). It is possible that the Board of Works were disgruntled with the use of external engineering consultants to advise on the refitting of the trawlers. Correspondence from these consultants to General Seán Mac Mahon in May 1923 referred to the Board of Works' proposals for equipping the trawlers as 'quite absurd' (ibid.).
17 Richard Mulcahy to Executive Council, 25 Sept. 1923 (IE/MA/DOD/A/7635).
18 Seán Mac Mahon to Richard Mulcahy, 15 Nov. 1923 (IE/MA/DOD/A/10023).
19 Alternative scheme of army organisation, 20 Dec. 1923 (IE/MA/DOD/A/11803).
20 'Memorandum on the development of the Force in the period 1923–1927', *c.*1927 (IE/MA/HS/A/876).
21 Report of the Army Organization Board, July 1926, pp 25–5 (IE/MA/AOB/Box 1).
22 Joseph Sweeney to Minister for Defence, [30 Sept.] 1929 (IE/MA/CREC/16).
23 Report of the Army Organization Board, July 1926 (IE/MA/AOB, Box 1).
24 'Defence policy memorandum', 13 Nov. 1925 (NAI, DT S4541).
25 Report of the Army Organization Board, July 1926 (IE/MA/AOB/Box 1).
26 Hugo MacNeill to Seán Mac Eoin, 21 July 1926 (UCDA, P151/314).
27 Daniel Hogan to Desmond FitzGerald, 'Confidential quarterly report No. 5', [June] 1928 (IE/MA/CREC/ 16).
28 Peadar MacMahon to Peter Hughes, 15 Oct. 1925 (IE/MA/CREC/7).
29 Memo by Capt O'Sullivan, *c.*Nov. 1927 (IE/MA/COD/3). Emphasis in original.
30 Extract from the constitution of the National Defence Association (*An tÓglách*, Aug. 1929).
31 Council of Defence minutes, 4 Jan. 1930 (IE/MA/COD/6).

Chapter 3 – 1932–9: Holding Pattern
1 Dept of Industry and Commerce, memo for government, 23 Oct. 1933 (NAI, DT S6327), quoted in Lar Joye, 'Frank Aiken and the Volunteer Force of the Irish Army, 1934–1939' in Bryce Evans and Stephen Kelly (eds), *Frank*

Aiken: nationalist and internationalist (Dublin, 2014).

2 *Dáil Debates*, vol. 55, col. 1795 (3 Apr. 1935).

3 Memo, 'Proposed completion of existing defence units and increase of defence vote by £1,500,000', Sept. 1936 (UCDA, P67/191).

4 Dan Bryan, 'Fundamental factors affecting Éire defence problem', May 1936 (IE/MA/ACS/189/11).

5 Memo, 'Estimate of the situation that would arise in the eventuality of a war between Ireland and Great Britain', Oct. 1934 (IE/MA/EDP/0020).

6 Michael Brennan to Frank Aiken, 22 Sept. 1936 (UCDA, P67/191). Brigades are subcomponents of divisions. In the Defence Forces, brigades typically consist of three battalions.

7 *Dáil Debates*, vol. 67, col. 720 (19 May 1937). As head of the government, De Valera was referred to as President of the Executive Council until 29 December 1937, the date on which the 1937 Constitution came into force. From that point onwards the leader of the government was referred to as Taoiseach, and deputy head of government as Tánaiste.

8 Memo, 'Present commitments, future policy and programme', *c.*June 1937 (UCDA, P71/27).

9 C.F. Russell, 'The Army Air Corps', *Aviation*, 1:6 (June 1935), p. 209. Quoted in Michael O'Malley, *Military aviation in Ireland, 1921–45* (Dublin, 2010), p. 101.

10 Memo, 'Proposed Completion of Existing Defence Units and Increase of Defence Vote by £1,500,000', Sept. 1936 (UCDA, P67/191 (5)).

11 M.J. Costello to Air Corps Investigation, 18 Feb. 1941 (quoted in O'Malley, *Military aviation in Ireland*, p. 134). During the 1930s Costello served as Commandant of the Military College (1932–7) and Assistant Chief of Staff (1937–9).

12 Bryan, 'Fundamental factors affecting Éire defence problem'.

Chapter 4 – 1939–45: The Emergency

1 *Dáil Debates*, vol. 77, col. 250 (27 Sept. 1939).

2 'Operation order 25/1940', 27 Dec. 1940 (IE/MA/EDP/E/3/1). 27 December 1940 was also the date of publication for the first issue of *An Cosantóir*, which has evolved to become the Defence Forces' official magazine.

3 Notes of a meeting between Dan McKenna and Éamon de Valera et al., 19 June 1940 (IE/MA/COS/1039).

4 'General report on the Army, for the year 1 Apr. 1940 to 31 Mar. 1941', 31 May 1941 (Michael Kennedy and Victor Laing (eds), *The Irish Defence Forces, 1940–1949: the Chief of Staff's reports* (Dublin, 2011), p. 40).

5 'General report on the Army, for the year 1 April 1940 to 31 March 1941', 31 May 1941 (Kennedy & Laing (eds), *The Irish Defence Forces, 1940–1949*, p. 44). Operation Green was planned as complementary to the planned invasion of Britain.

6 'No. 18 Mission: work of the mission', [1940] (IE/MA/18MM/1).

7 Michael Rynne to Joseph Walshe, 1 Sept. 1939 (https://www.difp.ie/volume-6/1939/memorandum-by-rynne/3001/#section-documentpage).

8 'Minutes of meeting between representatives of the Government of Éire and representatives of the Dominions Office and Service Departments of the United Kingdom', 23 May 1940 (NAI, DFA Secretary's Files, A3).

9 'No. 18 Mission: work of the mission', n.d. (IE/MA/18MM/1). One of the copies of the memo outlining 18MM's goals has some handwritten annotations, presumably by an Irish officer. The annotation to the 'proper co-operation' paragraph reads 'Impossible'.

10 [Col James Flynn], 'Notes on our position in relation to the British', 3 Jan. 1941 (IE/MA/18MM/1). Flynn was appointed Adjutant General in Jan. 1943, a post he held until Jan. 1949, and again from Jan. 1952 to Dec. 1954. He was Asst Chief of Staff from Jan. 1949 to Jan. 1952, and Jan. 1955 to Sept. 1961.

11 Memo by Capt Hewett, 'PAA passengers and British control', 20 May 1942 (IE/MA/18MM/1).

12 Memo by McKenna, 8 & 9 May 1941 (IE/MA/18MM/1).

13 'Training instructions issued to BTNI', memo by Lt Col R.A. Childers, 21 Oct. 1947 (IE/MA/18MM/22).

14 'General report on the Defence Forces, 1 Apr. 1942 to 31 Mar. 1943', 18 Apr. 1943 (Kennedy & Laing (eds), *The Irish Defence Forces, 1940–1949*, p. 196).

15 'General report on the Defence Forces, 1 Apr. 1942 to 31 Mar. 1943', 18 Apr. 1943 (Kennedy & Laing (eds), *The Irish Defence Forces, 1940–1949*, p. 184).

16 In 2013 the Irish government took the unprecedented step of issuing a blanket pardon to the soldiers who deserted during the Second World War and later enlisted in the armies of the Allied nations.

17 'General report on the Defence Forces, 1 Apr. 1943 to 31 Mar. 1944', 18 Apr. 1944 (Kennedy & Laing (eds), *The Irish Defence Forces, 1940–1949*, p. 337).

18 Dept. of External affairs memo submitted to the Taoiseach, *c*.1944 (quoted in Michael Kennedy, *Guarding neutral Ireland: the Coast Watching Service and military intelligence, 1939–1945* (Dublin, 2008), p. 271).

19 'General Report on the Army, 1 Apr. 1940 to 31 Mar. 1941', 31 May 1941 (Kennedy and Laing (eds), *The Irish Defence Forces, 1940–1949*, p. 78).

20 'General report on the Defence Forces, 1 Apr. 1941 to 31 Mar. 1942, 18 Apr. 1942 (Kennedy and Laing (eds), *The Irish Defence Forces, 1940–1949*, p. 326).

21 'General report on the Defence Forces, 1 Apr. 1944 to 31 Mar. 1945', 18 Apr. 1945 (Kennedy & Laing (eds), *Irish Defence Forces, 1940–1949*, p. 402).

22 'The position in regard to defence', *c*.1939 (IE/MA/ACS/189/11).

23 Report on air operations and intelligence, 17 Sept. 1940 (IE/MA/EDP/ADC/1/2).

24 Brian F. Maguire, 'Life in an A.A. outpost, 1939–46', *An Cosantóir* (Jan. 1974), p. 23.

25 Quoted in O'Malley, *Military aviation in Ireland, 1921–45*, p. 278.

26 O'Malley, *Military aviation in Ireland, 1921–45*, p. 285.

27 'General report on the Defence Forces, 1 Apr. 1944 to 31 Mar. 1945', 18 Apr. 1945 (Kennedy & Laing (eds), *The Irish Defence Forces, 1940–1949*, p. 410).

Beginnings: The Equitation School

1 Paul Rodzianko, *Tattered banners: an autobiography* (London, 1939), p. 277.

Chapter 5 – 1946–69: Stagnation and Revitalization

1 'Minutes of a meeting in the Taoiseach's office', 20 Sept. 1944 (IE/MA/COS/1039).

2 Gerry McMahon interview, Military Archives Oral History Project, 21 Dec. 2016 (IE/MA, MAOHP–004–F).

3 Attributed to an officer of the FCÁ, quoted in Terence O'Reilly, 'The FCÁ, 1946–2005', *History Ireland*, 19:4 (July/August, 2011).

4 'Annual report on the Defence Forces, 1 Apr. 1949 to 31 March 1950', [Apr. 1950] (IE/MA/COS/1344).

5 'Memo on proposed Defence Forces re-organisation', July 1958 (IE/MA/COS/1284).

6 'Ireland in a Major War', Annex D, *c*.1962 (IE/

MA/CO/S1026).

7 Memo, 'Army strength', 28 Jan. 1960 (IE/MA/COS/448).

8 'Ireland in a Major War', Annex B *c*.1962 (IE/MA/COS/1026).

9 'Ireland in a Major War', Annex E, *c*.1962 (IE/MA/COS/1026).

10 [Col Dan Bryan?], 'The North Atlantic Pact and Ireland', n.d. (Kennedy et al. (eds), *Documents on Irish Foreign Policy*, vol. IX (Dublin, 2014), (hereafter *DIFP*), p. 257).

11 Minute prepared by the Department of External Affairs, 9 Jan. 1962 (NAI, DT S16877 X62).

12 Frederick H. Boland to Seán Murphy, 7 Feb. 1949 (*DIFP IX*, p. 298).

13 'Annual report on the Defence Forces for the year ending 31 December 1953, [Jan. 1954] (IE/MA/COS/1348).

14 Memo by Lt Col J.R. Britten, 4 Jan. 1952 (TNA, DO 130/118).

15 Lt Gen G.C. Bucknall to Lt Gen A.E. Nye, 3 Jan. 1946 (TNA, WO 106/5900).

16 John Duggan, *A history of the Irish Army* (Dublin, 1991) p. 218.

17 Peadar MacMahon to Seán Mac Eoin (Minister for Defence), 9 Nov. 1956 (*DIFP X*, pp 660–2).

18 Eamonn Kennedy to Con Cremin, 'UN Observation Group in Lebanon', 23 June 1958 (*DIFP XI*, p. 180).

19 Telegram, Con Cremin to Frederick H. Boland, 24 June 1958 (*DIFP XI*, p. 181). For the background to and progress of Irish involvement with UN peacekeeping between 1958 and 1960, including a list of the 50 officers deployed in 1958, see Richard E.M. Heaslip, 'UNOGIL and UNTSO, 1958–60: the pre-Congo origins of Ireland's involvement in United Nations peacekeeping' in Michael Kennedy and Deirdre McMahon (eds), *Obligations and responsibilities: Ireland and the United Nations, 1955–2005* (Dublin, 2005), pp 79–116.

20 Department of External Affairs, memorandum for government: 'Request for Irish assistance in UN Military force in the Congo' 18 July 1960 (*DIFP XI*, p. 394). ONUC was the acronym given to the UN's mission, named Organization des Nations Unies au Congo.

21 Seán McKeown, 'The Congo (ONUC): the military perspective', *The Irish Sword*, 20:79 (1996), pp 43–4.

22 McKeown, 'The Congo (ONUC): the military perspective', p. 44. Leopoldville was renamed Kinshasa in 1966.

23 Foreword to '33 Infantry Battalion in the Republic of the Congo, August 1960 – January 1961' (IE/MA, UN Unit Histories).

24 Pte Michael Tighe interview, 19 Feb. 2021 (quoted in *Report of the Jadotville Independent Review Group* (Dublin, 2021), p. 95).

25 Minister for Defence, Gerald Bartley, in conversation with a Yugoslavian journalist, Dec. 1964 (quoted in NAI, DFA 98/3/288).

26 Dept of External Affairs memo, 2 Oct. 1964 (NAI, DFA 98/3/288).

27 Seán Mac Eoin to Michael Hilliard, 1 May 1968 (NAI, DFA 98/3/288).

28 Office of the Minister for Defence, memorandum for government, 19 June 1967 (NAI, 98/6/194).

29 *Irish Times*, 14 Nov. 1946.

30 Liam Egan to Seán Mac Eoin (Minister for Defence), 12 June 1954 (IE/MA/COS/161A).

31 Col James Flynn, 'Some observations on minute from OCSC dated 7/10/60', 24 Oct. 1960 (IE/MA/COS/161B).

32 Quoted in Aidan McIvor, *A history of the Irish Naval Service* (Dublin, 1994), p. 128.

33 Memo on conference held at Naval Base, 4 Oct. 1962 (IE/MA/COS/161B).

34 McIvor, *A history of the Irish Naval Service*, p. 128.

35 Seán Mac Eoin to Michael Hilliard, 10 Oct. 1966 (IE/MA/COS/161A).

36 Cabinet minutes, 8 Aug. 1967 (NAI, Taois 98/6/194).

37 *Dáil Debates*, vol. 199, col. (22 Jan. 1963). See also IE/MA/COS/134, 135, 136 & 137.

38 'Annual report on the Defence Forces, 1 Apr. 1951 to 31 Mar. 1952', [Apr. 1952] (IE/MA/COS/1346).

39 'Annual report on the Defence Forces for the year ending 31 December 1954' (IE/MA/COS/1349).

40 Quoted in Richard Cummins, *Air traffic services in the Irish Air Corps, 1922–1997* (Defence Forces Printing Press, 2013), p. 50.

41 'Annual report on the Defence Forces for the year ending 31 December 1954' (IE/MA/COS/1349).

42 Chief of Staff's branch, 'Defence Policy: Memorandum', October 1967 (IE/MA/COS/1070). The three memoranda referred to were: 'Ireland in a Major War' (1962), 'Memorandum on Defence Policy' (1963), and the 'Report of the Defence Review Board' (1966). Each can be consulted in Military Archives.

43 Chief of Staff's branch, 'Defence Policy: Memorandum', October 1967 (IE/MA/COS/1070).

44 Chief of Staff's branch, 'Defence Policy: Memorandum', October 1967 (IE/MA/COS/1070).

Chapter 6 – 1970–99: Guarding Borders and Breaking Boundaries

1 'Addendum to memo of 10 Feb. 1970, re Ministerial directive to Ceann Foirne', 11 Feb. 1970 (quoted in Michael Heney, *The arms crisis of 1970* (London, 1970)).

2 Brief for Chief of Staff, 5 June 1970 (IE/MA/SCS/18/1).

3 IE/MA/COS/1043.

4 The soldiers who died were Cpl Gerard O'Donovan, Pte Donal Nugent, Pte Cornelius Buckley, Pte Daniel O'Connell and Pte Anthony Hourihane (*An Cosantóir*, Sept. 2019, p. 31).

5 'Planning Assumptions', *c.*1973 (IE/MA/DOPS/Temp/2718).

6 'Memorandum: Northern Ireland', Apr. 1986. Cooney's aide memoire to the government, dated 7 Nov. 1985, stated that 'It was the unanimous view of the Council [of Defence] that the Defence Forces should not under any circumstances be ordered to intervene in Northern Ireland for the following reasons: a) They could not be given a clear mission in military terms, b) Their numerical strength and equipment are hopelessly inadequate, c) They may not operate outside the jurisdiction of the Republic except on United Nations duty.' Both memoranda are found at IE/MA/COS/1300.

7 Sgt Michael Jones interview, Military Archives Oral History Project, 16 Feb. 2019 (IE/MA, MAOHP, AC194).

8 Quoted in 'Unit History, 25 Infantry Group: Larnaca–Cairo–Sinai, Oct. 73–May 74' (Military Archives), p.2.

9 Revd Colm Matthews, CF, quoted in *An Cosantóir*, May 2008.

10 *Irish Times*, 30 Dec. 2017.

11 *Oireachtas Joint Committee on Justice, Defence and Equality Debate*, 16 May 2012. Chief of Staff Seán McCann issued an apology to the three families following publication of the report.

12 Tom Hodson, *The College: the Irish Military College, 1930–2000* (Dublin, 2016), pp 225–9.

13 Minister for Defence Seán Barrett, in reference to the work of the Defence Forces while on duty with UNIFIL (*Seanad Debates*, vol. 147, col. 131 (1 May 1996)).

14 Gerry McMahon, 'The Defence Forces and the United Nations', *Irish Sword*, 20 (1996), p. 7.

15 S. Duffy to Adjutant General, 22 Mar. 1979 (IE/MA/COS/1097).
16 *Report of the commission on remuneration and conditions of service in the Defence Forces*, 31 July 1990 (Dublin, 1990), chapter 1.
17 Recruiting survey, 1971 (IE/MA/COS/1097).
18 Recruiting survey, 1971 (IE/MA/COS/1097).
19 *Report of the commission on remuneration and conditions of service in the Defence Forces*, 31 July 1990 (Dublin, 1990), paragraph 3.7.13.
20 George Colley to Robert Molloy, 12 Sept. 1978 (IE/MA/DOPS/Temp/2648).
21 Brigid Lyons Thornton, 'Women and the Army', *An Cosantóir* (Nov. 1975), p. 364.
22 'First report of the committee on the establishment of a Women's Service Corps', 10 Feb. 1978 (IE/MA/COS/1448B).
23 'First report of the committee on the establishment of a Women's Service Corps', 10 Feb. 1978 (IE/MA/COS/1448B).
24 IE/MA/DOPS/Temp/5747. During its work, the board responsible for drafting the DFR made a number of assumptions relative to any future legislation, including that on enlistment cadets would be single, that a married woman may be enlisted in the ranks but would not be eligible for billeting in married quarters.
25 Tom McCaughren, reporting for RTÉ on the testing of a new service rifle for the Defence Forces, 12 Mar. 1987 (https://www.rte.ie/archives/collections/news/21242662-army-test-weapon/).
26 Department of Defence memo for government, 22 Apr. 1970 (NAI, DFA 10/2/478).
27 Irish Shipping Ltd acted as consultants to the Department of Defence in the procurement of the LÉ *Deirdre*. An outline specification was sent to approx 60 firms seeking expressions of interest. Nine firms eventually submitted quotations, reduced to three competitive offers. After negotiations, Verolme Cork Dockyard's quotation was accepted. Living conditions on *Deirdre* were said to be 'excellent by naval standards and the ship is capable of operating independently of base for long periods' (quotation in memorandum) (Dept of Defence memo for government, 25 Jan. 1974 (NAI, DFA 10/2/478).
28 *Report of the commission on remuneration and conditions of service in the Defence Forces*, 31 July 1990 (Dublin, 1990), chapter 1. The commission was chaired by Dermot Gleeson and is more commonly known as the Gleeson commission.
29 *Irish Times*, 30 Dec. 2021.
30 Thirty-one years later, in May 2022, a further major advance for representative associations was achieved when the Minister for Defence, Simon Coveney, granted temporary conditional consent for representative associations to apply for associate membership of the Irish Congress of Trade Unions for public sector pay talks. Permitting Defence Forces' representative bodies to pursue associate membership of ICTU had been one of the recommendations of the Commission on the Defence Forces (2022).
31 *Report of the commission on remuneration and conditions of service in the Defence Forces*, 31 July 1990 (Dublin, 1990), paragraph 1.5.1.
32 Extract from the 1991 EAG review of the Defence Forces/Department of Defence, quoted in the Department of Finance's submission on the White Paper on Defence, [Dec. 1998] (IE/MA/COS/2611).
33 The majority of the reduction in personnel was implemented through a voluntary early retirement scheme that ran between 1996 and 1998, and was availed of by more than 1,500 personnel at a cost of over £65m in retirement benefits (Department of Defence, *White Paper on Defence* (Dublin, 2000), p. 27).

Chapter 7 – 2000–22: Inflection Points

1 Department of Defence, *White Paper on Defence* (Dublin, 2000), p. 5.
2 Department of Defence, *White Paper on Defence* (Dublin, 2000), p. 77.
3 Fianna Fáil/Progressive Democrats programme for government, 'Action Programme for the Millennium', [1997] (Irish Election Manifesto Archive, http://michaelpidgeon.com/manifestos/about.html) (accessed 19 May 2021).
4 Department of Defence, *White Paper on Defence* (Dublin, 2000), passim.
5 Memo by Lt Col D. Betson, Director, Strategic Planning Office, 4 Feb. 2000 (IE/MA/COS/2063).
6 Lt Gen David Stapleton to Michael Smith, 24 Feb. 2000 (IE/MA/COS/2063). The meeting took place on 23 February. For reporting on the agreement (which incorporated the text of Stapleton's memo) see, e.g., *Irish Times*, 2 Mar. 2000.
7 Findings of the External Advisory Committee on bullying and harassment in the Defence Forces, quoted in *Irish Examiner*, 4 Apr. 2002.
8 Quoted in *Irish Examiner*, 4 Apr. 2002.
9 Independent Monitoring Group, *Second Report* (Dublin, 2008), p. 9.

10 *Report of the Special Group on Public Service Numbers and Expenditure Programmes* (Department of Finance, 2 vols, 2009) ii, 45–53.
11 'Report of the Steering Group on the Reserve Defence Forces', Aug. 1999.
12 Independent Monitoring Group, *Third Report* (Dublin, 2014), p. 5.
13 European Defence Agency data (https://eda.europa.eu/publications-and-data/defence-data) (Accessed 1 May 2022).
14 'Planning and Operations Branch, annual report 1962' (IE/MA/COS/1359).
15 *Report of the Commission on the Defence Forces* (Dublin, 2022), p. 15.
16 *Report of the Commission on the Defence Forces* (Dublin, 2022), p. 15.
17 *Report of the Commission on the Defence Forces* (Dublin, 2022), p. iv.
18 Minutes of meeting of the Commission on the Defence Forces, 22 Dec. 2020 (https://www.gov.ie/en/publication/039d2-commission-on-the-defence-forces-minutes-of-first-meeting/); *Irish Times*, 15 & 20 Dec. 2020.
19 *Report of the Commission on the Defence Forces* (Dublin, 2022), p. iv.
20 *Report of the Commission on the Defence Forces* (Dublin, 2022), p. vi.
21 *Report of the Commission on the Defence Forces* (Dublin, 2022), pp 55–6. At time of publication, legislation was in preparation to bring command and control structures in line with international best practice.
22 Department of Defence, *White Paper on Defence* (Dublin, 2015), p. 49.
23 Eunan O'Halpin, 'The challenges facing the Defence Forces in the next five years', *Defence Forces Review* (2011), p. 13.
24 Extract from a speech by Seán Clancy, Chief of Staff, to mark the centenary of the handover of Casement Aerodrome, 3 May 2022.

Beginnings: Military Archives
1 W.J. Brennan-Whitmore to M.J. Costello, 18 Nov. 1924 (IE/MA/HMA).
2 W.J. Brennan-Whitmore to M.J. Costello, 5 Oct. 1925 (IE/MA/HMA).
3 IE/MA/HS/A/884.
4 'General report on the Defence Forces, 1 Apr. 1948 to 31 Mar. 1949', [Apr. 1949] (Kennedy & Laing (eds), *The Irish Defence Forces, 1940–1949*, p. 799). For a detailed account of Military Archives, see Daniel Ayiotis, *Military Archives: a history* (Dublin, 2022).

Chapter 8 – 1922–2022: Memories of the Men and Women of the Defence Forces
1 For more on the Bureau of Military History, including online versions of the material it collected, see www.militaryarchives.ie/collections/online-collections/bureau-of-military-history-1913-1921. Military Archives also holds the Uinseann Mac Eoin Collection, acquired in 2018, which provides material complementary to the BMH from the perspective of those who took the anti-Treaty side, including 102 audio recordings of interviews conducted by Mac Eoin with Irish republicans, in which they discuss their activities between the Civil War and the end of the Emergency.
2 See https://www.militaryarchives.ie/collections/online-collections/oral-histories-project-20th-century.
3 Seán Mac Mahon's statement to the Army Inquiry Committee, 6 May 1924 (IE/MA, AMTY/3/27).
4 Oscar Traynor (1886–1963) took the anti-Treaty side during the Civil War. Twice served as Minister for Defence, 1939–48 and 1951–4.
5 Col Joseph V. Lawless, Bureau of Military History, Witness Statement No. 1,043, 9 Dec. 1954 (https://www.militaryarchives.ie/collections/online-collections/bureau-of military-history-1913-1921/reels/bmh/BMH.WS1043.pdf).
6 Seán Mac Mahon's statement to the Army Inquiry Committee, 6 May 1924 (IE/MA, AMTY/3/27).
7 Seán Mac Mahon's statement to the Army Inquiry Committee, 6 May 1924 (IE/MA, AMTY/3/27).
8 Gerry McMahon interview, Military Archives Oral History Project, 10 Feb. 2017 (IE/MA, MAOHP–001–H).
9 Seán Clancy (1901–2006) was a veteran of the Dublin Brigade of the IRA and joined the National Army in 1922. He retired from the Defence Forces in 1959 with the rank of Lt Col.
10 Michael Brennan (1896–1986), Chief of Staff of the Defence Forces, 1931–40.
11 During Operation Morthor, which began on 13 September 1961 when ONUC forces launched an offensive to take control of the secessionist state of Katanga, Magennis travelled alone into enemy territory to negotiate for the safe treatment of 28 captured Irish personnel. The Siege of Jadotville also occurred during Operation Morthor.
12 Gerry McMahon interview, Military Archives Oral History Project, 21 Dec. 2016 (IE/MA, MAOHP–004–F).

13 Joe Mallon interview, Military Archives Oral History Project, 15 Dec. 2017 (IE/MA, MAOHP–0010–E).

14 Joe Mallon interview, Military Archives Oral History Project, 15 Dec. 2017 (IE/MA, MAOHP–0010–B).

15 Joe Mallon interview, Military Archives Oral History Project, 15 Dec. 2017 (IE/MA, MAOHP–0010–G).

16 Trooper Anthony Browne, who was posthumously awarded the Military Medal for Gallantry, with distinction, died as a result of the Niemba ambush. His remains were found two years later, several kilometres from the site of the ambush.

17 Thomas Croke interview, Military Archives Oral History Project, 2 Dec. 2016 (IE/MA, MAOHP–0085–05).

18 Thomas Croke interview, Military Archives Oral History Project, 2 Dec. 2016 (IE/MA, MAOHP–0085–07).

19 In January 1974 members of the Provisional IRA hijacked a helicopter and dropped bombs – which failed to explode – on the RUC station in Strabane.

20 Dr Tiede Herrema, a Dutch businessman, was kidnapped by the Provisional IRA in Limerick on 3 October 1975. Following a major manhunt by the Gardaí with Defence Forces support, the kidnappers and Herrema were located in Monasterevin. Herrema was released unharmed after a two-week siege.

21 Michael Walsh interview, Military Archives Oral History Project, 7 Feb. 2017 (IE/MA, MAOHP–0017–E).

22 Maria O'Donoghue interview, Military Archives Oral History Project, 26 May 2021 (time stamp 0:24:10).

23 Staff College, Camberley, then the staff college for the British Army.

24 Royal Military Academy, Sandhurst.

25 Michael Jones interview, Military Archives Oral History Project, 16 Feb. 2019 (IE/MA, MAOHP, AC194). Time stamp: 0:43:50.

26 While on a UNIFIL supply mission on 18 April, just days after At Tiri, Pte Derek Smallhorne and Pte Thomas Barrett of 46 Battalion were abducted and murdered by members of the South Lebanon Army.

27 Maria O'Donoghue interview, Military Archives Oral History Project, 26 May 2021 (time stamp 0:42:10).

28 In May 2021 Maureen O'Brien was promoted to Major General, the second-highest rank in the Defence Forces, and appointed as military advisor on peacekeeping to the Secretary-General of the United Nations.

29 Michael Walsh interview, Military Archives Oral History Project, 7 Feb. 2017 (IE/MA, MAOHP-0017–E).

30 Tracey Walsh interview, Military Archives Oral History Project, 29 Sept. 2016 (IE/MA, MAOHP–0062–7).

31 Operation Grapes of Wrath was a campaign against Hezbollah by the Israeli Defence Forces, lasting sixteen days (11–27 April 1996). During the operation a UNIFIL compound at Qana was shelled by Israeli forces.

32 Jeremiah Carroll interview, Military Archives Oral History Project, 20 Sept. 2016 (IE/MA, MAOHP-009–H).

33 Jeremiah Carroll interview, Military Archives Oral History Project, 20 Sept. 2016 (IE/MA, MAOHP-009–3).

34 Ruairí de Barra interview, Military Archives Oral History Project, 10 Feb. 2017 (IE/MA, MAOHP-0097–06).

35 Ruairí de Barra interview, Military Archives Oral History Project, 10 Feb. 2017 (IE/MA, MAOHP-0097–09 & 10).

36 Ruairí de Barra interview, Military Archives Oral History Project, 10 Feb. 2017 (IE/MA, MAOHP-0097–10).

37 Ruairí de Barra interview, Military Archives Oral History Project, 10 Feb. 2017 (IE/MA, MAOHP-0097–11).

38 Maria O'Donoghue interview, Military Archives Oral History Project, 26 May 2021 (time stamp 1:28:20).

BIBLIOGRAPHICAL NOTE

There are few branches of the public sector as well served with archival material as the Defence Forces, or that have been the subject of so much historical study. Military Archives houses an extensive range of material – the vast majority unique and including both public and private collections – detailing the formation and evolution of all elements the Defence Forces from 1913 to the present day. Some of this material is available online, with the Bureau of Military History and the Military Service Pensions Collections the most well known. Other online collections include the 1922 Army Census, a vast corpus of maps, plans and drawings, and United Nations Unit Histories. As can be seen above, the Military Archives Oral History Project is an incredibly rich source. The main manuscript collections consulted for this book both from Military Archives and other repositories are listed below.

In addition to the vast corpus of archival material available, there is an abundance of secondary reading on Irish military topics. As the official periodicals of the Defence Forces, *An tÓglách* (1918–33) and *An Cosantóir* (1940–present) provide a wealth of contemporary and historical information. *An tÓglách* is accessible online at www. militaryarchives.ie, and some back issues of *An Cosantóir* can be viewed at www. dfmagazine.ie. Military Archives holds a set of both in hard copy.

The principal scholarly journals for military history and policy in Ireland are *The Irish Sword* and *Defence Forces Review*, both published annually. The latter is published by the Defence Forces Public Relations Branch, and a precursor to *Defence Forces Review*, known as *An Cosantóir Review*, was published in the 1990s. While more readily associated with the study of Irish foreign policy, *Irish Studies in International Affairs* contains much on the involvement of the Defence Forces in overseas operations.

Biographical studies of many of the principal figures within the Defence Forces, with a heavy focus on the first half of the twentieth century, can be found in the *Dictionary of Irish Biography* (Cambridge, 11 vols, 2009 & 2018) – now available as an open access, online database (www.dib.ie). *Documents on Irish Foreign Policy* (Royal Irish Academy, 13 vols, 1998–) is the main source for the study of Irish foreign policy, and publishes a wide range of material pertinent to Irish defence and the Defence Forces. At time of writing volumes I to IX (1919–51) are available in an online, open access database (www.difp.ie).

For the history of the Air Corps, Michael O'Malley's *Military aviation in Ireland, 1921–45* (Dublin, 2010), Donal MacCarron's *Wings over Ireland: the story of the Irish Air Corps* (Leicester, 1996), and Joe Maxwell's and Patrick Cummins' *The Air Corps: an illustrated guide* (Belfast, 2009) are indispensable. For the Naval Service the same may be said of Daire Brunicardi's prolific scholarship, available in a range of publications, while Aidan McIvor's *A history of the Irish Naval Service* (Dublin, 1994) is a good starting point.

John Duggan's *A history of the Irish Army* (Dublin, 1991), which focuses almost exclusively on the Army, offers an overview of its first seventy years and draws on the author's own experiences. Along with Karl Martin's *Irish Army vehicles: transport and armour since 1922* (2002), Ralph Riccio's *AFVs in Irish service since 1922* (Sandomierz, 2010), *The Irish Artillery Corps since 1922* (Sandomierz, 2012) and *Irish coastal landings, 1922* (Sandomierz, 2012), provide a comprehensive guide to the equipment of the Defence Forces over the past century. For studies of two further components of the Defence Forces, see Col Tom Hodson's *The College: the Irish Military College, 1930–2000* (Dublin, 2016), and Michael Slavin and Louise Parkes, *Ambassadors on horseback: the Irish Army Equitation School* (Dublin, 2010).

Aside from the sources mentioned above, there is a vast scholarship on the history of the Defence Forces, especially for the decade spanning the formation of the Volunteers in 1913 to the end of the Civil War. For the period after the Civil War, not only have the individual land, sea and air components of the Defence Forces been the subject of detailed historical study, so too have its reserves, its current and disbanded corps, battalions, brigades, and other units, as well as its equipment and built infrastructure. Many of these works can be found in the reference library at Military Archives. The list that follows the manuscript sources listed below is mostly confined to works that, when added to those mentioned above, have most heavily been relied on in compiling this book.

Manuscript Sources

Military Archives, Cathal Brugha Barracks, Dublin
IE/MA/18MM – 18th Military Mission
IE/MA/AC1 & AC2 – Air Corps Collections
IE/MA/ACS – Assistant Chief of Staff
IE/MA/ACM – Air Corps Museum
IE/MA/ADM – Administrative
IE/MA/AMTY – Army Inquiry Committee (1923–4)
IE/MA/AOB – Army Organisation Board (1925–7)
IE/MA/ASE – Army School of Equitation (1926–81)
IE/MA/CMA – Court Martial Administration (1922–4)
1E/MA/COD – Council of Defence (1925–74)
IE/MA/COS – Chief of Staff
IE/MA/CREC – Chief of Staff Reports to Executive Council (1923–30)
IE/MA/CW – Various Civil War Collections (OPS, CAPT)
IE/MA/DOD/A – Department of Defence A-series (1918–35)
IE/MA/DOD/2 – Department of Defence 2-series (1924–47)
IE/MA/DOD/3 – Department of Defence 3-series (1947–)
IE/MA/DOPS – Director of Operations
IE/MA/EDP – Emergency Defence Plans (1939–46)
IE/MA/HS – Historical Section
IE/MA/LE – Truce Liaison and Evacuation (1921–40)

IE/MA/MM – Military Mission and Temporary Plans Division (1924–8)
IE/MA/OS-ONUC – United Nations Operations in Congo Collection (1959–69)
Various Private Collections

Military Archives Online Collections
An tÓglách
Army Census, 1922
Bureau of Military History
Maps, Plans and Drawings
Military Service Pensions Collection
United Nations Unit Histories

National Archives, Dublin
Cabinet Minutes
Dáil Éireann papers
Department of Finance
Department of Foreign Affairs
Department of the Taoiseach

The National Archives, London
British Cabinet Minutes (CAB)
DO 130/118
WO 106/5900
WO 106/6043

National Archives and Records Administration, College Park, Maryland, US
RG 165

National Library of Ireland
J.J. O'Connell papers

University College Dublin, Archives
P7 – Richard Mulcahy papers
P24 – Ernest Blythe papers
P71 – Dan Bryan papers
P80 – Desmond Fitzgerald papers
P151 - Seán Mac Eoin papers

Select Secondary Sources

Ayiotis, Daniel, Gibney, John, and Kennedy, Michael, *The Emergency: a visual history of the Irish Defence Forces, 1939–1945* (Dublin, 2019).

Ayiotis, Daniel, *Military Archives: a history* (Dublin, 2022).

Bhreatnach, Aoife, 'Waxing and waning: garrison towns in independent Ireland', *Defence Forces Review* (2016), pp 37–45.

Borgonovo, John, *The battle for Cork: July–August 1922* (Cork, 2013).

Burke, Edward, 'Ireland's contribution to the United Nations mission in the Congo (ONUC)', in Kennedy and McMahon (eds), *Obligations and responsibilities*, pp 117–53.

Byrne, Susan, '"Keeping company with the enemy": gender and sexual violence against women during the Irish War of Independence and Civil War, 1919–1923', *Women's History Review*, 30:1 (2021), pp 108–25.

Campbell, Colm, *Emergency law in Ireland, 1916–1925* (Oxford, 1994).

Campbell, Liam, 'A historical analysis of Reserves in the Irish Defence Forces', *An Cosantóir Review* (1997), pp 22–35.

Clark, Gemma, *Everyday violence in the Irish Civil War* (Cambridge, 2014).

Clarke, Brian, 'An examination of civilian governance of the armed forces in Ireland and other neutral EU states', *Defence Forces Review* (2020), pp 46–54.

Connolly, Linda, 'Sexual violence in the Irish Civil War: a forgotten crime?', *Women's History Review*, 30 (2021), pp 126–43.

Crowley, John, Ó Drisceoil, Dónal, and Murphy, Mike (eds), *Atlas of the Irish Revolution* (Cork, 2017).

Cummins, Richard, *Air Traffic services in the Irish Air Corps, 1922–1997* (Defence Forces Printing Press, 2016).

Dorney, John, *The Civil War in Dublin: the fight for the capital, 1922–1924* (Newbridge, 2017).

Dorr, Noel, 'The development of UN peacekeeping over the past fifty years: an Irish perspective', *Irish Sword*, 20 (1996), pp 16–31.

Evans, Bryce, and Kelly, Stephen (eds), *Frank Aiken: nationalist and internationalist* (Dublin, 2014).

Farrell, Theo, '"The model army": military imitation and the enfeeblement of the army in post-revolutionary Ireland, 1922–42', *Irish Studies in International Affairs*, 8 (1997), pp 111–27.

–, 'Professionalisation and suicidal defence planning by the Irish Army, 1921–41', *The Journal of Strategic Studies*, 21:3 (1998), pp 67–85.

Flynn, Grace, Hogan, John and Feeney, Sharon, 'Whistleblowing in the Irish military: the cost of exposing bullying and sexual harassment', *Journal of Military Ethics*, 18:2 (2019), pp 129–44.

Gannon, Darragh, and McGarry, Fearghal (eds), *Ireland, 1922: independence, partition, civil war* (Dublin, 2022).

Gibney, John, Kennedy, Michael, and O'Malley, Kate, *Ireland: a voice among the nations* (Dublin, 2019).

Gibson, Andrew, 'Infrapolitics and role abeyance: how Irish military officers experience university', *Irish Journal of Sociology*, 29:2 (2021), pp 160–86.

Harvey, Dan, *Soldiering against subversion: the Irish Defence Forces and internal security during the Troubles, 1969–1998* (Dublin, 2018).

Heaslip, Richard E.M., 'UNOGIL and UNTSO, 1958–60: the pre-Congo origins of Ireland's involvement in United Nations peacekeeping', in Kennedy and McMahon (eds), *Obligations and responsibilities*, pp 79–116.

–, 'Ireland's first engagement in United Nations peacekeeping operations: an assessment', *Irish Studies in International Affairs*, 17 (2006), pp 31–42.

Hodson, Tom, 'Establishing the Irish Military College', *Defence Forces Review* (2016), pp 103–10.

Hopkinson, Michael, *Green against green: the Irish Civil War* (Dublin, 1988).

Ishizuka, Katsumi, *Ireland and international peacekeeping operations, 1960–2000* (Oxfordshire, 2013).

Joye, Lar, 'Frank Aiken and the Volunteer force of the Irish Army, 1934–1939' in Evans & Kelly (eds), *Frank Aiken: nationalist and internationalist*, pp 123–32.

Kavanagh, P.D., *Irish Defence Forces Handbook, 1974* (2nd ed., Dublin, 1974).

Kennedy, Michael, *Guarding neutral Ireland: the Coast Watching Service and Military Intelligence, 1939–1945* (Dublin, 2008).

Kennedy, Michael, and Laing, Victor, *The Irish Defence Forces, 1940–1949: the Chief of Staff's reports* (IMC, Dublin, 2011).

Kennedy, Michael, and Magennis, Art, *Ireland, the United Nations and the Congo* (Dublin, 2014).

Kennedy, Michael, and McMahon, Deirdre, *Obligations and responsibilities: Ireland and the United Nations, 1955–2005* (Dublin, 2005).

Kennedy, Padraic, 'Key appointments and the transition of the Irish Volunteers, the Irish Republican Army and the National Army, 1912–1933', *Defence Forces Review* (2016), pp 21–37.

Kinsella, Anthony, 'The Special Infantry Corps', *Irish Sword*, 20 (1997), pp 331–46.

Langton, James, *The forgotten fallen: National Army soldiers who died during the Irish Civil War* (Dublin, 2019).

Lavelle, Patrick, 'UNOGIL silver jubilee, 1958–83', *An Cosantóir* (June 1983), pp 189–93.

Long, Patrick, 'Organisation and development of the pro-Treaty forces, 1922–1924', *Irish Sword,* 82 (Winter, 1997), pp 308–30.

Longwill, Edward, 'The Niemba ambush: a reappraisal', *Defence Forces Review* (2010), pp 9–23.

Mac Eoin, Stephen, 'History, memory and commemoration – an archivist's perspective', *Defence Forces Review* (2016), pp 1–9.

Maguire, Brian F., 'Life in an A.A. outpost, 1939–1946', *An Cosantóir* (Jan. 1974), pp 23–6.

Mattimoe, Cyril, 'Cadets at Arlington', *An Cosantóir* (Sept. 1979), pp 274–9.

Meehan, Michael, 'A brief history and compendium of Survey Company C.O.E.' (Defence Forces Press, 1998, rev. 2018).

Murphy, Ray, 'The legal framework governing Irish participation in peace operations' in Kennedy and McMahon (eds), *Obligations and responsibilities*, pp 318–42.

O'Brien, Timothy, 'The evolution of Defence Forces peacekeeping operations', *Irish Studies in International Affairs*, 30 (2019), pp 119–29.

O'Donoghue, David, 'Army's Congo mission casts a long shadow', *Irish Studies in International Affairs*, 17 (2006), pp 43–59.

O'Halpin, Eunan, *Defending Ireland: the Irish state and its enemies since 1922* (Oxford, 1999).

O'Neill, John T., 'Ireland's participation in United Nations peacekeeping: a military perspective', in Kennedy and McMahon (eds), *Obligations and responsibilities*, pp 299–317.

O'Shea, Brendan, 'Punching above our weight: living, learning and leading the peacekeeping evolution', *Defence Forces Review* (2008), pp 1–10.

Parker, James, 'UNIFIL and peacekeeping: the Defence Forces experience', *Irish Studies in International Affairs*, 2 (1986), pp 63–77.

Regan, John, *The Irish counter-revolution, 1921–1936: Treatyite politics and settlement in independent Ireland* (Dublin, 1999).

Thornton, Brigid Lyons, 'Women and the Army', *An Cosantóir* (Nov. 1975), pp 364–5.

Tonra, Ben, 'Ireland and collective security', in Kennedy and McMahon (eds), *Obligations and responsibilities*, pp 281–98.

Treacy, John, 'Caveat emptor: building Ireland's small navy, 1945–49', *Defence Forces Review* (2016), pp 141–53.

Valiulis, Maryann, *Portrait of a revolutionary: General Richard Mulcahy and the founding of the Irish Free State* (Dublin, 1993).

Wood, Ian S., *Britain, Ireland and the Second World War* (Edinburgh, 2010).

Theses

Martin, Michael, 'Breaking ranks: the emergence of representative associations in the Irish armed forces, 1989–1992 (PhD, UCC, 2010).

Ó Confhaola, Padhraic, 'The naval forces of the Irish state, 1922–1977' (PhD, NUI Maynooth, 2009).

Ryan, Joseph, 'The Army School of Music, 1922–1940 (MA, 2 vols, NUI Maynooth, 1987).

Valiulis, Maryann Gialanella, 'The Irish Army mutiny of 1924' (PhD, Loyola University of Chicago, 1977).

Irish Defence Forces/Government of Ireland Reports

Commission on remuneration and conditions of service in the Defence Forces, *Report* (Dublin, 1990).

Commission on the Defence Forces, *Report* (Dublin, 2022).

Department of Defence, *White Paper on Defence* (Dublin, 2000).

—, *White Paper on Defence* (Dublin, 2015).

—, *White Paper on Defence: Update 2019* (Dublin, 2019).

Department of Defence and Irish Defence Forces, *Annual Reports* (Dublin, 2006–19).

Irish Defence Forces, *Annual Reports* (Dublin, 2002–5).

—, *Defence Force Regulations*, vols 1–6 (1923–55).

—, *General Routine Orders*, vols 1–5 (1922–55).

—, *Medals of the Irish Defence Forces* (1st ed., 2010).

Ombudsman for the Defence Forces, *Annual Reports* (Dublin, 2005–20).

IMAGE CREDITS

Every effort has been made to trace the copyright holder of the images reproduced in this book, and to ensure the accuracy of all captions. An asterisk (*) at the start of an image credit indicates that the caption draws on Daniel Ayiotis, John Gibney and Michael Kennedy (eds), *The Emergency: a visual history of the Irish Defence Forces, 1939–1945* (Dublin, 2019). Where appropriate, archival references are given in brackets.

Introduction
10 Courtesy of Military Archives (IE/MA/BMH/CD/023/2)
12 Courtesy of Military Archives (IE/MA/HS/A/33)
15 Courtesy of Military Archives (*An tÓglach* Collection)
16 Courtesy of Military Archives (IE/MA/058)

Chapter 1: 1922–3
21 Image courtesy of the National Library of Ireland (NLI, HOGW135)
23 Image courtesy of the National Library of Ireland (NLI, HOGW174)
24–5 Reproduced by kind permission of UCD Archives (UCDA, P80/PH/160)
27 Image courtesy of the National Library of Ireland (NLI, HOGW55)
28 Courtesy of Military Archives (IE/MA/PRCN0004/02/59)
30 Reproduced by kind permission of UCD Archives (UCDA, P80/PH/156)
31 Courtesy of Military Archives (IE/MA/DOD/A/6852)
32 Reproduced by kind permission of UCD Archives (UCDA, P7/B/73)
33 Reproduced by kind permission of UCD Archives (UCDA, P7a/50)
36 Courtesy of Military Archives (IE/MA/DOD/A/12004)
37 Irish Air Corps Archives, 105 Squadron, Photographic and Airborne Imaging
38 Reproduced by kind permission of UCD Archives (UCDA, P7/B/10)
39 Reproduced by kind permission of the Hugh Lane Gallery
40 Courtesy of Military Archives (IE/MA/AL/IMG/252)
41 Courtesy of Military Archives (IE/MA/DOD/A/7092)
42 Irish Air Corps Archives, 105 Squadron, Photographic and Airborne Imaging
43 Reproduced by kind permission of UCD Archives (UCDA, P80/PH/23)
44 Courtesy of Military Archives (IE/MA/ACC2012/07)
45 Reproduced by kind permission of UCD Archives (UCDA, P80/PH/26)
46 Image courtesy of the National Library of Ireland (NLI, HOGW60)
48 Image courtesy of the National Library of Ireland (NLI, HOGW26)
49 Image courtesy of the National Library of Ireland (NLI, HOGW37)
50 Courtesy of Military Archives (IE/MA/PC253)
51 Image courtesy of the National Library of Ireland (NLI, HOGW39)
52 Courtesy of Military Archives (IE/MA/Barry Family Collection)
54 Courtesy of Military Archives (IE/MA/MSPC/4P66 – Joseph O'Brien)

Specialist Corps of the Civil War
56 Courtesy of Military Archives (IE/MA/MPD/AD134227-005)
57 Courtesy of Military Archives (IE/MA/GPN/034/015)
58 Image courtesy of the National Library of Ireland (NLI, HOGW9)
59 Courtesy of Military Archives (IE/MA/GPN/048/002)

Chapter 2: 1923–32
62 Reproduced by kind permission of UCD Archives (UCDA, P80/PH/65)
65 Courtesy of Military Archives (IE/MA/AMTY/2/1)
66 Courtesy of Military Archives (IE/MA/AMTY/3/8)
67 Courtesy of Military Archives (IE/MA/AMTY/2/2)

68 Courtesy of Military Archives (IE/MA/OGLA)
70–71 Courtesy of Military Archives (IE/MA/AMTY/2/1)
74 Courtesy of Military Archives (IE/MA/CREC/6)
77 Courtesy of Military Archives (IE/MA/016/056)
78 Courtesy of Military Archives (IE/MA/016/065)
80 Courtesy of Military Archives (IE/MA/PRCN/0066/1737)
81 Irish Air Corps Archives, 105 Squadron, Photographic and Airborne Imaging
82 Courtesy of Military Archives (IE/MA/Recruitment Posters)
83 Courtesy of Military Archives (IE/MA/PC Major Seán Cotter)
84 Courtesy of Military Archives (IE/MA/GPN/023/015)
87 Courtesy of Military Archives (IE/MA/MPD/AD119294–003)
88 Courtesy of Military Archives (IE/MA/GPN/056/004)
89 Courtesy of Military Archives (IE/MA/GPN/022/035)
90 Courtesy of Military Archives (IE/MA/GPN/023/017)
92 Courtesy of Military Archives (IE/MA/PRCN/0016/01/09)
93 Courtesy of Military Archives (IE/MA/AMTY/3/66)
94 Courtesy of Military Archives (IE/MA/GPN/028/012)
96 Courtesy of Military Archives (IE/MA/GPN/059/018)
98 Reproduced by kind permission of UCD-OFM Partnership (UCDA, P151/384 (5))

The Cartoons and Cartoonists of An tÓglách
100–102 Reproduced courtesy of Military Archives (IE/MA/OGLA).

Chapter 3: 1932–9
107 Courtesy of Military Archives (IE/MA/ACC2018/02)
108 Courtesy of the Irish Defence Forces
109 Courtesy of Military Archives (IE/MA/GPN/067/003)
110 Courtesy of Military Archives (IE/MA/GPN/067/012)
111 Courtesy of the Irish Defence Forces
112 Courtesy of Military Archives (IE/MA/Recruitment Posters)
113 Courtesy of Military Archives (IE/MA/ACPS/GPN/301)
114 Courtesy of the Irish Defence Forces
115 Courtesy of Military Archives (IE/MA/PC Major Seán Cotter)
116 Reproduced by kind permission of UCD Archives (UCDA, P71/22)
117 Courtesy of Military Archives (IE/MA/PC Major Seán Cotter)
118 Courtesy of Military Archives (IE/MA/ACPS/GPN/19/24)
119 Courtesy of Military Archives (IE/MA/PRCN/0066–1740)
120 Courtesy of Military Archives (IE/MA/ACPS/GPN/267/2)
121 Courtesy of Military Archives (IE/MA/PC72)
122 Courtesy of Military Archives (IE/MA/ACPS/GPN/276)
123 Courtesy of Military Archives (IE/MA/PRCN/0013/03/01)
124 (top)* Reproduced by kind permission of UCD-OFM Partnership (UCDA, P150/2536)
124 (bottom)* Courtesy of Military Archives (IE/MA/PC94/002)
125 Courtesy of Military Archives (IE/MA/MPD/AD134243–008)
126 Courtesy of Military Archives (IE/MA/GPN/054/007)
127* Courtesy of Military Archives (IE/MA/D8/238/1/38)

Beginnings: The Defence Forces School of Music
128–30 Reproduced by kind permission of the Defence Forces School of Music
131 Courtesy of Military Archives (IE/MA/HMV C_2191)

Chapter 4: 1939–45
135 Courtesy of Military Archives (IE/MA/18MM/2)

136* Courtesy of Military Archives (IE/MA/PC179)
137 Courtesy of Military Archives (IE/MA/MPD/AD134134–004)
138–9 Courtesy of Military Archives (IE/MA/Recruitment Posters)
140 Courtesy of Military Archives (IE/MA/18MM/14)
141 Courtesy of Military Archives (IE/MA/18MM/15)
142 Courtesy of Military Archives (IE/MA/IE/MA/GPN/BOX/063/031)
143* Courtesy of Military Archives (IE/MA/Emergency Photographs)
144* Courtesy of Military Archives (IE/MA/PC94 (2))
145 Image kindly supplied by Comdt Lar Joye (Reserve Defence Forces)
146* Courtesy of Military Archives (IE/MA/Divisional Manoeuvres/MAP/B/Cork & Lismore)
148* Courtesy of Military Archives (IE/MA/G77)
151* Courtesy of Military Archives (IE/MA/083/005)
152 Courtesy of the Irish Defence Forces
154* Courtesy of Military Archives (IE/MA/P241)
155* Courtesy of Military Archives (IE/MA/Photos/092/045)
156* Courtesy of Military Archives (IE/MA/Naval Service Photographer 2015/1/B&W/negatives/Ships/Misc)
158 Courtesy of Military Archives (IE/MA/PRCN/0020/003/005)
159 Courtesy of Military Archives (IE/MA/AVCN/P2/L10/1090)
161 Courtesy of Military Archives (IE/MA/18MM/25)
162 Courtesy of Military Archives (IE/MA/PC72)
163 (top) Courtesy of Military Archives (IE/MA/PC72)
163 (bottom) Irish Air Corps Archives, 105 Squadron, Photographic and Airborne Imaging
164 Courtesy of Military Archives (IE/MA/MPD/AD119392–007)
165 Courtesy of Military Archives (IE/MA/ACPS/GPN/050/1–4)

Beginnings: The Equitation School
167 Courtesy of Military Archives (IE/MA/GPN/004/020)
168–9 Images courtesy of the RDS Library & Archives

Chapter 5: 1946–69
172 Courtesy of Military Archives (IE/MA/ACC2019/04)
173 Courtesy of Military Archives (IE/MA/ACC2019/04)
174 UN Photo Library (UN7511421)
177 Courtesy of Military Archives (IE/MA/PRCN/0006/08/06)
179 UN Photo Library (UN7730864)
181 UN Photo Library/Irish Times (UN7681072)
185 UN Photo Library/JH (UN7660613)
186 UN Photo Library/JH (UN7731152)
187 Courtesy of Military Archives (IE/MA/PRCN/006/08/25)
188 Courtesy of Military Archives (IE/MA/OS/ONUC/35INFBN/03/06)
189 Courtesy of Military Archives (IE/MA/PRCN/006/08/42)
190 Courtesy of Military Archives (IE/MA/OS/ONUC/33INFBN/04/04)
191 UN Photo Library (UN7464499)
192 Courtesy of Military Archives (IE/MA/ACC2020/07)
193 UN Photo Library/BZ (UN7731225)
194 Courtesy of Military Archives (IE/MA/PC/Cadet School)
195 (top) UN Photo Library/BZ (UN7768310)
195 (bottom) UN Photo Library/BZ (UN7768312)
196 UN Photo Library/DB (UN7677914)
197 Courtesy of the Irish Defence Forces
198 Courtesy of Military Archives (IE/MA/GPN/012/002)
200 Courtesy of Military Archives (IE/MA/GPN/015/008)
202 Courtesy of Military Archives (IE/MA/PRCN/0066/1742)

203 Irish Air Corps Archives, 105 Squadron, Photographic and Airborne Imaging
204 Irish Air Corps Archives, 105 Squadron, Photographic and Airborne Imaging

The Defence Forces on the Silver Screen
206 Courtesy of Military Archives (IE/MA/COS/370)
207 Courtesy of Military Archives (IE/MA/PRCN/0066/2653)
208 Courtesy of Military Archives (IE/MA/PRCN/0066/2648)

Chapter 6: 1970–99
212 PA Images/Alamy Stock Photo
214 Alan Le Garsmeur, 'The Troubles' Archive/Alamy Stock Photo
215 Alan Le Garsmeur, 'The Troubles' Archive/Alamy Stock Photo
216 Courtesy of Military Archives (IE/MA/MPD/AD119315–009)
218 Courtesy of Military Archives (IE/MA/COS/1300)
219 Courtesy of Military Archives (IE/MA/ACC2019/04)
220 Courtesy of Mediahuis Ireland (Independent Newspapers Ireland/NLI Collection)
221 Courtesy of Military Archives (IE/MA/ACC2019/05)
222 Courtesy of the Irish Defence Forces
223 Courtesy of Military Archives (IE/MA/PC96)
225 Courtesy of Military Archives (IE/MA/ACC2020/01)
226 UN Photo Library/Yutaka Nagata (UN7739852)
227 Courtesy of Military Archives (IE/MA/PC96)
228 Courtesy of Military Archives (IE/MA/PC96)
229 UN Photo Library/John Isaac (UN7719938)
230 UN Photo Library/John Isaac (UN7719850)
232 UN Photo Library/John Isaac (UN7771979)
235 Courtesy of Military Archives (IE/MA/Cadet Class Photos/1st and 2nd Female Cadet Class 1980–81)
236 Courtesy of Military Archives (IE/MA/Photos/070/005)
237 Courtesy of Mediahuis Ireland (Independent Newspapers Ireland/NLI Collection)
238 Courtesy of Military Archives (IE/MA/An Cosantóir Photos)
239 Courtesy of Military Archives (IE/MA/PC339)
240 Irish Air Corps Archives, 105 Squadron, Photographic and Airborne Imaging
243 Irish Air Corps Archives, 105 Squadron, Photographic and Airborne Imaging
245 Irish Air Corps Archives, 105 Squadron, Photographic and Airborne Imaging

Beginnings: An Cosantóir
246–7 Courtesy of Military Archives (*An Cosantóir* collection)

Chapter 7: 2000–22
250 UN Photo Library/Evan Schneider (UN7768224)
251 Courtesy of the Irish Defence Forces
252 UN Photo Library/Mark Garten (UN7442238)
253 Courtesy of the Irish Defence Forces
254 Courtesy of the Irish Defence Forces
255 UN Photo Library/Pasqual Gorriz (UN7383353)
256 UN Photo Library/Pasqual Gorriz (UN7310242)
257 Courtesy of the Irish Defence Forces
258 Courtesy of the Irish Defence Forces
259 UN Photo Library/Martine Perret (UN7288318)
260 Courtesy of the Irish Defence Forces
261 UN Photo Library/Evan Schneider (UN7197058)
262 Courtesy of the Irish Defence Forces
264–5 Courtesy of the Irish Defence Forces

266 UN Photo Library/Pasqual Gorriz (UN 7111282)
267 Courtesy of the Irish Defence Forces
268 Courtesy of the Irish Defence Forces
269 Courtesy of the Irish Defence Forces
270 **(top and bottom)** Courtesy of the Irish Defence Forces
271 Courtesy of the Irish Defence Forces
272 Courtesy of the Irish Defence Forces
273 Courtesy of the Irish Defence Forces
274 Courtesy of the Irish Defence Forces
275 Courtesy of the Irish Defence Forces
276 All photos reproduced by kind permission of Amelia Stein (IE/MA/ACC2021/04)

Beginnings: Military Archives
278 Courtesy of the Irish Defence Forces
279 Courtesy of the Irish Defence Forces

Chapter 8: Witness History
282 Image courtesy of the National Library of Ireland (NLI, HOG101)
285 Reproduced by kind permission of UCD Archives (UCDA, P80/PH/51)
286 Reproduced by kind permission of UCD Archives (UCDA, P80/PH/77)
287 Reproduced courtesy of the National Museum of Ireland (NMI, HE-EW-1809)
289 Reproduced by kind permission of UCD Archives (UCDA, P80/PH/87)
290 Reproduced by kind permission of UCD Archives (UCDA, P80/PH/122)
291 Courtesy of Military Archives
292 **(top)** Courtesy of Military Archives
292 **(bottom)** Courtesy of Military Archives (IE/MA/PRCN/0006/03/06 (3))
293 Courtesy of Military Archives (IE/MA/PRCN/ACC2015/16)
294 Courtesy of Military Archives (IE/MA/PRCN/ACC2018/02)
295 Reproduced by kind permission of Cpl Michael J. Whelan
296 Courtesy of Military Archives (IE/MA/PRCN/0066/2656)
297 Courtesy of Military Archives
299 Irish Air Corps Archives, 105 Squadron, Photographic and Airborne Imaging
300 Courtesy of Military Archives
301 Reproduced by kind permission of Cpl Michael J. Whelan
303 Courtesy of Military Archives (IE/MA/MAOHP/AC193)
307 Courtesy of the Irish Defence Forces
308 Reproduced by kind permission of FQMS Tracey Walsh
309 **(top)** Courtesy of the Irish Defence Forces
309 **(bottom)** Irish Air Corps Archives, 105 Squadron, Photographic and Airborne Imaging
310 Reproduced by kind permission of Sgt Maj Keith Caffrey
311 Reproduced by kind permission of CPO Ruairí de Barra
313 Courtesy of the Irish Defence Forces
314 Courtesy of the Irish Defence Forces
315 **(top)** Reproduced by kind permission of UCD Archives (UCDA, P80/PH/57)
315 **(bottom)** Reproduced by kind permission of UCD Archives (UCDA, P80/PH/81)
316 Image courtesy of the National Library of Ireland (NLI, HOGW20)
317 Courtesy of Military Archives (IE/MA/GPN/053/025)
318 Courtesy of Military Archives (IE/MA/GPN/033/012)
330 Courtesy of Military Archives (IE/MA/GPN/033/007)

INDEX

*Page numbers in **bold** refer to image captions*

FORT WESTMORELAND
...LAND DEFENCES 1943
DESIGN OF EMPLACEMENT FOR 9 INCH EL. MK VII...
TO BE ERECTED ON Nos. 2 AND 4 BASTIONS

the second machine and we intended starting
yesterday, but the weather was unfit for flying. the
weather was as bad this morning and a report I got
through from Castle Townwich stated that it was
raining along the route. Also on account of the holiday
there is no one at the Depot there to supply petrol
I expect to start to morrow morning.